ARTHUR DRO
and the Histor
School of the
JAMES D. TABC
Testament at the University of North Carolina,
Charlotte.

A Noble Death

A Noble Death

SUICIDE AND MARTYRDOM
AMONG CHRISTIANS AND JEWS
IN ANTIQUITY

Arthur J. Droge

James D. Tabor

HarperSanFrancisco
A Division of HarperCollins*Publishers*

A NOBLE DEATH. *Suicide and Martyrdom Among Christians and Jews in Antiquity.* Copyright © 1992 by Arthur J. Droge and James D. Tabor. All rights reserved. Printed in the United States of America. No part of this book may be used or reproduced in any manner whatsoever without written permission except in the case of brief quotations embodied in critical articles and reviews. For information address HarperCollins Publishers, 10 East 53rd Street, New York, NY 10022.

FIRST EDITION

Library of Congress Cataloging-Publication Data

Droge, Arthur J.
    A Noble Death : suicide and martyrdom among Christians and Jews
in antiquity / Arthur J. Droge, James D. Tabor.—ed.
    p. cm.
    Includes bibliographic references and index.
    ISBN 0–06–062095–1
    1. Suicide—Moral and ethical aspects—History. 2. Suicide—
Mediterranean Region—History. 3. Social History—To 500.
4. Suicide—Religious aspects—Christianity. 5. Martyrdom (Christianity)
6. Suicide—Religious aspects—Judaism. 7. Martyrdom (Judaism)
I. Tabor, James D. II. Title.
HV6543.D76 1991
394'.8—dc20   91-55280
                                                 CIP

92 93 94 95 96 ❖ RRD(H) 10 9 8 7 6 5 4 3 2 1

This edition is printed on acid-free paper that meets the American
National Standards Institute Z39.48 Standard.

For Robert M. Grant

οὐκ ἔστιν μαθητὴς ὑπὲρ τὸν διδάσκαλον.
ἀρκετὸν τῷ μαθητῇ ἵνα γένηται ὡς ὁ διδάσκαλος αὐτοῦ.

Contents

Viele sterben zu spät, und Einige sterben zu früh.
Noch klingt fremd die Lehre: "stirb zur rechten Zeit!"
Stirb zur rechten Zeit: also lehrt es Zarathustra.

Nietzsche, *Also Sprach Zarathustra* 1.21

Preface

As the manuscript of this book was nearing completion, a national stir was created when a Michigan pathologist, Dr. Jack Kevorkian, used his "suicide machine" to assist an Oregon woman suffering from Alzheimer's disease to end her life. The episode was widely reported and discussed in all the major media and served to focus attention yet again on the vexing question of whether and in what circumstances an individual has the right to die. The question is certainly not new, but within the last two decades it has come to occupy a prominent place in the national consciousness. Whether theologians, medical ethicists, pollsters, talk-show hosts, or the public at large, all are participants in the debate, each seeking to influence and control the discourse on suicide.

For the most part, however, the recent debate about suicide betrays a lamentable ignorance of the history of the question. An article that appeared in the Chicago *Tribune* (June 17, 1990), in response to the Kevorkian episode, typified this nescience. It stated, "Much to the dismay of religious leaders, an increasing number of people now consider suicide a personal right, not the shameful, sinful act against God that it has been regarded since biblical times" (p. 18). The author of this article, and no doubt most of his readers, would be surprised to learn that the Bible nowhere proscribes suicide. In fact, there are at least seven individuals in the Bible who take their own lives, and none of them is condemned for the act.

A problem that besets the recent discussion of suicide is that many, like the author of the *Tribune* article, bring to it a vague notion that the so-called Judeo-Christian tradition speaks decisively against the act of suicide, but just what that objection is, when it developed, and what came before it are mostly not known. Again, many would be surprised to discover the diverse and sometimes conflicting evaluations of suicide in Western antiquity and that no consensus was reached until the fifth century of our era, and then only after a protracted intellectual struggle. Part of our intention in this book is to trace the extraordinary twists and turns in the debate about voluntary death among Jews and Christians in the ancient world, a debate still little understood in a society so obsessed with the problem of suicide.

There is another side to our project, perhaps more fundamental. The question of whether and in what circumstances an individual has the right to die is a remarkably revealing one for the historian of religion, for when this question is put to a particular religious tradition the answer(s) given say much about the character of that religion: its conception of God, salvation, the nature of life and death, personhood, free will, and determinism. By investigating the problem of voluntary death in antiquity, we intend to say something about Judaism and Christianity.

Our project could not have been completed without the support of a number of individuals. We owe a debt of gratitude to Hans Dieter Betz, John J. Collins, Eugene V. Gallagher, Jon D. Levenson, Bernard McGinn, John M. Rist, and Brian K. Smith, who read all or parts of the manuscript in various stages. Their perceptive criticisms, useful suggestions, and constant encouragement have made this book possible. Needless to say, they bear no responsibility for the errors or wrongheadedness that remain.

Our thinking about the problem of voluntary death has benefited enormously from Dr. Michael Borowitz, who graciously allowed us to make use of an unpublished paper in the introductory chapter.

A special word of thanks is due to four graduate students at the University of Chicago: Andrew Eulass, J. Andrew Foster, Dorothy Goehring-Somalwar, and Colleen Stamos, all of whom gave generously of their time to the project and improved both its substance and style. *Salus ubi multi consiliarii.*

Finally, this book has been a collaborative enterprise, with all the advantages and liabilities that such an endeavor entails. Each of us has read, commented upon, and criticized the other's work. Consequently, each page of our study bears the imprint of two hands, at times the direct result of seemingly endless editing and revision, at other times the indirect result of conversations too numerous to recall. However, given the wide range of texts and traditions over which we ranged, it was necessary to divide the project between us. Aside from the introductory chapter and conclusion, both coauthored in the strict sense, Mr. Tabor is responsible for chapters three and four, Mr. Droge for the remaining four chapters.

Arthur J. Droge
James D. Tabor
Chicago and Charlotte
October 1, 1991

A Noble Death

❦

CHAPTER 1

The Distance We Have Traveled

On 7 March A.D. 203 a small group of North African Christians, victims of the persecution of Septimius Severus, were led into the amphitheater at Carthage to fight with wild animals.[1] Among them were Vibia Perpetua, twenty-two years of age, newly married, and the mother of an infant son; Perpetua's slave girl Felicitas; two young men named Saturninus and Secundulus; a Christian slave named Revocatus; and a young catechumen named Saturus. Their deaths have been recorded in the famous *Acts of Perpetua and Felicitas*, written by an anonymous Christian of North Africa (perhaps Tertullian) allegedly from the martyrs' own words as recorded in the diaries that they kept in prison.[2]

This firsthand narrative is remarkable for many reasons, not the least of which is its vivid description of how some early Christians chose death rather than compromise their religious convictions. During the interrogation by the Roman governor, Hilarianus, Perpetua remained unmoved. "Have pity on your father's grey head," he exhorted her, "have pity on your infant son. Offer the sacrifice for the welfare of the emperors" (6.3). Perpetua refused: *"Non facio."* "Are you a Christian?" asked the governor. *"Christiana sum,"* was her reply (6.4). Whereupon Hilarianus passed judgment on all of them: they were condemned to the beasts as part of the games to be held in honor of the birthday of Geta, the emperor's younger son (6.6; cf. 7.9; 16.3).

We do not know how these Christians came to the attention of the Roman governor, whether they were hunted down as criminals, or whether, like so many other martyrs, they deliberately provoked the authorities to arrest them. From the Roman point of view this was not a persecution; it was the prosecution of individuals deemed to be a threat to the state. But for Perpetua and her circle this was a religious act par excellence. The night before she was to face the beasts Perpetua had a vision in which she realized "that it was not with wild animals that I would fight but with the Devil, but I knew that I would win the victory" (10.14). Victory, for Perpetua, signified immortality; death meant entry into life.

Saturus, too, had a vision. "We had died and put off the flesh, and we began to be carried toward the east by four angels. . . . And when we were free of the world, we first saw an intense light. And I said to Perpetua (for she was at my side): 'This is what the Lord promised us' " (11.2–4). The angels brought them first to a luscious garden, where they were greeted by their fellow martyrs, and then before the throne of God himself (11.5–12.6). Saturus's vision concludes with an exultant Perpetua declaring, "Thanks be to God because I am happier here now than I was in the flesh" (12.7). So resolute were these martyrs that, in the words of the narrator, when "the day of their victory dawned, they marched from the prison to the amphitheater joyfully as though they were going to heaven, with calm faces, trembling, if at all, with joy rather than fear" (18.1).

Throughout the *Acts* emphasis is placed on the *voluntary* nature of the martyrs' impending deaths. "We came to this of our *own free will*," Perpetua declared, "that our *freedom* should not be violated" (18.5). Even after being knocked down in the amphitheater by a "mad heifer," Perpetua modestly adjusted her tunic to cover her thighs, and then asked for a pin to fasten her hair, "for it [is] not right that a martyr should die with her hair in disorder, lest she seem to be mourning in her hour of triumph" (20.3–5). When the hostile crowd of onlookers demanded that the victims be brought out into the open, in order to witness their throats being slashed by the gladiator, "the martyrs got up and went to the spot *of their own accord* . . . , and kissing one another sealed their martyrdom with the ritual kiss of peace" (21.7).

In the *Acts* there is not the slightest hint that these condemned Christians either hesitated in the face of death or felt compelled in any way by their executioners. On the contrary, they embraced death willingly and in a manner that must have struck the Roman authorities as utterly reckless. Lucian, an educated pagan of the second century, expressed what must have been a typical Greek and Roman attitude when he wrote of the Christians, "The poor wretches have convinced themselves, first and foremost, that they are going to be immortal and live forever, in consequence of which they despise death and even *willingly* give themselves over to arrest."[3] Despite its condescending and condemnatory tone, Lucian's description is accurate and, indeed, confirmed by the account of the death of Perpetua herself:

> The others took the sword in silence and without moving, especially Saturus, who being the first to climb the stairway was the first to die. . . . Perpetua, however, had yet to taste more pain. She screamed as she was struck on the bone; then she took the hand of the young gladiator and guided it to her throat. It was as though so great a woman, feared as she was by the unclean spirit, *could not be killed unless she herself was willing* (21.8–10).

This account illustrates the ambiguity and complexity of the phenomenon of self-killing, whether understood positively as martyrdom or negatively as suicide. What sort of death did Perpetua die? Was she officially executed by the state or did she kill herself? When does a martyr become a suicide? To answer these questions it will be necessary to excavate the attitudes and reactions to various forms of voluntary death among Jews and Christians, Greeks and Romans in the ancient world.

Whether one considers Plato's interpretation of the "suicide" of Socrates in the *Phaedo*, or Josephus's account of the "martyrdoms" at Masada in *The Jewish War*, or even the statement attributed to Jesus in the Gospel of John, "No one takes my life, I lay it down of my own free will," the religious and philosophical issues involved in these forms of voluntary death were as diverse as they were complex. This much, however, is clear: in Western antiquity the problem of voluntary death was conceived of altogether differently from the way it is understood today.

On the subject of suicide the modern West is still the intellectual heir of Augustine, who slammed the door shut on the right of individuals to kill themselves by condemning the act as a form of murder and therefore an unpardonable sin. So influential was the Augustinian condemnation that it remained largely unchallenged until 1647, when the door was opened again with the publication of John Donne's treatise *Biathanatos: A Declaration of the Paradox or Thesis That Self-Homicide Is Not So Naturally a Sin That It May Never Be Otherwise.* Our concern in this book is the period bounded by the towering figures of Socrates and Augustine—roughly 400 B.C. to A.D. 400—a period in which one finds a surprisingly open discussion of voluntary death but that concludes with a rigidly drawn distinction between suicide and martyrdom.

In the last hundred years a considerable amount of literature has been devoted to the topics of suicide and martyrdom in the ancient world. Most studies, however, fail to examine the conceptual categories typically employed to discuss the phenomenon of voluntary death, and most fail to integrate the views of Jews and Christians, Greeks and Romans. The standard work in English on Jewish and Christian martyrdom contains only three passing references to suicide in more than six hundred pages[4]—and this despite the fact that some Jews and Christians deliberately killed themselves rather than betray their religious convictions. Conversely, while there exists a rich bibliography on suicide in Greco-Roman antiquity, only a few studies explore its association with martyrdom, and fewer still are concerned with Judaism and Christianity.

Part of the problem, of course, is that the categories typically employed to discuss the phenomenon of voluntary death—suicide and martyrdom—continue to determine what the modern interpreter is able or willing to see. In conventional parlance, *suicide* is a pejorative term, *martyrdom* a positive one. By definition, therefore, Jews and Christians who died for their religion, even by their own hand, cannot be considered suicides (unless, of course, they were "heretics"). By contrast, Greeks and Romans who died for their beliefs cannot be considered martyrs, except in a vague sense and then only by association with Christian martyrdom.

An example from the recent past will illustrate this. During World War II enemy attacks undertaken without regard to the cost in lives were often described as "suicidal" in a pejorative sense. The Americans spoke of Japanese "suicide pilots," emphasizing the barbarity of the strategy. It was the *other* that behaved in this fashion, in contrast to the "sacrificial" acts of heroism displayed by American soldiers. In Japanese, however, the term *kamikaze* does not mean "suicide pilot," a popular Western understanding, but "divine wind," connoting a divinely sanctioned death.[5]

A similar prejudice can be found in descriptions of current events in the Middle East. The Western press likes to speak of Islamic (fundamentalist) "suicide squads"; the Arab side, however, prefers "holy martyrs." Depending, therefore, on the perspective—or bias—of the observer, the act of taking one's life or allowing it to be taken can be described negatively as "suicide" or positively as "martyrdom." This distinction—a polemical one, as we shall argue—is unique to the West and a result of the enduring legacy of Augustine.

Ironically, the term *suicide* was first coined to provide an alternative or morally neutral designation for the act of voluntary death. Almost immediately, however, it came to have decidedly pejorative connotations: suicide is "sinful," "self-centered," "irrational," and more recently a "symptom" of psychological and social disorder. Martyrdom, by contrast, has enjoyed a uniformly positive meaning for more than two thousand years: it is "heroic," "sacrificial," "noble," and "ennobling." Part of our intention in this book is to question this distinction by tracing the extraordinary twists and turns in the debate about voluntary death in Western antiquity, and above all within Judaism and Christianity.

In this book we have deliberately avoided using the word *suicide*, a recent innovation and pejorative term, preferring instead the designation *voluntary death.* By this term we mean to describe the act resulting from an individual's intentional decision to die, either by his own agency, by another's, or by contriving the circumstances in which death is the known, ineluctable result.[6] This definition is intended to be morally neutral, since our enterprise is not one of moral (or clinical) judgment but an attempt to understand the ways in which voluntary death was evaluated in antiquity. For the purposes of our investigation a definition is required that neither glorifies nor condemns the act of taking one's life for whatever reasons or in whatever circumstances. Whether one is a "martyr" or a "fanatic," a "hero" or a "fool," is a matter of commitment.

Given this definition, our intention is to examine significant instances of voluntary death in antiquity, attending whenever possible to the explicit rationale underlying such acts, the circumstances in which they were committed, and the manner in which they were carried out. By considering the different and sometimes conflicting evaluations of voluntary death in antiquity, we may derive a clearer understanding of our own relationship to the problem and of the distance we have traveled.

The idea that killing oneself is both a sin and a crime is a relatively late Christian development, taking its impetus from Augustine's polemics against the "self-destructive mania" of the Donatists in the late fourth and early fifth centuries and acquiring the status of canon law in a series of church councils during the sixth century. Throughout antiquity, the act of taking one's life had been respected, admired, and even on occasion sought after as a means of attaining immortality. Now it became the focus of intense Christian opposition. It is a profound irony of Western history that later Christian theologians condemned the act of voluntary death as a sin for which Christ's similar act could not atone.

As we shall see, Augustine's case against voluntary death was based on a selective reading of Plato, not the Bible. It was the Donatists who could cite biblical precedent for their acts of self-destruction. Aside from his appeal to the sixth commandment, "Thou shalt not kill," Augustine took over the Pythagorean argument of Plato in the *Phaedo* that to sever the bonds of body and soul prematurely was to usurp a privilege that belonged only to God. To deliberately take one's life, therefore, meant that the individual had acted, in his last moment of life, in direct opposition to the divine will—had, in a strict sense, murdered himself.[7]

Augustine's condemnation of voluntary death was transformed into canon law as a result of a series of three church councils in the sixth century. At the Council of Orléans in 533 it was decreed that funeral rites would be denied to individuals who killed themselves having been accused of crime, though the church permitted these rites for "ordinary" criminals (canon 15). It was the Council of Braga in 563, however, that took the decisive step: *anyone* who killed himself would be denied the usual funeral rites of the Eucharist and the singing of psalms (canon 16). In 578 the Council of Auxerre reaffirmed and strengthened these penalties. The door had been shut. To Augustine's theological arguments there now corresponded a system of ecclesiastical laws to punish and deter.[8]

In the centuries between Augustine and the Renaissance voluntary death was condemned by the church as an act of murder, a sin considered unredeemable along with the sin of apostasy. The ecclesiastical proscription of suicide was eventually incorporated into secular law by the emerging nation-states in the early modern period. Suicide was seen not only as a violation of the divine commandment but also as a crime against the state. In canon law the person who killed himself was denied proper Christian burial; in secular law this was extended to include the dishonoring of the corpse. The Elizabethan lawyer Fulbrecke, writing in 1601, offered the following description of what was to be done to the corpse of an individual who had killed himself: "[The body] is drawn by a horse to the place of punishment and shame, where he is hanged on a gibbet, and none may take the body down but by the authority of the magistrate." Another legal authority, Blackstone, wrote that the burial of a suicide was "in the highway, with a stake driven through the body."[9] Not only was the corpse disfigured (indeed, treated as if the individual had been a vampire!), but the deceased forfeited all his personal goods and property to the state.

The peculiar logic of secular law can be seen in the penalty for *attempted* suicide. The punishment, paradoxically, was death. The absurdity of executing a man who had sought death by his own hand was described by the Russian exile Nicholas Ogarev in a letter written to his mistress from England in about 1860:

> A man was hanged who had cut his throat, but who had been brought back to life. They hanged him for suicide. The doctor had warned them that it was impossible to hang him as the throat would burst open and he would breathe through the aperture. They did not listen to his advice and hanged their man. The wound in the neck immediately opened and the man came back to life again although he was hanged. It took time to convoke the aldermen to decide the question of what was to be done. At length the aldermen assembled and bound up the neck below the wound until he died. Oh my Mary, what a crazy society and what a stupid civilization.[10]

This morbid anecdote illustrates how seriously the state of England reckoned the threat of suicide. Since an individual was the subject of the state, the state owned the individual's body, and only the state could dispose of it. Suicide was an act of rebellion, not only against God but also against the state, that must be suppressed at all costs.

By 1900 most of the horrific medieval laws had been repealed in England, but attempted suicide was still a crime punishable by fine or imprisonment up to two years. And the successful suicide was still denied funeral rites if he took his life while "of sound mind." Only in 1961 did Parliament, with the approval of the Anglican church, declare suicide—or attempting it—no longer a crime. At the same time Parliament added a footnote: abetting another's suicide would be punishable by up to fourteen years in jail.[11]

One way to gauge the history of the evaluation of voluntary death is to trace the vocabulary used to describe the act: from morally neutral expressions in antiquity, to terms of condemnation in the Middle Ages, and finally to a more moderate language with the rise of humanism. The term *suicide*, a composite of "self" and "killing," is a relatively new word, unattested before the mid-seventeenth century. Though it gives the impression of coming straight from Latin, there was no Latin *suicidium,* and its construction is contrary to the rules of Latin word building.[12]

In the ancient world there was no comprehensive term analogous to our word *suicide.* Instead one finds a variety of expressions to denote the act of taking one's life. In Greek, for example, descriptions of the act were numerous: "to grasp death" (*lambano thanaton*), "to end life" (*teleutao bion*), "to die voluntarily" (*hekousios apothneisko*), "to remove oneself from life" (*exagein heauton tou biou*), "to kill oneself" (*kteinein heauton*), "to destroy oneself" (*diaphtheirein heauton*). An early adjective for a person who committed suicide was *autocheir* ("own-handed" or "acting with one's own hand"). Later, in the first century A.D., one finds the adjective *autothanatos* ("dying through oneself"). The nominal expression for suicide in general, *exagoge* ("removal"), to which might be attached the adjectives *eulogos* ("rational") and *paralogos* ("irrational"), dates only from the second century A.D., though it appears to have derived from earlier Cynic and Stoic debates about voluntary death and its various aspects.

Similar terminology was used in classical Latin: "voluntary death" (*mors voluntaria*), "to inflict death upon oneself" (*mortem* or *necem sibi consciscere*), "to remove oneself from life" (*e vita excedere*), "to bring one's hand against oneself" (*manus sibi inferre*), and "to inflict violence on oneself" (*vim sibi adfere*). These are but a sampling of the Greek and Latin vocabulary for voluntary death; new terms were constantly being coined. The point worth emphasizing is the absence in antiquity of a uniformly negative term to denote the act of self-killing.[13]

The term *suicide,* despite its popular pejorative connotation, seems to have been coined in an attempt to get away from accusing references to "murder." The *Oxford English Dictionary* dates its first appearance to Walter Charleton's *The Ephesian Matron* of 1651, though the word can be found slightly earlier in Sir Thomas Browne's *Religio Medici,* written in 1635 and published in 1642.[14] The term was still considered enough of a neologism for Dr. Johnson to exclude it from his *Dictionary* of 1755. Instead of "suicide" one finds condemnatory expressions, such as "to murder oneself," "to destroy oneself," "to slaughter oneself," and "to assassinate oneself." John Donne, the first to compose a formal defense of voluntary death in English, cleverly entitled his treatise *Biathanatos,* a slightly garbled rendering of the Greek *biaiothanatos* ("one who dies violently"), to avoid the pejorative association of the act with murder. Throughout his treatise Donne employed, and perhaps coined, the term *self-homicide,* an intentionally neutral designation, since the word *homicide* could apply to criminal acts as well as to justifiable and even commendable ones.[15]

Drawing on a wealth of classical references, Donne attempted to defend the morality of certain forms of voluntary death against Aquinas's arguments that the act violated the law of nature, the law of the state, and the law of God.

Against the first argument, Donne maintained that in certain circumstances people naturally desire death. Against the second, he argued that voluntary death would be justified if the intention of the act were not self-promoting. Against the third, he noted that the Bible nowhere condemns voluntary death.

Donne's treatise did little to overturn the church's religious and moral condemnation of suicide. The traditional arguments were reiterated in Jeremy Taylor's classic of Anglican casuistry, *The Rules of Conscience* (1660), and John Locke's *Second Treatise* (1690) argued that even in a state of nature, where one is free to dispose of one's personal possessions, one is not at liberty to destroy oneself.

Donne's successors, among them such luminaries as Hume, Montesquieu, Voltaire, and Rousseau, fared little better, despite introducing some important new themes.[16] It took the work of the social sciences, launched by Enrico Morselli and Emile Durkheim, to change the situation. The phenomenon of suicide was now seen not as a moral or religious problem but as a psychological and social one, reducible to statistical analysis. In the early nineteenth century, when statistics began to be collected, it was believed that, with a sufficiently large collection of data, the mechanistic laws determining the behavior of human society could be deduced. The use of statistics was applied to the problem of suicide in an attempt to understand and control it.[17]

Using statistics as his mode of analysis, Morselli attempted to explain suicide by means of a curious admixture of psychological and social theory. Morselli was professor of psychological medicine at the Royal University of Turin and physician-in-chief to the Royal Asylum of the Insane. His study *Il suicidio: Saggio di statistica morale,* published in 1879, was quickly translated into English, French, and German. Durkheim based much of his classic work *Le suicide: Etude de sociologie* (1897) on Morselli's research, though their interpretations differed considerably, a point often overlooked.

Morselli believed that suicide was not the self-conscious choice of the individual. "The motive of every suicide," he wrote, "is not alone that which is apparent; there are other more secret causes whose existence and influence elude even the suicide himself, because they act upon him almost unconsciously" (p. 8).[18] According to Morselli, the natural laws ("secret causes") underlying suicide could be identified through the analysis of statistics, which laid bare "the indications of the prophylactics and therapeutics of suicide against which laws and philosophy show themselves powerless" (p. 10).

Morselli located the cause of suicide in a kind of Darwinian struggle for existence. "Suicide is an effect of the struggle for existence and of human selection, which works according to the laws of evolution among civilized people" (p. 354). The struggle for existence in the civilized world, according to

Morselli, was no longer a struggle based on brute strength but one based on the relative strengths of individual minds: "He conquers in whom the cerebral development is highest" (p. 359). Those who fail to compete successfully in the intellectual struggle for existence, who are biologically unprepared for the battle, are defeated, and their brains deteriorate pathologically:

> It is . . . obvious that the first and evil effect of defeat is felt on the organ which is destined to be the instrument of the battle, and as the instrument is destroyed in weak and inexperienced hands, so the brain breaks down under the excessive weight of a struggle to which its forces and faculties are unequal. This amounts to saying that in the exercise of the brain power some morbid aberration takes place which comes out in madness, or in that unsatisfied desire which terminates in voluntary death (p. 362).

For Morselli, suicide and madness were symptoms of the pathology of the individual, specifically, the maldevelopment of the brain: "One whose morbid sensibility and whose faculties are incapable of striving against the cruel experience of practical reality soon arrives at the two roads in which Goethe places his hero in *Werther*: suicide or madness" (p. 373). Since it was impossible to alter nature—to eliminate the struggle for existence—there could be no final cure for suicide. The most that could be done, according to Morselli, would be to ameliorate the conditions of that struggle and better equip individuals for it: "The whole cure is . . . to neutralize the inequality placed by nature between the various combatants . . . and to develop in man the power of well-ordered sentiments and ideas by which to reach a certain aim in life; in short, to give force and energy to the moral character" (p. 374).[19]

In contrast to Morselli, Durkheim argued in his classic study *Le suicide* that the cause of suicide was to be found not in the pathology of the individual but in the pathology of society. Durkheim maintained that a *scientific* theory of suicide would have to account for the change in the rate of suicides not only between different geographical regions and ethnic groups but also over time. Once again, the mode of analysis was statistics. Durkheim used statistical arguments to discount other explanations of suicide such as race, heredity, climate, and so on, since none of these factors could account for the statistical variation. In particular, Durkheim rejected the view of those, like Morselli, who claimed that suicide was caused by mental illness. "No psychopathic state bears a regular and indisputable relation to suicide," Durkheim wrote. "Admittedly, the degenerate is more apt to commit suicide than the well man; but he does not necessarily do so because of this condition. This potentiality of his becomes effective only through the action of other factors which we must discover" (p. 81).[20]

Durkheim identified three major types of suicide: altruistic, egoistic, and anomic. An individual is prone to *altruistic* suicide when completely subordinated to the group. Where group attachments make an excessively powerful claim on the individual to fulfill his social obligations, the individual is inclined to view his life as secondary to the claims of the group. In a world of total social integration individuals place relatively little value on their lives; indeed, they are prone to taking their lives on the smallest of provocations for the benefit of the whole. The French army was an example. Statistics, Durkheim argued, revealed a much higher rate of suicide among soldiers, and, among soldiers, officers had the highest rate of all. This is because in the army an individual is completely subordinated to the will of the group. A soldier will voluntarily sacrifice his own life based on the command of his superior.

An individual is prone to *egoistic* suicide when freed from group control. When individuals are integrated into society through family, social community, and religion, the rate of suicide is low. When these ties begin to break down, however, the fabric of society begins to unravel, and the rate of suicide increases. Again, according to Durkheim, statistics indicated that suicide was more common among people who were single in comparison to those who were married. Suicide was more common in families that had no children than in those that did. Suicide was more common among Protestants than Catholics, because the latter had a more cohesive religious community. Put simply, Durkheim argued that the rate of "suicide varies inversely with the degree of integration of religious society, domestic society, and political society" (p. 208). Durkheim believed that this form of suicide was common because of the individualizing tendencies in modern European society ("hypercivilization," as he called it), which separated people from the constraints of community and traditional religion.

Individuals are prone to commit *anomic* suicide when social regulation that controls human desires breaks down. That is, according to Durkheim, when individuals enter new situations with no rules to guide and direct them, they are freed from the traditional constraints that hold the suicidal impulse in check. For example, Durkheim maintained that anomic suicide increases in times of economic crisis, but it also increases in times of economic prosperity and social unrest. These are situations when an individual's wants are no longer in accord with the possibility of their fulfillment. The disparity between aspirations and their satisfaction leads to anomic suicide. Anomic suicide differs from the other two types "in its dependence, not on the way in which individuals are attached to society, but on how it regulates them. Egoistic suicide results from man's no longer finding a basis for existence in life; altruistic suicide, because this basis for existence appears to man situated beyond life itself.

The third sort of suicide . . . results from man's activity lacking regulation and his consequent sufferings" (p. 258).

Durkheim's sociological typology of suicide, which he claimed was valid for all societies (including those of the past), stands in sharp contrast to Morselli's, for Durkheim opposed the social Darwinism implicit in Morselli's work. Although both used statistics to uncover the cause of suicide, Durkheim did not locate the cause in the degeneration of the individual in the face of the Darwinian struggle for existence. Rather, he explained suicide as the failure of society to integrate and regulate individuals. Of Morselli's theory, Durkheim wrote, "Just as suicide does not proceed from man's difficulties in maintaining his existence, so the means of arresting its progress is not to make the struggle less difficult and life easier" (p. 386). The cure, for Durkheim, was to reincorporate the individual into the social collective. At the end of *Le suicide* he sets forth a program of suicide prevention, urging that the integrative powers of occupational groups or labor communities be strengthened and regulated to take the place of the traditional basis of communal life and social organization—church, family, politics—which had irretrievably lost their power to bind individuals together. Only through such a reform could a sense of collective personality and a common bond be restored to modern society and the problem of suicide be controlled.

Durkheim's explanation of suicide turned outward toward society to find the cause, whereas the psychological and medical explanation looked within the individual. Durkheim's theory was developed when psychiatry was still in its infancy and making its transition from a pathological-anatomic model to a psychological one. When Durkheim wrote, psychiatry could not explain suicide, as can be seen in Durkheim's own critique of psychological explanations for suicide. The development of a more refined psychological psychiatry (specifically, psychoanalysis) gave medicine the power to try to dominate the explanation of suicide. But Durkheim's work, refined by later sociologists, remained as a counterdiscourse that could not easily be refuted.[21]

Both the psychological and sociological explanations of suicide can be seen as a form of "medicalization," for both operate on the pathological distinction between the normal and the abnormal. Both attempt to explain the cause of disease not as an individual choice but as driven by something over which the individual has little control. In medical discourse, it is psychic derangement that compels an individual to suicide; in sociological discourse, it is the degree of social integration. Both, however, wrest control of the act of suicide away from the individual, denying the suicide agency. From this perspective, suicide is seen as a "symptom," of both individual psychopathology and social disorganization, and less as a religious and moral problem.[22]

There were, of course, certain advantages in the medical and social-scientific explanations of suicide. Eventually, suicide was decriminalized: successful suicides could now be buried, and their families were no longer disinherited; unsuccessful suicides were spared execution. Yet, as Alfredo Alvarez has observed, something was also lost:

> The Church's condemnation of suicide, however brutal, was based at least on a concern for the suicide's soul. In contrast, a great deal of modern scientific tolerance appears to be founded on human indifference. The act [of suicide] is removed from the realm of damnation only at the price of being transformed into an interesting but purely intellectual problem, beyond obloquy but also beyond tragedy and morality. . . . Despite all the talk of prevention, it may be that the suicide is rejected by the social scientist as utterly as he was by the most dogmatic Christian. . . . The implication is clear: modern suicide has been removed from the vulnerable, volatile world of human beings and hidden safely away in the isolation wards of science.[23]

To recognize that Alvarez is correct, one need only consider the following. In the most recent edition of the *Encyclopaedia Britannica* there is no "Macropaedia" entry under suicide; it merits only a column and a half in the "Micropaedia." Upon consulting the index, however, one discovers that suicide *is* treated, but only here and there and exclusively under the following headings: depressive reactions, Durkheim's social views, elderly people, life insurance policies, manic-depressive psychosis, medico-legal status, Sartre's existentialist view, and sedative-hypnotic drugs. In other words, suicide has become the domain of medicine and social science and has been removed from the "vulnerable and volatile" world of human beings—in short, has ceased to be seen as an enduring moral and religious question.

It should be noted that the medical hegemony over suicide is currently under siege. Having fought a long battle with theology to take control of the discourse on suicide, medicine now faces a lay movement that is creating a new discourse by appropriating a term from antiquity: *rational suicide* (cf. the Stoic expression *exagoge eulogos*). However, this new understanding of suicide should not be equated with the conception of suicide in antiquity. Although defenders of "rational suicide" call upon an ancient vocabulary and cite ancient examples as evidence against the medical model of suicide, their arguments are an outgrowth of medicine itself.

In both medical and sociological discourse suicide is "irrational," a "symptom" either of mental illness or of a diseased society. To carve out a space for "rational" suicide, modern proponents delimit their concern to those cases that have passed medical scrutiny, to those individuals who are deemed "normal" and thus able to *decide* their fates. The so-called right-to-die movement is *not* concerned with the question of whether an individual has the right to die; rather it is concerned primarily with those persons afflicted with terminal illnesses and secondarily with the elderly, who have enjoyed the full measure of life and are prepared to die.[24]

There are several curious aspects to the new right-to-die movement. The first is the disguised language it uses to discuss suicide. Indeed, the term is rarely used. Instead, suicide is replaced by expressions such as *death with dignity, accelerated death, death by design,* and *deliverance from evil.* A second curious feature of the right-to-die movement is its limited scope. No one in the movement argues that there is a right to suicide in general. The discourse is restricted only to the terminally ill. The argument is not that people have a right to take their lives, but that medicine has become too powerful, too intrusive, and has wrested control of death away from the individual. The right-to-die movement, therefore, is an attempt to free humanity from the dehumanizing technology of medicine.

The right-to-die movement may, however, have a less obvious motive than restoring individual autonomy. The reader may recall the 1984 speech of Richard Lamm, then governor of Colorado, in which he advocated that elderly people who are terminally ill have a "duty to die and get out of the way."[25] At issue here is the problem of "cost containment": the elderly are absorbing increasing proportions of health-care resources. Books and articles have appeared in recent years that argue for the establishment of limits in the rationing of health care—that is, that health care should be directed away from the elderly, who are close to death, and given to the young. For example, Daniel Callahan has argued for an age limit on major medical care.[26] A recent article in the journal *Ethics* argues that we should inculcate an obligation among the elderly to commit suicide.[27] We leave to others more competent than ourselves the task of assessing the ethical and public policy issues raised by the right-to-die movement. Clearly, however, we are witnessing in our own day the reevaluation of voluntary death, even if its meaning and significance are as yet difficult to discern.

In this century there has been an outpouring of books and articles on suicide.[28] The subject has been approached from nearly every conceivable angle, yet, as David Cannadine laments in his review of Olive Anderson's monumental study *Suicide in Victorian and Edwardian England,* virtually all of the research has been "ahistorical":

> Like childhood and adolescence, sexuality and homosexuality, madness and old age, suicide is undeniably one of the central moral and medical issues in our society today. But, like them again, it is also as much a historical as a contemporary phenomenon. Yet compared with these other subjects, very little attempt

has been made to understand suicide in time or over time. We are all vaguely aware that ancient Greece, imperial Rome, feudal Japan, Christian Europe and premodern India had their own customs of self-destruction. But almost nothing is known about the history of suicide, even in the post-Enlightenment West.[29]

No historian could do for the Greco-Roman world what Anderson has done for Victorian and Edwardian England. We simply do not have the kind of evidence—statistical data and personal records—that she had at her disposal. Nearly all the evidence that can be of any real help to us, in giving even tentative answers to our questions, comes from a tiny minority of the population of the ancient Mediterranean world, the literate members of the upper classes. The limited nature of the data also prevents us from applying the theories of Morselli, Durkheim, and their epigones. But it is not our intention to set forth or defend a general theory of suicide. Our main purpose in this book is to try to describe, through a process of historical re-enactment, how Jews and Christians in the ancient world understood the problem of voluntary death. This process "is not a passive surrender to the spell of another's mind; it is a labor of active and therefore critical thinking. The historian not only re-enacts past thought, he re-enacts it in the context of his own knowledge and therefore, in re-enacting it, criticizes it, forms his own judgment of its value, corrects whatever errors he can discern in it."[30] Ours is not an attempt to find ancient answers to modern questions; rather, by interrogating the ways in which self-killing was understood in the ancient world, we ourselves may choose to conceptualize suicide differently.

NOTES

1. The precise day and year of the martyrdoms have been disputed. For convenience, we have given the traditionally accepted date. On this, see T. D. Barnes, "Pre-Decian *Acta Martyrum*," *Journal of Theological Studies* 19 (1968): 522–23.

2. For the Latin text and English translation of the *Acts* we have followed H. Musurillo, *The Acts of the Christian Martyrs*, Oxford Early Christian Texts (Oxford: Clarendon Press, 1972). With Musurillo, we take this text to be a fairly accurate reflection of the period of persecution in North Africa c. 200, though one need not assume that it is accurate in every detail or that the author has quoted verbatim the words of the martyrs themselves.

3. Lucian, *The Death of Peregrinus* 13.

4. W. H. C. Frend, *Martyrdom and Persecution in the Early Church: A Study of a Conflict from the Maccabees to Donatus* (Oxford: Blackwell, 1965). Frend refers to suicide on pp. 47, 52, and 293. In each instance the term is used in a pejorative sense.

5. See David Daube, "The Linguistics of Suicide," *Philosophy and Public Affairs* 1 (1972): 435, where he notes that the term *kamikaze* "originally denoted the storms by which, in the late thirteenth century, the national deities saved Japan: the Mongol fleet which attacked in overwhelming strength was miraculously dispersed."

6. On those occasions when we do use the term *suicide* (mainly in tracing the history of the discussion), we imply no pejorative connotation. Our definition of voluntary death deliberately includes cases in which the decision to die is carried out by *other* persons. Compare our definition with Durkheim's famous standard of suicide: "the term suicide is applied to all cases of death resulting *directly or indirectly* from a positive or negative act of the victim himself, which he knows will produce this result" (*Suicide: A Study in Sociology* [Glencoe, IL: Free Press, 1951], p. 44).

7. The relevant texts are *Against Gaudentius* (a Donatist bishop) and the *City of God* 1.17–27. Augustine's views will be examined in detail in chap. 7.

8. On this, see H. R. Fedden, *Suicide: A Social and Historical Study* (London: Davies, 1938), pp. 133–35.

9. Both quotations are from Glanville Williams, *The Sanctity of Life and the Criminal Law* (New York: Knopf, 1957), p. 233.

10. We owe this reference to Alfredo Alvarez, *The Savage God: A Study of Suicide* (New York: Random House, 1970), p. 45.

11. See the report in *Time* magazine (Aug. 18, 1961), p. 23.

12. If understood in accordance with the rules of Latin word building, "suicide" would suggest "the killing of a pig" (*sus, suis*)! See Daube, "Linguistics of Suicide," p. 422.

13. The vocabulary of voluntary death in Hebrew will be discussed in chaps. 3 and 4.

14. "Herein are they in extremes, that can allow a man to be his own assassin, and so highly extol the end and suicide of Cato" (Sect. XLIV); available in Sir Thomas Browne, *Religio Medici and Other Writings*, Everyman's Library (New York: Dutton, 1965). About seventy-five years later the term *suicide* found its way into French literature, replacing phrases like *meurtre de soi-meme*. German has remained unaffected: the most common term for suicide is still *Selbstmord*. See David Daube, "Suicide," in *Studi in onore di Giuseppe Grosso* (Torino: G. Giappichelli, 1971), pp. 119–27.

15. See Daube, "Linguistics of Suicide," pp. 419–20. Donne's treatise was composed in 1607 or 1608 but not published until c. 1647, after the author's death and against his wishes. Prior to Donne, Sir Thomas More and Michel de Montaigne had expressed some support for suicide (and euthanasia).

16. Among the many noteworthy studies of suicide in this period, see L. G. Crocker, "Discussion of Suicide in the Eighteenth Century," *Journal of the History of Ideas* 13 (1952): 47–72; John McManners, *Death and the Enlightenment* (Oxford: Oxford Univ. Press, 1981), pp. 409–37; Michael MacDonald, "The Secularization of Suicide in England," *Past and Present* 111 (1986): 50–100; and Tom L. Beauchamp, "Suicide in the Age of Reason," in Baruch A. Brody (ed.), *Suicide and*

Euthanasia: Historical and Contemporary Themes, Philosophy and Medicine, no. 35 (Dordrecht, Boston, and London: Kluwer Academic Publishers, 1989), pp. 183–219.

17. On this development in the social sciences, see Jack Douglas, *The Social Meanings of Suicide* (Princeton, NJ: Princeton Univ. Press, 1967), pp. 3–13. The discussion of Morselli and Durkheim that follows is informed by an (as yet) unpublished paper by Dr. Michael Borowitz, "Some Ruminations on Suicide: A History of Its Problematization" (Mar. 1988).

18. This and other quotations are taken from the abridged English translation of Morselli's work, *Suicide: An Essay on Comparative Moral Statistics* (London: Paul, 1881).

19. See further Borowitz, "Some Ruminations on Suicide," pp. 27–29. For a survey of recent materials on the psychological approach to suicide, see E. S. Shneidman, N. L. Farberow, and R. E. Litman (eds.), *The Psychology of Suicide* (New York: Science House, 1970). A more technical treatment, which surveys the history of interpretation into the twentieth century, is Gabriel Deshaies, *Psychologie du suicide* (Paris: Presses Universitaires de France, 1947).

20. This and other quotations are taken from the English translation of Durkheim's work, *Suicide: A Study in Sociology* (Glencoe, IL: Free Press, 1951).

21. See further Borowitz, "Some Ruminations on Suicide," pp. 29–36; and Douglas, *Social Meanings of Suicide*. Durkheim's use of statistics and his program for prevention have been repeatedly criticized, but his general theory of suicide has remained virtually unchallenged by sociologists. For the subsequent discussion and refinement of Durkheim's theory, see Steve Taylor, *Durkheim and the Study of Suicide* (London: Macmillan, 1982).

22. We owe this point to Borowitz, "Some Ruminations on Suicide," pp. 36–37.

23. Alvarez, *Savage God*, p. 74.

24. See Borowitz, "Some Ruminations on Suicide," pp. 49–52, where he illustrates this point by examining a recent article in *Life* magazine, "The Liberation of Ellen and Marvin Gronsky" (Dec. 1986), pp. 70–76. The author of the article gives a sympathetic account of the "rational suicide" of this elderly couple, each of whom suffered from terminal illness.

25. See the report in *The New York Times* (March 29, 1984), p. A16.

26. Daniel Callahan, *Setting Limits: Medical Goals in an Aging Society* (New York: Simon & Schuster, 1987).

27. Margaret Battin, "Age Rationing and the Just Distribution of Health Care: Is There a Duty to Die?" *Ethics* 97 (1987): 317–40.

28. See Ann E. Prentice, *Suicide: A Selective Bibliography of Over 2,200 Items* (Metuchen, NJ: Scarecrow Press, 1974), and John C. McIntosh, *Research on Suicide: A Bibliography* (Westport, CT: Greenwood Press, 1985).

29. David Cannadine, review of Olive Anderson, *Suicide in Victorian and Edwardian England* (Oxford: Clarendon Press, 1987), in *The New York Times Book Review* (June 16, 1988), p. 13.

30. R. G. Collingwood, *The Idea of History* (Oxford: Clarendon Press, 1946), p. 215.

CHAPTER 2

❧

The Death of Socrates
and Its Legacy

"There is but one truly serious philosophical problem, and that is suicide." This is the famous opening line of Albert Camus's essay *The Myth of Sisyphus*.[1] Camus's remark is descriptive not only of the modern existentialist debate about "suicide" but also of the discussion of this problem in Greek and Roman antiquity. In general, ancient society did not discriminate against the person who took his own life, nor did it attach any particular disgrace to the act itself, provided there was sufficient justification for it. This was the question to which the philosophers turned their attention. What concerned them more than the act itself were the reasons for which an individual might justifiably choose death.[2]

It has been customary for historians to regard the debate about voluntary death in antiquity as a distinctly Stoic phenomenon, yet this should not cause us to lose sight of the fact that nearly all the philosophical schools of the Greco-Roman period had worked out their own positions on the "one truly serious philosophical problem." Admittedly, in the Roman period, many of the famous examples of voluntary death were adherents of the Stoic school, and in the writings of Seneca in particular the act of taking one's life was extolled as the greatest triumph of an individual over fate. But the phenomenon was by no means limited to Stoics. The remark of E. R. Dodds that "in these centuries a good many persons were consciously or unconsciously in love with death" may be an exaggeration, but for a point.[3] As Arthur Darby Nock observed, the first century A.D. witnessed the rise of what can only be described as a "suicide cult."[4]

ACHILLES AND AJAX

The literary legacy of the ancient Greeks is full of examples of individuals who not only chose to die but also did so by their own hand. Accounts of self-inflicted death can be found in Greek literature as early as Homer, who regarded the act of voluntary death as something natural and usually heroic.[5] To the ancient Greeks, Achilles was the paradigm for human aspiration, the embodiment of what it meant to be a "good man," an *agathos*. This evaluation was based in part upon Achilles' ability to choose between two alternatives: to leave Troy for a long, but obscure, life in "fertile Phthia," or to remain at Troy and win great glory, never to return.[6] At the time of his decision Achilles had withdrawn in anger from the battle, having been dishonored by Agamemnon. When his friend and dependent Patroclus was killed in battle, Achilles resolved to put his anger aside and return to the fray. At this point, Thetis, Achilles' mother, advised him to consider his options carefully: "Then I must lose you soon, my child, by what you are saying, since it is decreed that your death must come soon after Hector's."[7] Achilles responded in the following way: "I must die soon, then; since I did not stand by my companion. . . . Now I shall go, to overtake that killer of dear life, Hector; then I will accept my own death, at whatever time Zeus wishes to bring it about. . . . Now I must win great glory."[8]

Achilles' choice is one he may have later rued, for when Odysseus encountered him among the feckless shades of the underworld, Achilles lamented, "O shining Odysseus, never try to console me for dying. I would rather follow the plow as thrall to another man, one with no land allotted him and not much to live on, than be a king over all the perished dead."[9] Although Achilles bemoaned his status as a shade in the underworld, he never explicitly repudiated his decision to remain at Troy. Death, as Achilles himself noted, was inevitable, the fate of all mortals. The only real choice Achilles had, therefore, was in determining when and under what conditions he was to die. His decision reflects the view that the content of a person's life is more important than its duration. To prolong life at the expense of personal fame and glory was not a desirable end for a Homeric hero.

This understanding of life and death is also reflected in the figure of Sophocles' Ajax:

> It is a shameful thing [*aischron*] to want to live forever
> When a man's life gives him no relief from trouble.
> What joy is there in a long file of days,
> Edging you forward toward the goal of death,
> Then back a little? I wouldn't give much for a man
> Who warms himself with the comfort of vain hopes.
> Let a man live nobly, or die nobly.[10]

Ajax, the son of Telamon and a hero second only to Achilles in prowess, was a tragic figure. Upon the death of Achilles, a dispute arose between Ajax and Odysseus over which of them was to be awarded the armor of Achilles. The Greeks eventually decided in favor of Odysseus. At this point the details of the myth diverge. In one version, known to Pindar, Ajax immediately killed himself as a result of being dishonored.[11] In the version of Sophocles a more detailed account is given of the circumstances that led Ajax to destroy himself. Angered at having been slighted, he resolved to take vengeance on the Greeks and reclaim his prize. To prevent this, Athena drove him mad, and Ajax slaughtered a herd of animals that, in his condition, he mistook for the Greeks. When Ajax came to his senses and realized what he had done, he killed himself because he could not bear the shame associated with his actions. In neither version of the myth, however, is Ajax censured for his decision to destroy himself.

One must exercise caution in attempting to extract a theory of voluntary death from this kind of source, but it is important to note the way in which Sophocles treats the death of Ajax. The fact that Ajax killed himself is never seen to be a smudge upon his excellence (arete). The manner of his death is irrelevant in determining whether or not he was a good man (agathos). This is revealed in the dispute between Menelaus, Agamemnon, and Teucer. After Ajax's body was discovered, Menelaus and Agamemnon attempted to prevent its burial, a proposal that Teucer (and later Odysseus) firmly rejected. What is significant is the rationale Menelaus and Agamemnon offer for their proposal:

> When we brought Ajax here from Greece,
> We thought he would be our ally and friend:
> On trial we have found him worse than any Trojan—
> Plotting a murderous blow at the whole army,
> A night attack, to naïl us with his spear.
> And unless some God had smothered that attempt,
> We should have met the end that he met. . . .
> But God changed
> His criminal heart to fall on sheep and cattle.
> Therefore I say, no man exists on earth
> Who has the power to give him burial.[12]

Clearly, Menelaus was concerned only with Ajax's criminal intentions, not with the particular manner of his death. The only one who did protest Ajax's death was Tecmessa, his consort. When she realized that Ajax was about to kill himself, she begged him to change his mind. The reason for her appeal, however, was not that such an act was wrong but that it would bring misfortune on Tecmessa and, as a result, shame on Ajax:

> For this is certain: the day you die
> And by your death desert me, that same day
> Will see me outraged too, forcibly dragged
> By the Greeks, together with your boy, to lead a slave's life.
> And then some one of the lord class,

> With a lashing word, will make his hateful comment:
> "There she is, Ajax's woman;
> He was the greatest man in the whole army.
> How enviable her life was then, and now how slavish!"
> Some speech in that style. And my ill fate
> Will be driving me before it, but these words
> Will be a reproach to you and all your race.[13]

Tecmessa did not attempt to restrain Ajax because she thought that voluntary death was morally wrong, but because such an act would bring misfortune on herself and thus irrevocable shame on Ajax. Her appeal was not ethical (at least in the modern sense); it was an expression of the Homeric system of values, which were concerned almost exclusively with shame and honor, with success and failure. Depending on the circumstances, in such a system of values voluntary death could be praised as a noble and ennobling act.[14]

Achilles and Ajax are only two among many examples in myth and history of individuals who decided to take their lives or allow them to be taken. In antiquity Greeks (and Romans) appealed to the noble deaths of Achilles and Ajax, of Heracles and Antigone, as precedents for their acts of self-destruction. Nevertheless, it was Plato who provided the starting point for, and remained central to, the *philosophical* discussion of voluntary death throughout antiquity, and it is that discussion that we wish to pursue in this chapter.

PLATO

In the *Phaedo* the condemned Socrates asserts that "those who pursue philosophy aright study nothing but dying and being dead" (64a). Indeed, according to Socrates, the philosopher should welcome death, since he may expect to attain "the greatest blessings" (64a). But Socrates goes even further: he urges everyone with a worthy interest in philosophy "to come after me as quickly as he can" (61b; cf. 61c). The "death wish" of Socrates is by no means hyperbolic; on the contrary, it is the logical result of his view of the body and material existence as impediments to the philosophical pursuit of truth. "So long as we have the body, and the soul is contaminated by such an evil, we shall never attain completely what we desire, that is, the truth" (66b; cf. 64e).

No doubt realizing the provocative nature of his remarks, Socrates is quick to issue a disclaimer: "Perhaps," he says, "[the philosopher] will not take his own life, for *they* say that is not permitted" (*ou themiton*, 61c). Socrates is referring here to the Pythagoreans, the only philosophers in antiquity to deny that an individual had the right to take his life under *any* circumstances. The apparent contradiction only serves to confuse the issue among Socrates' disciples, so that one of them, Cebes, asks, "What do you mean by this, Socrates, that it is not permitted to take one's life, but that the philosopher would desire to follow after your dying?" (61d). Socrates responds to Cebes' question by appealing first to the Pythagorean doctrine that individuals are placed in a kind of prison (the body) from which they must not set themselves free or run away (62b).[15] The Pythagoreans argued that, since the soul is placed in the body as a punishment for sins committed in a previous existence, voluntary death was an unjustified revolt against God by the individual, who must wait until God sets him free.[16]

Socrates confesses, however, that "the doctrine that is taught in secret about this matter, that we men are in a kind of prison and must not set ourselves free or run away, seems to me to be weighty and not easy to understand" (62b). In its place, therefore, he offers Cebes a simpler principle: "The gods are our guardians and we humans are one of the possessions of the gods. . . . If one of your possessions should kill itself when you had not wished it to die, would you not be angry with it and punish it if you could?" (62bc). By this analogy Socrates implies that an individual, who is one of the gods' possessions, ought not to take his own life because that would mean usurping a privilege that belongs only to the gods. This statement, in particular, has led some modern interpreters to conclude that Socrates (or Plato) condemned suicide.[17] But Socrates' argument is less straightforward and more subtle than it may appear at first glance. On the one hand, his "sweetly reasonable tone repudiates suicide, yet at the same time he makes death infinitely desirable; it is the entry into the world of ideal presences of which earthly reality is a mere shadow."[18] This is confirmed by Socrates' last words in the *Phaedo* (118a): "Crito, we ought to offer a cock to Asclepius. See to it, and don't forget." Asclepius was the preeminent healer god among the Greeks. The cock was a thank offering that those who were ill made upon being cured. In other words, Socrates implies that death (in this case, self-inflicted) is the "cure" for life.

As John M. Rist and others have noted, Socrates left one point obscure, and this point remained at the center of the discussion of voluntary death throughout antiquity, to appear again in the first book of Augustine's *City of God*.[19] Socrates concludes that "perhaps from this point of view it is not unreasonable to say that a person must not kill himself until god sends some necessity [*anangke*] upon him, such as now has come upon me" (62c).[20] With this "loophole" Plato implies that Socrates' drinking of the poison was truly a voluntary act, despite his having legally received the death penalty.[21]

As the *Crito* makes clear, Socrates could have gone into *voluntary* exile, thus obviating the need for a trial. Or, having been condemned to death, he could have proposed exile as an alternative punishment. He could even have escaped illegally with the assistance of his friends.[22] But, as Socrates himself says, attempting to console the jurors who voted for his acquittal, "This present experience of mine has not come about mechanically [or 'by chance,' *apo tou automatou*]; I am quite certain that the time has come when it is better for me to die and be released from troubles. That is why my sign [i.e., the *daimonion*] never turned me back."[23]

The importance of the *Phaedo* for the subsequent discussion of voluntary death can hardly be exaggerated. As we shall see, the death of Socrates served as the paradigm and justification for numerous other acts of self-destruction. At the same time, however, and owing to their playfully ambiguous character, the statements attributed to Socrates in the *Phaedo* were also used as a way of moderating against an excessive fascination with death.

In the *Phaedo* the problem of voluntary death is discussed from a religious point of view, namely, an individual's responsibility to God. Plato concedes the legitimacy of voluntary death, but only when God brings some necessity or compulsion (*anangke*) to bear on an individual. Elsewhere he discusses the problem in the light of an individual's responsibility to the city-state. In the ninth book of the *Laws* (873cd) Plato outlines the appropriate punishments to be inflicted on the corpse of a person who takes his or her own life for the *wrong* reasons (that is, out of mere indolence or cowardice). "For those thus destroyed," Plato writes, "the tombs shall be, first, in an isolated position with not even one adjacent, and, secondly, they shall be buried in those borders of the twelve districts which are barren and nameless, without note, and with neither headstone nor name to indicate the tombs" (873d). This penalty notwithstanding, Plato recognizes at least three circumstances in which voluntary death is permissible: (1) if one has been ordered to do so by the *polis*; (2) if one has encountered devastating misfortune; and (3) if one is faced with intolerable shame (873c). As Rist has observed, "These reasons are . . . the ones commonly invoked by most Greeks who speak of suicide, and they are mentioned by historical as well as fictional characters as providing grounds for their acts of self-destruction."[24] In light of the *Phaedo*, each of these reasons could be understood as a form of *anangke*, or "divine compulsion." Certainly that is how Plato interpreted Socrates' death. Plato did not condemn voluntary death per se; rather he condemned the taking of one's life only when such an act was performed without sufficient justification. Then, and only then, had a crime that the state had the right to punish been committed.[25]

ARISTOTLE

Aristotle appears to adopt a similar position in the fifth book of the *Nicomachean Ethics* by insisting that the man who kills himself in a fit of anger is guilty of a crime punishable by the state:

> He who through anger voluntarily stabs himself does this contrary to the right rule of life, and this the law does not allow; therefore he is acting unjustly. But

towards whom? Surely towards the state, not towards himself. For he suffers voluntarily, but no one is voluntarily treated unjustly. This is also the reason why the state punishes; a certain loss of civil rights attaches to the man who destroys himself, on the ground that he is treating the state unjustly (*N.E.* 1138a9–13).

The topic of voluntary death does not come up elsewhere in Aristotle's extant political and ethical writings, and this brief passage in the *Nicomachean Ethics* is notoriously difficult to interpret because it results in a paradox. Aristotle maintains on the one hand that the person who kills himself in anger acts unjustly with respect to the state, yet on the other hand that he cannot be acting unjustly with respect to himself because he suffers knowingly and willingly, and Aristotle has already argued (1136b3–12) that no one can knowingly and willingly be treated unjustly. So conceived, the person who kills himself acts unjustly toward the state but not toward himself.

Whether or not this paradox can be resolved, Aristotle's remarks should not be construed as a blanket condemnation of voluntary death. His special regulations have been correctly explained by Rudolf Hirzel as directed against the person who took his own life while still able to bear arms—that is, while his fellow citizens still had the right to expect some service from him.[26] Can we go further? John M. Rist has plausibly suggested that Aristotle, like Plato, appears to have recognized circumstances in which voluntary death was permissible, and perhaps even justified. Since in another passage Aristotle points out that the taking of one's life to escape poverty, passion, or pain is cowardly (*N.E.* 1116a12–14), it seems that he would have endorsed "the normal Greek view" that there are other situations in which an individual might justifiably choose death.[27] In other words, both Plato (in the *Laws*) and Aristotle maintain that the question of life or death must be evaluated finally in light of an individual's civic responsibilities.

Voluntary death was a much discussed topic among the three principal schools of philosophy in Hellenistic and Roman times: Cynics, Epicureans, and Stoics. A different perspective emerges, however, in part a result of the catastrophic social and political changes that occurred during this period. Absent, in particular, is the mention of civic duty as a restraining factor in the matter of voluntary death.

CYNICS

The Cynic "school" of philosophy was founded by Diogenes of Sinope (c. 400–c. 325 B.C.), who was given the epithet "the dog" (*ho kuon*) because he rejected all social conventions and advocated a life according to nature.[28] The

Cynics were never organized in a school like the Epicureans and Stoics were and never worked out a systematic philosophical system. Eschewing the study of logic and physics, the Cynics devoted their attention exclusively to ethics and preached a "gospel" of simplicity and independence as a means of attaining virtue (and therefore happiness). Governed solely by reason (*logos*), the true wise person will strive after "freedom" (*eleutheria*) and "self-sufficiency" (*autarkeia*) by renouncing all material possessions and social entanglements and will live a life "according to nature" (*kata physin*). For the Cynics, virtue was the only good, and everything else either evil or totally indifferent. The Cynics were totally indifferent to death and were prepared to recommend it as a "cure" for any kind of failure to live rationally.

The texts and anecdotes that survive about the Cynics offer little evidence that they possessed a fully worked out theory of voluntary death—at least anything approaching the subtle and complex theory of Plato. It appears that the Cynics, in contrast to Plato, were prepared to recommend voluntary death on the slightest provocation. "For the conduct of life," Diogenes says, "we need either reason [*logos*] or the noose [*brochos*]."[29] Likewise, his most famous disciple, Crates of Thebes, advised that if *eros*, a stumbling block to virtue, could not be curbed by fasting or the passage of time, then the noose was always available.[30]

These sayings are borne out by the numerous examples of Cynic acts of self-destruction. It is reported of Diogenes that at the age of ninety "he died voluntarily by holding his breath."[31] Presumably, Diogenes thought that old age was a hindrance to maintaining a Cynic way of life and so took himself out.

Metrocles (c. 300 B.C.), the brother-in-law of Crates, had been a disciple of Theophrastus, Aristotle's pupil. While rehearsing a speech one day, he inadvertently farted. Metrocles was so ashamed by this that he "shut himself up at home, intending to starve himself to death."[32] When Crates learned of this, he first prepared a meal of beans (!) for Metrocles and then persuaded him that he had done nothing wrong—that is, nothing contrary to nature. Metrocles changed his mind and from that time on became a disciple of Crates and a Cynic philosopher.

The point of this anecdote is not that Crates thought self-killing wrong, only that it was wrong to take one's life for the wrong reason, in this case, for having violated some trivial social convention. In fact, Metrocles eventually did take his own life by choking himself.[33] The reason, we are told, was "because of old age." In other words, when the Cynic life could no longer be maintained, life itself was no longer worth living, and Metrocles was free to take himself out.

Menippus of Gadara, a disciple of Metrocles, hanged himself in despair after he was robbed of all his possessions. In view of the deaths of Diogenes and

Metrocles, this sounds like voluntary death for the *wrong* reason. Possessions were supposed to be of no consequence to the true Cynic. Diogenes Laertius, who preserved the anecdote of Menippus's hanging, appears to have recognized this, for he composed the following little poem:

> Perhaps you know Menippus, Phoenician by birth,
>   but a Cretan hound [*kuon*, "Cynic"].
> A moneylender by day—so he was called—
>   at Thebes when his house was broken into and he lost all,
> Not understanding what it is to be a Cynic,
>   he hanged himself.[34]

In the second century A.D. Demonax of Cyprus is reported to have starved himself to death at the ripe old age of one hundred. His biographer, Lucian of Samosata, provides the following account:

> When Demonax realized that he was no longer able to wait upon himself, he quoted to those who were with him the verses of the heralds at the games: "Here ends a contest awarding the fairest of prizes. Time calls, and forbids us delay." Then refraining from all food, he took leave of life in the same cheerful humor that people he met always saw him in.[35]

The point, once again, is that the wise person should try to live not as long as he can but as long as he ought. When circumstances (in this case, old age) make the Cynic life no longer possible, voluntary death is the required cure.

Lucian also gives an extraordinary, though this time sarcastic, account of how the Cynic philosopher Proteus Peregrinus, who had been a Christian prior to his conversion to Cynicism, burned himself to death in A.D. 165 at the Olympic Games.[36] Peregrinus was regarded by some as highly as Epictetus, the well-known slave turned Stoic philosopher. Lucian dismissed Peregrinus as a charlatan. The reason for Peregrinus's act of self-destruction is not clear. Lucian condemned it as a publicity stunt, but Peregrinus may have styled his death on that of Herakles, a revered figure among the Cynics.[37] According to Peregrinus's disciples, he was emulating the "Brahmans"—the "naked philosophers" (Gymnosophists) of India—who had thrown themselves into the fire in order to make a protest against Alexander the Great.[38]

These reports seem to indicate that for the Cynics the only justification necessary for voluntary death was the inability to preserve a Cynic way of life. If the Cynics considered voluntary death unjustifiable in certain circumstances, they did so without appealing to the religious and civic arguments of Plato and Aristotle. When Crates dissuaded Metrocles from starving himself, he did so by arguing that humiliation resulting from the violation of some trivial social convention was not a sufficient reason for killing oneself. But Metrocles did kill himself when old age made living freely, self-sufficiently, and in accord with nature impossible. If a person could no longer live such a life, then voluntary death was the best thing for him. Only in this way did the Cynics justify voluntary death. They made no claim that the body was a prison from which the soul must escape; they never spoke of the soul being set free in order to attain immortality.

Still, the body was the crucial problem for the Cynics. With Plato and Aristotle we saw that one could not dispose of the body without first considering the question of ownership. Both the gods and the state were believed to exercise certain rights over an individual's body. The Cynics, however, regarded themselves as completely independent and autonomous beings, free from divine or civic control. Freedom, in the sense of complete independence from external compulsions, whether natural or supernatural, was the distinguishing characteristic of the wise person, or true Cynic. That is what Diogenes meant when he said that he esteemed nothing so highly as freedom.[39] True Cynics, therefore, were at all times free to take their own lives.

EPICUREANS

Like Cynicism, the philosophy of Epicurus (c. 341–270 B.C.) was primarily a system of ethics.[40] His epistemology rested on the validity of sense impressions. His physics—the doctrine of atoms and void—was an attempt to explain the workings of the cosmos without recourse to the activity of the gods. The gods existed, according to Epicurus, but they lived in eternal bliss removed from the world of human beings, neither imparting blessings nor inflicting evil. Their undisturbed tranquility (*ataraxia*) was the full realization of the life to which humans should aspire, but the gods themselves could not help humans attain it. If humans were to attain *ataraxia*, they must do so in this life, for the human soul was dissolved at death into its constituent atoms and had no further existence either to fear or desire.

The Epicurean goal of existence is happiness, understood not as self-indulgence or the hedonistic pursuit of pleasure but as a state of tranquility impervious to the vicissitudes of life. Two themes lie at the heart of Epicurean ethics: (1) the supreme goal of life is pleasure, properly understood as the avoidance of pain and disturbance, and (2) pleasure can be attained only by freeing oneself from fear of the gods and fear of death and by suppressing the agitation caused by desires.

Before examining the Epicurean position on voluntary death, it is essential to understand how the Epicureans viewed death itself.[41] Most people are inclined to see mortality as a severe limitation on the possibility of happiness, but for Epicurus and his followers death was a source of consolation, for after death the individual could be completely confident that there was nothing to fear. "Accustom yourself," Epicurus advises,

> to think that death is nothing to us, for good and evil imply sentience, and death is the privation of all sentience; therefore a right understanding that death is nothing to us makes mortality of life enjoyable, not by adding to life an illimitable time, but by taking away the yearning after immortality. For life has no terrors for him who has thoroughly apprehended that there are no terrors for him in ceasing to live. Foolish, therefore, is the man who says that he fears death, not because it will pain him when it comes, but because it pains in the prospect. Whatsoever causes no annoyance when it is present, causes only a groundless pain in the expectation. Death, therefore, the most awful of evils, is nothing to us, seeing that, when we are, death is not come, and, when death is come, we are not. It is nothing, then, either to the living or to the dead, for with the living it is not and the dead exist no longer.[42]

Once the fear of death is removed, human beings are free to enjoy the fullness of pleasure (that is, the absence of pain) in the present. How can one overcome the fear of death? If one's opinions about the gods are false, then evils will follow: fear of divine retribution, superstition, and above all fear of death. If, in contrast, one holds true opinions about the gods (that they exist in undisturbed tranquility, neither caring about nor intervening in human affairs), this will be the source of very great pleasure. Since the soul is merely the confluence of certain atoms that are dissolved at the moment of death, death entails the end of all sensation. "The magnitude of pleasure," according to Epicurus, "reaches its limit in the removal of all pain."[43] Thus, death no longer holds any terror, for "unlimited time and limited time afford an equal amount of pleasure, if we measure the limits of that pleasure [i.e., the absence of pain] by reason."[44]

Given this understanding of death, it is not surprising that the Epicureans did not oppose the right of an individual to take his own life when circumstances warranted it. Nevertheless, the decision to take oneself out should not to be made capriciously or irrationally:

> In the world, at one time men shun death as the greatest of all evils, and at another time choose it as a respite from the evils of life. The wise man does not deprecate life nor does he fear the cessation of life. The thought of life is no offense to him, nor is the cessation of life regarded as an evil. And even as men

choose of food not merely and simply the larger portion, but the more pleasant, so the wise seek to enjoy the time which is most pleasant and not merely that which is longest.[45]

Epicurus exhorted his followers to consider carefully whether they would prefer death to come to them, or would themselves go to death.[46] According to Lucretius, the famous poet of the sect, "for fear of death men are seized by hatred of life and of seeing the light, so that with sorrowing heart they devise their own death, forgetting that fear is the fountain of their cares."[47] Voluntary death should not be undertaken for trivial reasons, such as, paradoxically, the fear of death.

Among the collection of Epicurean maxims preserved by Diogenes Laertius there is the following injunction: "Even when [the wise person] has lost his sight, he will not withdraw himself from life." [48] This is not a condemnation of voluntary death per se; it is only pointing out that losing one's sight is not so devastating a blow that one should therefore kill himself. But there are circumstances in which an individual may legitimately take his or her own life. Cicero states the Epicurean position on voluntary death as follows: "For Epicurus represents the wise man as always happy. Death he disregards; he has a true conception, untainted by fear of the immortal gods. If it be expedient to depart from life, he does not hesitate to do so."[49] This is confirmed by another saying of Epicurus: "It is wrong to live under constraint [necessitas]; but no man is constrained to live under constraint."[50] Cicero summarizes the Epicurean position by means of the following analogy:

> For my part I think we should observe the rule which is followed at Greek banquets: "Let him either drink," it runs, "or leave!" And rightly; for either he should enjoy the pleasure of drinking with the others or get away early, that a sober man may not be a victim to the violence of those who are heated with wine. Thus by running away one can escape the assaults of Fortune which one cannot face. This is the same advice as Epicurus gives.[51]

Epicurus himself did not commit suicide but chose to endure the agony of his final illness. Writing to Idomeneus near the end of his life, Epicurus said, "My continual sufferings . . . are so great that nothing could augment them; but over against them all I set happiness at the remembrance of our past conversations."[52] The happiness that is a complete absence of pain from both body and mind is the happiness of the gods; human beings enjoy it insofar as they are able. The Epicurean wise person, Cicero tells us, "is schooled to encounter pain by recollecting that pains of great severity are ended by death, and slight ones have frequent intervals of respite; while those of medium intensity lie within our own control. We can bear them if they are endurable, or if they are not, we may serenely quit life's theater, when the play has ceased to please us."[53] Epicurus was able to endure what others apparently could not. Among his followers, Lucretius died by his own hand, as did also Cassius, Atticus the friend of Cicero, Petronius, and the philosopher Diodorus.

STOICS

The Stoics had much in common with the Epicureans. Both schools rejected the idealism of Plato and conceived of reality in materialistic terms, reviving earlier conceptions of matter: the Epicureans, as we have seen, the "atomism" of Leucippus and Democritus; the Stoics, the notions of fire and breath of Heraclitus and other pre-Socratic thinkers. Both schools sought to ground the good in human happiness, namely, peace of mind and tranquility (*ataraxia*). The difference between them was in the means by which this could be achieved. The Epicureans sought to free themselves from nature's law, while the Stoics sought to submit to it.

The Stoic school was founded by Zeno of Citium (335–263 B.C.), who had been a disciple of the Cynic philosopher Crates. From him Zeno learned the Cynic ideals of freedom, self-sufficiency, and life according to nature. Unlike the Cynics, however, the Stoics had an elaborate philosophical system, comprising logic, physics, and ethics. Their ethics were integrally related to their conception of how the universe worked. According to the Stoics, the formative and guiding principle in the universe is the impersonal Logos (Reason), sometimes identified in the language of popular religion as Zeus, which manifests itself as fate or necessity (*heimarmene*) and providence (*pronoia*). In a special way it also manifests itself in human reason (*logos*). Human nature (the microcosm), therefore, is one with the essential nature of the universe (the macrocosm).

To be virtuous, for the Stoic, is to live in harmony with R(r)eason. Since the course of the universe and every human being in it is determined, an individual's freedom consists solely of accepting that which is ordained for him or her, that is, in bringing the individual's own will into harmony with the rational purpose of the universe. This purpose is not blind fate; on the contrary, the universal Logos ordained all things in wisdom and for the good of all. Thus, the individual who lives in accord with nature (the Logos directing the universe) is completely independent of the vicissitudes of human existence: pain and pleasure, wealth and poverty, success and misfortune.[54]

The Stoics recognized the right of an individual to take his own life, but what concerned them more than the act itself was the context and manner in which it might be performed. Above all, the decision to take one's life must be done rationally (*eulogos*).[55] Diogenes Laertius reports that the Stoics "tell

us that the wise man will for reasonable cause make his own exit from life
[*exagein heauton tou biou*], on his country's behalf or for the sake of friends,
or if he suffer intolerable pain, mutilation, or incurable disease."[56] There is
little that is new here; indeed, this list is very similar to the one Plato gave in
the *Laws*.[57]

Although Diogenes Laertius mentions only certain circumstances when the
Stoic wise person *may* commit suicide, according to Chrysippus, there are occasions when the wise person *will* commit suicide, when it will be an appropriate
act (*kathekon*):

> When a man's circumstances contain a preponderance of things in accordance
> with nature, it is appropriate for him to remain alive; when he possesses or sees
> in prospect a majority of the contrary things, it is appropriate for him to depart
> from life. This makes it plain that it is on occasion appropriate for the wise man
> to quit life although he is happy, and also of the foolish man to remain in life
> although he is miserable. . . . For the Stoic view is that happiness, which means
> life in harmony with nature, is a matter of seizing the right moment. So that wis-
> dom itself on occasion bids the wise man to leave it. Hence, as vice does not pos-
> sess the power of furnishing a reason for voluntary death, it is clear that even for
> the foolish, who are also miserable, it is appropriate to remain alive if they pos-
> sess a preponderance of those things which we pronounce to be in accordance
> with nature. And since the fool is equally miserable when departing from life and
> when remaining in it, and the undesirability of his life is not increased by its pro-
> longation, there is good ground for saying that those who are in a position to
> enjoy a preponderance of things that are natural ought to remain in life.[58]

According to Chrysippus, there are occasions when the wise person should
kill himself and the fool remain alive. Nevertheless, the decision to live or die
should not be based on happiness or unhappiness but on whether or not individuals can expect their lives to contain "a preponderance of things in accordance with nature." There will be circumstances when the wise person,
although happy, should choose death, and the fool, though miserable, should
go on living. Happiness, for the Stoics, meant life according to nature. When
circumstances render such a life no longer possible, then the wise person will
take himself out. Voluntary death, therefore, is a matter of "seizing the right
moment."

The first half of Chrysippus's proposition, that there are occasions when
the wise individual will reason in favor of a self-inflicted death, echoes earlier
statements, but the second half of the proposition presents a new twist. It is
precisely the opposite of the Cynic view that if one cannot live rationally he is
better off dead. Chrysippus argues to the contrary, that it may be appropriate
for the fool to remain alive.[59]

Quoting Chrysippus directly, Plutarch notes that the Stoics were in the habit of restraining the foolish from taking their own lives:

> In the books on Exhortation where he attacks Plato for saying that one who has not learned or does not know how to live had better not be alive [*Clitophon* 408a], he has the following statement word for word: "Such an assertion is self-contradictory and also least effective as exhortation. For in the first place by indicating that it is best for us not to be alive and in a sense requiring us to die it would exhort us to do something other than philosophize, for it is not possible to philosophize without being alive nor possible either to have become prudent without having survived a long time in vice and ignorance. . . . For in the first place virtue all by itself is no reason for our living, and so neither is vice any reason why we need to depart this life."[60]

Chrysippus seems to have concerned himself with the question of whether the "fool" is ever able to justify taking his own life, but his position cannot be determined with absolute precision. The sources are garbled and on occasion contradictory. It is telling that Chrysippus did not kill himself. If he thought that only the wise man may take his own life, this may be the reason why he did not take his own. He did not regard himself as a wise man.[61]

To understand better the Stoic position on voluntary death, it is instructive to examine the biographies of the Stoics. According to the traditions preserved by Diogenes Laertius, both Zeno and Cleanthes took their own lives when old age and illness came upon them. At the age of seventy-two Zeno was leaving his school one day when he fell and broke his toe (or finger). Striking the ground with his fist, he proceeded to quote the following line from a (lost) tragedy of Timotheus, the *Niobe*: "I come, I come, why do you call for me?" Zeno then killed himself by holding his breath.[62]

Why did Zeno kill himself? The answer is not given explicitly in the anecdote but may be inferred. It seems, as Adolf Bonhoeffer observed, that Zeno interpreted this "accident" as a divine summons, hence the quotation from the *Niobe*.[63] Bonhoeffer's explanation may strike the modern reader as ludicrous, but it is even more ludicrous to claim, as is often done, that Zeno killed himself *because* he broke his toe. More likely, as John Rist has noted, Zeno killed himself because he thought he had received the divine signal to depart.[64] Zeno supposed that the time for his departure had come, perhaps because his philosophical work was complete or, as seems more likely, because old age no longer allowed him to live according to nature. In either case, the account of Zeno's death echoes the rationale of Socrates in the *Phaedo*. Like Socrates, Zeno believed that God gives the signal for an individual's departure.[65]

The account of the death of Cleanthes, Zeno's successor, admits of a similar interpretation. Cleanthes refused to resume eating after a physician had

prescribed a two-day fast to cure an inflammation of the gums: "Declaring that
he had already gotten too far down the road, Cleanthes went on fasting the rest
of his days until his death at the same age as Zeno's."[66] Like Zeno's broken
toe, Cleanthes' inflammation of the gums was taken to be a sign indicating
death.

These stories may not be demonstrably historical, but they were meant to
be plausible. The evaluation of voluntary death contained in these anecdotes
no doubt reflects the views of the individuals who composed and preserved
them rather than the actual beliefs of Zeno or Cleanthes. In any case, we see
here an appropriation of the Socratic position on voluntary death. This is
understandable if we remember that for the Stoics the cosmic deity was the
Logos of which human reason was a part. An individual's logos, therefore,
would allow him to determine the divinely (or, more strictly, rationally)
appointed time for his exit from life.

There is another point worth considering. Earlier we noted that Chrysippus
was concerned with the question whether the fool could ever justifiably kill
himself. According to Chrysippus, only the wise person could be the judge of
when "to seize the right moment." Now there is no evidence that Zeno and
Cleanthes ever thought of themselves as wise. Does this indicate that they
viewed voluntary death as more widely justifiable for the foolish than did
Chrysippus? If anything can be deduced from the accounts of their deaths, it
may be that Zeno and Cleanthes (or whoever composed the accounts of their
deaths) believed that the foolish could, on occasion, be informed as to the
appropriate moment for death by some direct intervention of providence.[67]

The views of the later Stoics betray much more clearly the influence of the
Socratic tradition on voluntary death. For evidence we must rely on Cicero,
who seems to have considered the Stoic and Socratic views of voluntary death
to be analogous in several respects.

In *Tusculan Disputations* 1.71–75 Cicero recounts the death of Socrates
and then compares it with the death of Cato of Utica (95–46 B.C.), the famous
opponent of Julius Caesar:

> Cato departed from life with a feeling of joy in having found a reason for death;
> for the God who is master within us forbids our departure without permission.
> When, however, God himself has given a valid reason, as he did in the past to
> Socrates and in our day to Cato and to many others, then with certainty your
> true wise man will joyfully go forth from the darkness here into the light
> beyond. All the same, he will not break the bonds of his prison house—the law
> forbids it—but as if in obedience to a magistrate or some lawful authority, he
> will go forth at the summons and release of God. For the whole life of the
> philosopher, as the same wise man says, is a preparation for death.[68]

As this passage makes clear, Cicero holds that an individual may depart from life only when a signal to do so has been received from the deity. When such a sign is given, death should be entered into joyfully, since it is a haven and refuge from life's troubles. This understanding of voluntary death appears later in the *Tusculans*, although Cato is not mentioned:

> For our part, if it happens that it seems a sentence delivered by God, that we depart from life, let us obey joyfully and thankfully and consider that we are being set free from prison and loosed from our chains, in order that we may pass on our way to the eternal home which is clearly ours, or else be free of all sensation and trouble.[69]

A similar view is expressed in Cicero's *Dream of Scipio*, where the question is raised, as in the *Phaedo*, if death is a gain, why not die at once? The answer is much the same: until God permits, a person must continue his earthly tasks:

> For unless that God, whose temple is everything you see, has freed you from the prison of the body, you cannot gain entrance there. . . . Wherefore you, Publius, and all good men, must leave that soul in the custody of the body, and must not abandon human life except at the behest of him by whom it was given you, lest you appear to have shirked the duty imposed upon man by God.[70]

Cicero's tone and language are Platonic, and it remains to be seen to what extent his view follows the theory and practice of earlier Stoics. In a passage from *On Duties* Cicero portrays Cato as the ideal Stoic sage and martyr and seems to justify Cato's act of self-destruction solely on the ground that Cato was a wise man (*sapiens*). For others in Cato's position voluntary death would have been wrong:

> Diversity of character carries with it so great a significance that death may be for one man a duty, for another under the same circumstances not a duty. Did Marcus Cato find himself in one predicament, and were the others who surrendered to Caesar in Africa, in another? And yet, perhaps, they would have been condemned if they had taken their lives; for their mode of life had been less austere and their characters more pliable. But Cato had been endowed by nature with an austerity beyond belief, and he himself had strengthened it by unswerving consistency and had remained ever true to his purpose and fixed resolve; and it was for him to die rather than to look upon the face of a tyrant.[71]

Cicero argues that in similar circumstances one man (in this case, Cato) ought to kill himself, whereas another ought not. Cato's circumstances after the triumph of Caesar were the same as those of other men, but it was Cato's character that set him apart. Cicero's description of Cato—his austerity, constant resolve, and manner of life—fits the model of the ideal Stoic sage. If this is the case, then Cicero appears to be justifying Cato's death solely on the ground that he was a wise man. The decision of the wise man to take his own life will, as a matter of course, be a rational decision. This runs parallel to the view the early Stoics and, in particular, Chrysippus held regarding voluntary death, namely, that the wise man—and only the wise man—will be able to determine the appropriate time for his departure. For everyone else—the foolish—a divine signal will be necessary. In other words, Cicero's views on voluntary death appear to weave together the Socratic and Stoic positions.[72]

When we turn to Seneca in the first century A.D., we encounter a distinct shift in perspective, in part a result of the new political reality of the Roman Empire. Whereas for the early Stoics voluntary death remained in the background of philosophical discussion, with Seneca the problem assumes center stage.[73] Indeed, Seneca extols voluntary death as the act par excellence of the free man.[74] Instead of invoking the Socratic and earlier Stoic view that an individual should not take his own life until God gives the signal to depart, Seneca emphasizes the right to die in general. He repeatedly refers to voluntary death as the path to liberty, as proof that an individual cannot be held against his will:

> In any kind of slavery the way lies open to freedom. If the soul is sick and because of its own imperfection unhappy, a man may end its sorrows and at the same time himself. . . . In whatever direction you turn your eyes, there lies the means to end your woes. Do you see that cliff? Down there is the way to freedom. Do you see that ocean, that river, that well? There sits freedom at the bottom. Do you see that tree . . . ? From its branches hangs freedom. Do you see that throat of yours, that stomach, that heart? They are ways of escape from slavery. Do you ask what is the path to freedom? Any vein in your body![75]

Like Cicero, Seneca frequently mentions the Republican hero Cato as an example of how to die nobly. But Seneca's Cato would have made Cicero's blush! One passage in particular is worth quoting at length:

> I do not know what nobler sight Jupiter could find on earth . . . than the spectacle of Cato, after his cause had already been shattered more than once, nevertheless standing erect amid the ruins of the republic. "Although," said he, "all the world has fallen under one man's sway, although Caesar's legions guard the land, his fleets the sea, and Caesar's troops beset the city gates, yet Cato has a way of escape; with one single hand he will open a wide path to freedom. This sword, unstained and blameless even in civil war, shall at last do good and noble service: the freedom that it could not give to his country it shall give to Cato! Essay, my soul, the task long planned; deliver yourself from human affairs. Already Petreius and Juba have met and lie fallen, each slain by the other's hand. Their compact with fate was brave and noble, but for my greatness such

would be unfit. For Cato it were as ignoble to beg death from any man as to beg life." I am sure that the gods looked on with exceeding joy while that hero, most ruthless in avenging himself, took thought for the safety of others and arranged the escape of his departing followers; while even on his last night he pursued his studies; while he drove the sword into his sacred breast; while he scattered his vitals, and drew forth by his hand that holiest spirit, too noble to be defiled by the steel.[76] I should like to believe that this is why the wound was not well-aimed and efficacious—it was not enough for the immortal gods to look but once on Cato. His virtue was held in check and called back that it might display itself in a harder roll; for to seek death needs not so great a soul as to reseek it. Surely the gods looked with pleasure upon their pupil as he made his escape by so glorious and memorable an end![77]

According to Seneca, Cato *proved* his freedom by taking his life. And although Seneca still compares Cato to Socrates (as Cicero had), he intentionally ignores any suggestion that God provided a particular sign indicating death. This represents a considerable shift in Stoic thinking about voluntary death: "To allow for suicide in certain circumstances is one thing, to exalt it is quite another."[78] Still, the difference may be one of degree, for Socrates had also emphasized the benefits, and hence desirability, of death in general (though for clearly different reasons).

Quoting Epicurus, Seneca advises the long-suffering Lucilius to " 'think on death.' In saying this, Epicurus bids us to think on freedom."[79] An earlier letter to Lucilius concludes with another quote from Epicurus: " 'It is wrong to live under constraint, but no man is constrained to live under constraint.' Of course not! On all sides lie many short and simple paths to freedom."[80] Seneca's famous *70th Epistle*, which for all intents and purposes is a panegyric to death (or freedom), begins with the maxim that "the wise man will live as long as he ought, not as long as he can," and continues by insisting that the wise man will consider death long before he is under extreme compulsion (*in necessitate ultima*).[81] Seneca's use of the term *necessitas* here is a deliberate, albeit distorted, allusion to the Socratic theory of the *anangke*, the divine sign indicating death. Seneca maintains that an individual has the right to take his life irrespective of any divine signal. For Seneca, voluntary death is the assertion of human freedom.

In the same letter Seneca emphatically opposes philosophers who condemn voluntary death (i.e., the Pythagoreans) as those who "shut off the path to freedom."[82] It is the deity who has arranged things so that individuals can never be kept in this life against their wills:

Above all, I [God] have taken pains that nothing should keep you here against your will. The way is open. If you do not choose to fight, you may run away.

Therefore, of all things I have deemed necessary for you, I have made nothing easier than dying. I have set life on a downward slope: if it is prolonged only observe and you will see what a short and easy path leads to freedom.[83]

Thus, it is by no means contrary to the will of God if at any time an individual chooses to end his life. It is precisely because of the divine order of things that one is at all times free to die.[84] Furthermore, as John Rist perceptively notes, "it seems that not only is the choice of suicide open to everyone, it is also particularly ennobling—a wholly novel concept for a Stoic. Apparently the fool can be transformed into a sage by a well-judged and opportune death. Here indeed is the concept of the *ambitiosa mors.*"[85]

It is true that Seneca recognizes factors that may keep an individual from killing himself,[86] but his emphasis on voluntary death as the supremely free act and his neglect of the requirement of a divine call represent a considerable alteration in the typical Stoic position. It may be that his attitude reflects the appropriation of earlier Stoic views to his own day, when voluntary death was an almost daily occurrence and a common means of protest among the philosophical opposition to the Roman emperors. In any case, it is not clear how Seneca would have defended his own self-inflicted death as a supremely free act, since it was carried out at the command of Nero in the spring of A.D. 65. [87] As the Roman historian Tacitus remarked on the forced suicide of a certain Asiaticus during the reign of the emperor Claudius (A.D. 47), his freedom consisted only of the *means* of his death![88]

Seneca's fascination with voluntary death strikes the modern reader as exaggerated and extreme—indeed, pathological—but it would be a serious historical misjudgment to dismiss it as such. The "lust for death" in this period was widespread and, as Arthur Darby Nock suggests, had various causes: the aura surrounding voluntary death in legend and life, a certain stridency of self-expression, a desire for theatrical prominence, and the popular notion of the body as the prison of the soul.[89] The self-immolation of Peregrinus is a good example. Seneca himself recognized a *libido moriendi* so widespread among his contemporaries that even he was critical of it. Similarly, Epictetus (c. A.D. 55–c. 135), the well-known slave turned Stoic philosopher, knew of a death wish among his young Greek students so strong that he felt obligated to rein it in. These young men appealed to him in the following manner:

Are we not akin to God, and have we not come from him? Allow us to go back whence we came; allow us to be freed from these chains that are fastened to us and weigh us down. Here there are thieves and robbers, and courts of law, and those who are called tyrants. They think that they have some power over us because of this paltry body and its possessions. Let us show them that they have no power over us.[90]

The death wish of these Greeks has two causes: first, a longing to escape from earthly troubles and, in particular, from the prison of the body, and, second, an equally strong desire to return "home," to attain immortality by reuniting with the deity.[91] In an attempt to restrain these men, Epictetus addressed them in language reminiscent of Socrates in the *Phaedo*: "Men, wait upon God. When he shall give the signal to depart and set you free from this service, then you shall depart to him. But for the present endure to remain in the place where he has stationed you."[92] Epictetus goes on to refer to the example of Socrates and freely paraphrases his words in the *Apology* (28e, 29c) where Socrates speaks of being given a post that must not be deserted.[93]

In view of these passages, it should come as no surprise that Epictetus displays considerably more moderation than Seneca on the problem of voluntary death. Epictetus is concerned more with the problem of death in general, and he insists repeatedly on its indifferent status. "Of things," Epictetus declares, "some are good, others bad, and still others indifferent [*adiaphora*]. Now the virtues and everything that shares in them are good, while vices and everything that shares in vice are bad, and what falls in between these, namely, wealth, health, life, death, pleasures, pain, are indifferent."[94] Elsewhere, he asks, "What is death? A terrifying mask. Turn it around and learn what it is. See, it does not bite. The paltry body must be separated from the bit of spirit, either now or later, just as it existed apart from it before. Why are you grieved, then, if it be separated now? For if it be not separated now, it will be later."[95] Once again Epictetus appeals to the example of Socrates who, in the *Phaedo*, exposed death as nothing more than a terrifying mask (*mormolukeion*).[96]

Absent from Epictetus is the exaggerated fascination with voluntary death as the free act par excellence. According to Epictetus, an individual ought not to give up on life irrationally or for frivolous reasons. Like Socrates, Epictetus maintains that God provides the sign indicating that an individual should remove himself. "Only let me not give up my life irrationally," he declares,

> only let me not give up my life faintheartedly, or from some casual pretext. For again, God does not so desire; for he has need of such a universe, and of such men who go to and fro upon earth. But if he gives the signal to retreat, as he did to Socrates, I must obey him who gives the signal, as I would a general.[97]

This statement is a far cry from Seneca's position. Whereas Seneca argued that it was precisely because of the divine order of things that individuals are always free to kill themselves, Epictetus maintains that voluntary death is justified only when a divine signal has been received. Epictetus's position is consistent with the views of the earlier Stoics: Zeno and Cleanthes, Chrysippus, and Cicero.

Nevertheless, on occasion Epictetus neglects the idea of voluntary death at God's command and approaches the Cynic position: if the trials and hardships of life cannot be endured, then one simply gives up. "Death is my harbor," Epictetus says. "And this is the harbor of all men, even death, and this their refuge. That is why none of the things that befall us in our life is difficult. Whenever you wish, you walk out of the house, and are no longer bothered by the smoke."[98]

In another passage Epictetus likens human existence to a game in which moral principles are the rules. If one is compelled to break a rule—"to do something foolish or unseemly"—then one stops playing the game.[99] But simple adversity is usually not a sufficient ground for self-killing. In general it is warranted only in cases when it is no longer possible to live according to nature, or, more specifically, when a divine signal has been received:

> For this reason the good and excellent man, bearing in mind who he is, and whence he has come, and by whom he was created, centers his attention on this and only this: how he may fill his place in an orderly fashion and with due obedience to God. Is it your will that I should still remain? I will remain as a free man, as a noble man, as you wish it; for you have made me free from hindrance in what was my own. And now have you no further need of me? Be it well with you. I have been waiting here until now because of you and none other, and now I obey you and depart. How do you depart? Again, as you wish it, as a free man, as your servant, as one who has perceived your commands and your prohibitions. But so long as I continue to live in your service, what manner of man would you have me be? An official or a private citizen, a senator or one of the common people, a soldier or a general, a teacher or the head of a household? Whatsoever station and post you assign me, I will die ten thousand times, as Socrates says, or else abandon it. And where would you have me be? In Rome, or in Athens, or in Thebes, or in Gyara? Only remember me there. If you send me to a place where men have no means of living in accordance with nature, I shall depart this life, not in disobedience to you, but as though you were sounding the recall for me. I do not abandon you—far be that from me!—but I perceive that you have no need of me. Yet if there be vouchsafed a means of living in accordance with nature, I will seek no other place than that in which I am.[100]

In his *Meditations*, the Stoic emperor Marcus Aurelius (A.D. 161–80) presents a number of differing views on voluntary death, some of them contradictory. On the one hand, he quotes Epictetus and refers to death as a way out when circumstances make it impossible for an individual to live rationally;[101] on the other hand, he recommends endurance in the face of pain and hardship.[102] In one place Marcus approaches the Cynic position. "Who is there," he asks, "to hinder you from being good and sincere? Resolve then to live no longer if such you cannot be. For neither does reason [*logos*] in that case insist that you should."[103] It is either reason or the noose.

In another passage Marcus implies that it may be prudent to kill oneself *before* one's powers of reasoning fail:

> If a man has entered upon his dotage, there will still be his the power of breathing, digestion, thought, desire, and all such faculties; but the full use of himself, the accurate appreciation of the items of duty, the nice discrimination of what presents itself to the senses, and a clear judgment on the question whether it is time for him to end his own life, and all such decisions, as above all require well-trained powers of reasoning—these are already flickering out in him.[104]

If a person is going to kill himself, then he should do so in a dignified manner and above all without theatrics (*atragodos*). The latter, according to Marcus (or a scribe), was the hallmark of the Christian martyrs:

> What a soul is that which is ready to be released from the body at any requisite moment, and be quenched or dissipated or hold together! But the readiness must spring from a man's inner judgment, and not be the result of mere obstinance [as is the case with the Christians]. It must be associated with deliberation and dignity and, if others too are to be convinced, without theatrics.[105]

Although the Stoics shared many assumptions about when it was appropriate for an individual to abandon life, there was no single Stoic theory of voluntary death. Nor did the Stoics devote much attention to evaluating critically the assumptions on which their views were based. For this we must go outside the school to the Platonists of late antiquity and, in particular, to Plotinus.

NEOPLATONISTS

Our knowledge of the life of Plotinus (A.D. 205–69/70) comes from his biographer and most accomplished disciple, Porphyry. It was Porphyry who was responsible for collecting and editing Plotinus's writings in six *Enneads*, or groups of nine, and publishing them sometime between A.D. 300 and 305. The essays that comprise the *Enneads* range over the whole field of ancient philosophy and form the basis of the philosophical movement known as Neoplatonism, a new synthesis of Platonic, Pythagorean, Aristotelian, and Stoic elements.[106] Neoplatonism was the dominant philosophy of the Greek and Roman world from the middle of the third century down to the close of antiquity, and it exerted a strong influence on Christian theology.

In a fragment of Plotinus not found in the *Enneads* but preserved by a later Aristotelian commentator, we have a summary of Plotinus's argument against the Stoic position on voluntary death:

> Plotinus writes a single treatise about reasonable departure [*peri eulogou exagoges*] and does not accept any of these five ways.[107] He says that just as God does not leave off taking thought for us . . . ; and just as the sun dispenses its light equally . . . ; so the philosopher must imitate God and the sun and not neglect his body altogether in caring for his soul, but take thought for it in the appropriate way until it becomes unfit and separates itself from its community with the soul. It is all wrong to take oneself out before the right time, when he who bound body and soul together looses the bond.[108]

This is a clear reference to the Pythagorean argument of Socrates in the *Phaedo* (62c). What is interesting about this passage is that it attempts to demonstrate that voluntary death is "irrational" in Stoic terms.

In *Ennead* 1.9 Plotinus argues that individuals who do violence to themselves inevitably fall prey to the passions of disgust, grief, or anger. In other words, and against the Stoics, Plotinus holds that it is impossible to decide *rationally* to kill oneself. This argument is supported by an appeal to fate (*heimarmene*). "If each man has a destined time allotted to him," Plotinus says, "it is not a good thing to go out before it, unless, as we maintain, it is necessary." But the point of the treatise is to demonstrate that it is never necessary to kill oneself, for "if each man's rank in the other world depends on his state when he goes out, one must not take out the soul as long as there is any possibility of progress." As Rist notes, "It seems unlikely that Plotinus thought that anyone was good beyond all possibility of improvement, and hence withdrawal is to be rejected."[109]

Plotinus's position on voluntary death is illuminated by what Porphyry tells us in his biography. As a young man Porphyry suffered a serious bout of melancholy and decided to take his own life, but he was dissuaded by Plotinus:

> He once noticed that I, Porphyry, was thinking of removing myself from this life. He came to me unexpectedly while I was staying indoors in my house and told me that this lust for death did not come from a settled rational decision but from a melancholic disease, and urged me to go away for a holiday. I obeyed him and went to Sicily. . . . So I was brought to abandon my longing for death.[110]

Here Plotinus employs a Stoic argument to dissuade Porphyry from killing himself, for the claim that his decision had not been made "rationally" is, strictly speaking, Stoic. This would seem to imply that voluntary death could, in certain circumstances, be rationally defended. Is this what Plotinus meant?

In *Ennead* 1.4.16 Plotinus states that the wise man "must give to his bodily life as much as it needs and he can, but he is himself other than it and free to abandon it, and he will abandon it in nature's good time, and, besides, has the right to decide about this for himself." The answer to our question, then, appears to be yes, an individual does have the right to decide whether or not to kill himself.

Other passages in the *Enneads* support this view. "The way lies open to depart," Plotinus declares, "if it is not possible to live well."[111] Similarly, he says, "If you have come by now to dislike the world, you are not compelled to remain a citizen of it."[112] A problem arises when we attempt to reconcile these passages with Plotinus's views in *Ennead* 1.9 and the Elias fragment, both of which condemned voluntary death. In the former passage Plotinus had said that "it is not a good thing to go out before the time allotted him, unless, as we maintain, it is necessary" (*anangkaion*). This sounds Platonic, for Socrates had argued that one should not kill himself until God brings some *anangke* (necessity) to bear on him (*Phaedo* 62c). If we evaluate the phrase "unless it is necessary" in light of other passages in which Plotinus holds open the possibility of voluntary death, then it would appear that he did allow for suicide in certain extreme situations. But this may be to "stoicize" Plotinus in a way that does not do justice to all the passages in which he treats voluntary death.

John M. Rist has shown the way to a correct interpretation.[113] In various passages of the *Enneads* Plotinus maintains that the soul has the right to decide whether to remain in the body or not, but—and this is the crucial point—the good soul should always choose to remain. Support for this interpretation is to be found in *Ennead* 1.8.6, where Plotinus offers an exegesis of a passage in Plato's *Theaetetus* (176a). Plotinus argues that the Platonic notion of "flight to the beyond" does not mean leaving this life but rather means living in accordance with the precepts of justice, holiness, and wisdom.[114] It is incorrect to maintain that Plotinus thought that voluntary death was ever *in practice* justifiable.[115] Although an individual can choose for or against voluntary death, the good individual will always choose against it. Plotinus sets forth a reconciliation of the Platonic and Stoic traditions on voluntary death. He learned from the Pythagorean argument of Socrates in the *Phaedo* that to kill oneself was to abandon one's post, but he was also aware of the Stoic view that an individual has the right to choose between life and death. From these two positions Plotinus fashioned his own independent view.

The arguments of the later Platonists against voluntary death are nicely summarized in Macrobius's *Commentary on the Dream of Scipio*. Macrobius flourished at the end of the fourth and beginning of the fifth centuries and has been identified by some with a contemporary Macrobius who held high governmental positions.[116] In the first book of his *Commentary* he devotes an entire chapter to the problem of voluntary death (1.13).[117] Macrobius discusses this problem in relation to the response of Aemilius Paulus, Scipio's father, in Cicero's *Dream of Scipio*. Having seen his dead father, Scipio begins to desire death:

> I beg you, most revered and best of fathers, since this is truly life, . . . why do I linger on earth? Why do I not hasten hither to you? You are mistaken, he replied, for until that God who rules all the region of the sky at which you are now looking has freed you from the fetters of your body, you cannot gain admission here (1.13.3).

Macrobius maintains that this is consistent with the view of Plato in the *Phaedo* (1.13.5–8) and also of Plotinus, who developed Plato's doctrine more fully (1.13.9–16).[118]

But what of the person who is completely purified? Should he not take his own life, since there is no reason for him to remain in the body? Macrobius's answer is no, for

> the very act of summoning death ahead of time in the hope of enjoying blessedness ensnares a man in a net of passion, since hope is a passion as well as fear. . . . This explains why Aemelius Paulus forbade his son, hoping for a truer life to hasten him. He did not want Scipio's rash yearning for freedom and resurrection to bind him and hold him back the more because of his passion (1.13.17–18).[119]

His rejection of voluntary death notwithstanding, Macrobius admits to one exception. He concludes the chapter by reminding the reader that Scipio's father "did not tell him that he *could not die* unless a natural death overtook him, but that he could not gain admission there: *for until God . . . has freed you from the fetters of your body, you cannot gain admission here*" (1.13.18–19). According to Macrobius, the only exception to the prohibition against dying voluntarily is the explicit command of God to do so. Despite eight centuries of philosophical debate, the Socratic "loophole" has not been closed—nor, for that matter, has the problem of how to recognize that the command is divine been resolved.[120]

SUMMARY

The preceding survey has endeavored to treat most of the major texts in which the philosophical discussion of voluntary death appears. Brief and attenuated as many of these passages are, they are sufficiently numerous to allow us to sketch the history of the problem. We have tried to indicate where the most important philosophical schools stood on the question of voluntary death and what significance they attached to it. Here it was observed that a passage from Plato's *Phaedo* attracted considerable attention and came to serve both as a justification for and as a means of moderating against the act of taking one's life.

With the exception of the Pythagoreans (and their intellectual heirs, the Neoplatonists), no philosophical school in antiquity condemned the practice of voluntary death.[121] What concerned the philosophers more than the act itself were the reasons for which an individual might justifiably choose death. The justifications varied from school to school and from philosopher to philosopher, but the general direction of the discussion took its orientation from the Platonic theory of *anangke*. Indeed, the entire philosophical discussion of voluntary death in antiquity can be understood as an attempt to solve the problem of how to recognize the *anangke*.

While the conception of death influenced the position various philosophical schools took on the problem of voluntary death, it was not the determining element in the discussion. Paradoxically, the two schools with the strongest belief in an afterlife (the Pythagoreans and Platonists) expressed the strongest opposition to voluntary death. In contrast, the Cynics and Epicureans, who did not believe in an afterlife, were prepared to defend the right of an individual to take his own life. In fact, it appears that the Cynics were prepared to die on the slightest provocation.

The Stoics occupied a middle position. For them, death meant either nonexistence or eternal bliss, but in either case their view of the afterlife was not of primary importance in their justification of voluntary death.[122] It was their conceptions of human freedom, nobility, and dignity that controlled the discourse on this problem.

Although none of the schools (again, with the exception of the Pythagoreans) absolutely condemned voluntary death, at least four arguments were advanced in an attempt to moderate against the practice. These arguments were by no means mutually exclusive, and it is possible to find one or more of them employed by particular schools and particular philosophers.

First, there was the religious argument of the Pythagoreans that voluntary death was an unjustified rebellion against God, who had joined body and soul together, and who alone had the authority to separate them. For an individual to take his own life meant to arrogate to himself a right that belonged only to God. This argument was appropriated by Plato, who qualified it by maintaining that an individual must not kill himself unless and until God brings some compulsion to bear upon him.

Second, there was the civic argument of Plato and Aristotle, which held that voluntary death was an unjustified abandonment of one's responsibilities to the state. Nevertheless, it appears that Plato and perhaps also Aristotle admitted circumstances in which an individual might justifiably choose death, for example, if one were ordered to do so by the *polis*, or if one suffered devastating misfortune or intolerable shame.

Third, there was the admonition to endurance. Both the Epicureans and Stoics admitted the right of the individual to end his or her life, but more often they counseled endurance in the face of pain, suffering, and misfortune. If these could not be endured, then voluntary death was a way out, but one that should be taken rationally and in an appropriate matter.

Finally, there was the "quietist" position of the Neoplatonists. In response to the Stoics, they argued that the decision to take oneself out could never be rational, since the individual who does violence to himself inevitably falls prey to the passions of disgust, grief, and anger.[123]

The identification of these four arguments should not lead us to assume that the discussion of voluntary death was more coherent and consistent than it was. There was considerable variety and, at times, contradiction, even within the writings of individual philosophers. The chief problems the philosophers faced, but were unable to resolve, were how to distinguish between (1) allowing oneself to be killed, (2) seeking to be killed, and (3) simply killing oneself. Cato is a good example of this conceptual confusion about the nature of voluntary death. Why did Cato choose to kill himself instead of waiting to be killed? Why did he believe that a self-inflicted death was nobler than suffering death at the hands of Caesar's henchmen? If we are to believe Seneca, the reason Cato killed himself was that it would have been a "shameful thing" (*turpe*) to beg death from any person. Cato's virtue, greatness of soul, and freedom were demonstrated by his act of self-destruction. To have allowed himself to be killed would have been an affront to his dignity as a free man. Is the crucial issue, then, a particular conception of nobility?

If we return to the example of Perpetua with which we began in the first chapter, a different set of questions emerges. Could Perpetua have killed herself? She certainly provoked her own death and, having provoked it, embraced it willingly. Indeed, she guided the sword to her throat! But the sword was first and foremost in the hand of the gladiator. How far does provocation count as seeking to be killed?

The question may be put in yet another way. Those who preserved the memory of Cato revered him as the ideal Stoic sage and martyr. Would Perpetua, or for that matter any Christian, have regarded Cato as a martyr? Would she and her coreligionists have allowed themselves the option of doing what Cato did, but "for Christ"? In both cases—Cato's and Perpetua's—concepts of human freedom and nobility informed their decisions to die. Both their deaths, moreover, smacked of the same kind of theatricality. But would either have admitted that the other suffered a *noble* death? At this stage in our investigation we can only raise these questions; it would be premature to try to answer them here. First we must explore the other great cultural tradition of which Christianity was an heir: Judaism.

NOTES

1. Albert Camus, *The Myth of Sisyphus and Other Essays*, trans. by Justin O'Brien (New York: Random House, 1955), p. 3.
2. The classic study of suicide in antiquity is still R. Hirzel, "Der Selbstmord," *Archiv für Religionswissenschaft* 11 (1908): 75–104, 243–84, 417–76 (reprinted separately as *Der Selbstmord* [Darmstadt: Wissenschaftliche Buchgesellschaft, 1967]). For a relatively complete bibliography, see Y. Grisé, *Le suicide dans la Rome antique* (Montreal: Bellarmin, 1982), pp. 299–308.
3. E. R. Dodds, *Pagan and Christian in an Age of Anxiety: Some Aspects of Religious Experience from Marcus Aurelius to Constantine* (Cambridge: Cambridge Univ. Press, 1965), p. 135.
4. A. D. Nock, *Conversion: The Old and the New in Religion from Alexander the Great to Augustine of Hippo* (Oxford: Clarendon Press, 1933), p. 197. See the list of Roman suicides compiled by Grisé, *Le suicide dans la Rome antique*, pp. 34–52. By far the greatest number occurs between 100 B.C. and A.D. 100.
5. See, for example, *Odyssey* 11.271–80 (Epicaste), 11.543–67 (Aias), and 15.353–59 (Antikleia, the mother of Odysseus; cf. 11.200–3); cf. the lament of Andromache in *Iliad* 6.405–14. See further the list of famous "suicides" in Greek legend and history assembled in A. W. Mair, "Suicide (Greek and Roman)," in J. Hastings (ed.), *Encyclopaedia of Religion and Ethics*, vol. 12 (1921), pp. 26–29.
6. Homer, *Iliad* 9.410–16.
7. Homer, *Iliad* 18.95–96.
8. Homer, *Iliad* 18.98–121. Unless otherwise indicated, translations from Greek and Latin authors are from the *Loeb Classical Library*. On occasion, however, we have altered these translations if they were not sufficiently literal or precise for our purposes.
9. Homer, *Odyssey* 11.488–91.
10. Sophocles, *Ajax* 473–80.
11. Pindar, *Nemean Ode* 7.26, 8.25; *Isthmian Ode* 4.35.
12. Sophocles, *Ajax* 1053–63.
13. Sophocles, *Ajax* 496–505.
14. A similar debate between Heracles and Theseus occurs in Euripides' *Heracles* (1246–1351). Like Ajax, Heracles decided to kill himself rather than endure his misfortune. In this case, however, Theseus convinced him that it would be more shameful to take himself out. There is a self-conscious air to the debate, but it does not introduce any new criteria for determining when and if voluntary death is appropriate. Although Heracles reached the conclusion opposite to that of Ajax, his decision was based on the same criteria: shame and honor. The fact, however, that Euripides has Heracles choose to live may indicate a desire on the

part of the poet to restrict the circumstances in which voluntary death was praise-
worthy. On this, see the excellent discussion in Arthur W. H. Adkins, "Values in
Euripides' *Hecuba* and *Hercules Furens*," *Classical Quarterly* 16 (1966): 193–219,
esp. 214–19.

15. In the *Cratylus* (400c) this view is said to be Orphic. The related doctrine of the
"body" (*soma*) as the "tomb" (*sema*) of the soul appears from the *Cratylus* passage and from *Gorgias* 493a to have been Pythagorean rather than Orphic.

16. Socrates attributes this view to the Pythagorean Philolaus (*Phaedo* 61de; see
Diels-Kranz 44 B 14). Cf. Ludwig Edelstein: "Among all Greek thinkers the
Pythagoreans alone outlawed suicide and did so without qualification. . . . Even
in later centuries the Pythagorean school is the only one represented as absolutely
opposed to suicide" (in O. Temkin and C. L. Temkin, eds., *Ancient Medicine:
Selected Papers of Ludwig Edelstein* [Baltimore, MD: Johns Hopkins Univ. Press,
1967], p. 17).

17. See, for example, David Novak, *Suicide and Morality: The Theories of Plato,
Aquinas and Kant and Their Relevance for Suicidology* (New York: Scholars
Studies Press, 1975), pp. 7–19; and David J. Melling, *Understanding Plato*
(Oxford and New York: Oxford Univ. Press, 1987), p. 65.

18. A. Alvarez, *The Savage God: A Study of Suicide* (New York: Random House,
1970), p. 60.

19. J. M. Rist, *Stoic Philosophy* (Cambridge: Cambridge Univ. Press, 1969), p. 234; cf.
Hirzel, "Der Selbstmord," p. 245, n. 2.

20. Cf. *Phaedo* 67a: in order to acquire knowledge the philosopher must keep the soul
separate from the body as much as possible "until God himself sets us free."

21. See R. Hackforth, *Plato's Phaedo* (Cambridge: Cambridge Univ. Press, 1952), p.
36, n. 4; and R. G. Frey, "Did Socrates Commit Suicide?" *Philosophy* 53 (1978):
106–8. The depiction of the death of Jesus in the Gospels is similar. For example,
the author of the Fourth Gospel has Jesus say, "No one takes [my life] from me,
but I lay it down of my own accord" (John 10:18). See our discussion in chap. 5,
pp. 114–19.

22. See *Crito* 45a–46a. Note that Aristotle, when he was charged with impiety, went
into voluntary exile rather than let the Athenians "sin twice against philosophy"
(Diogenes Laertius, *Lives of the Eminent Philosophers* 5.5).

23. *Apology* 41d. On this, see the comments of Nietzsche in "The Problem of
Socrates," *Twilight of the Idols*, trans. by R. J. Hollingdale (Harmondsworth:
Penguin Books, 1968), p. 34.

24. Rist, *Stoic Philosophy*, p. 236.

25. It should also be noted that Plato's discussion of suicide in the *Laws* is more ideal
than real. At no time did Athenian law (or, for that matter, Roman law) define
suicide as a *penal* offense. See Mair, "Suicide (Greek and Roman)," p. 30. It is
true that in Athens the corpse of one who had killed himself was buried with its
right hand amputated, but this measure seems to have been designed not so
much as a punishment for the act as an attempt to render harmless the soul of a
victim of violent death, even though a self-inflicted one.

26. Hirzel, "Der Selbstmord," pp. 264, 271.

27. Rist, *Stoic Philosophy*, p. 236; see further John M. Cooper, "Greek Philosophers on Euthanasia and Suicide," in Baruch A. Brody (ed.), *Suicide and Euthanasia: Historical and Contemporary Themes*, Philosophy and Medicine, no. 35 (Dordrecht, Boston, and London: Kluwer Academic Publishers, 1989), pp. 19–23.

28. The literature on Cynicism is enormous. The best introduction in English is still D. R. Dudley, *A History of Cynicism from Diogenes to the Sixth Century* A.D. (London: Methuen, 1937). There are a number of shortcomings in Dudley's book, however, one of which is its failure to discuss the Cynic position on voluntary death. Some interpreters, both ancient and modern, credit Antisthenes (a disciple of Socrates) with establishing the Cynic school. At a minimum it appears that Antisthenes influenced the philosophy of Diogenes.

29. Diogenes Laertius 6.24. Diogenes' collection of "lives" is the first extant attempt to write the history of Greek philosophy. Composed in the late second or early third century A.D., it is based upon much earlier sources. The entire sixth book is devoted to the Cynic school.

30. Diogenes Laertius 6.86.

31. Diogenes Laertius 6.76–77 (though there are several different accounts of his death).

32. Diogenes Laertius 6.94.

33. Diogenes Laertius 6.95.

34. Diogenes Laertius 6.100.

35. Lucian, *Demonax* 65. Earlier Lucian had commented, "[Demonax] had trained his body and hardened it for endurance and in general he made it his aim to require nothing from anyone else. Consequently, when he found out that he was no longer sufficient unto himself, he voluntarily took his departure from life, leaving behind him a great reputation among the Greeks of culture" (*Demonax* 4).

36. Lucian, *Death of Peregrinus* 20–41.

37. See Hirzel, "Der Selbstmord," pp. 283–84. According to legend, Heracles cremated himself on Mt. Oeta with the help of his son Philoctetes and with the hope of attaining immortality.

38. Lucian, *Death of Peregrinus* 20–25, 38–39. Peregrinus's self-immolation actually took place at Harpina, two miles from Olympia, and on the day after the Games concluded (20). Lucian is probably wrong, therefore, that Peregrinus's death was merely an attempt to achieve notoriety.

39. Diogenes Laertius 6.71. It was above all Heracles whom the Cynics regarded as embodying this ideal. See Rist, *Stoic Philosophy*, p. 237.

40. For an instructive survey of Epicureanism, see J. M. Rist, *Epicurus: An Introduction* (Cambridge: Cambridge Univ. Press, 1972).

41. On this, see F. D. Miller, "Epicurus on the Art of Dying," *Southern Journal of Philosophy* 14 (1976): 169–77.

42. Diogenes Laertius 10.124–25. Cf. 10.139: "Death is nothing to us; for the body, when it has been resolved into its elements, has no feeling, and that which has no feeling is nothing to us" (*Kyriai Doxai* 2).

43. Diogenes Laertius 10.139 (*Kyriai Doxai* 3).

44. Diogenes Laertius 10.145. See further Rist, *Epicurus*, pp. 119–20.

45. Diogenes Laertius 10.125–26.

46. See Seneca, *Epistle* 26.8–10, for a summary of the view of Epicurus.

47. Lucretius, *On the Nature of Things* 3.79–82.

48. Diogenes Laertius 10.119.

49. Cicero, *On the Ends of Goods and Evils* 1.62. In the same treatise Cicero reports that the Epicureans permitted voluntary death in cases of extreme physical suffering (cf. 1.49).

50. Preserved by Seneca, *Epistle* 12.10.

51. Cicero, *Tusculan Disputations* 5.118.

52. Diogenes Laertius 10.22. That Epicurus chose to endure the pain of his final illness is probably the reason why the Epicureans had the reputation of opposing voluntary death in general.

53. Cicero, *On the Ends of Goods and Evils* 1.49.

54. What we have presented here is just a rough sketch of Stoic philosophy, without taking into account the various developments in the history of the school (viz. the Old, Middle, and Late Stoa). All the writings of the early Stoics (notably Zeno, Cleanthes, and Chrysippus) have not survived and are preserved for us only in "fragments" (collected by von Arnim) and from accounts of later writers, especially Diogenes Laertius. See further Rist's valuable survey *Stoic Philosophy*.

55. See the fragments collected by Hans von Arnim, *Stoicorum Veterum Fragmenta*, 4 vols. (Leipzig: Teubner, 1905–24), 3.757–68; the discussion in Grisé, *Le suicide dans la Rome antique*, pp. 180–84, 193–223; and Rist, *Stoic Philosophy*, pp. 238–55. Our analysis is indebted to Rist at several points.

56. Diogenes Laertius 7.130.

57. Similar lists are found elsewhere. The best example is cited by von Arnim, *Stoicorum Veterum Fragmenta* 3.768: "Rational departures [*eulogoi exagogai*] occur in the following five ways: Either (1) on account of a great necessity, as when the Pythia commands that someone sacrifice himself on behalf of his polis . . . , or (2) because tyrants, acting as uncontrolled revellers, compel us to do base things or speak the unspeakable; or (3) because terrible sickness in the entire body prevents the soul from making use of the body; . . . or (4) because of poverty; . . . or (5) because of a trivial matter" (trans. by J. Andrew Foster).

58. Preserved by Cicero, *On the Ends of Goods and Evils* 3.60–61. Cf. Plutarch, *Stoic Self-Contradictions* 1042d, where this view is ascribed to Chrysippus himself.

59. Plutarch, *On Common Conceptions* 1063d: "The Stoics speed many sages from life on the ground that it is better for them to have done being happy and restrain many base men from dying on the ground that they ought to live on in unhappiness."

60. Plutarch, *Stoic Self-Contradictions* 1039de. Plutarch goes on, however, to state that Chrysippus contradicted himself by endorsing the view of Antisthenes that

one needs either "intelligence" (*nous*) or the "noose" (*brochos*). A similar remark is attributed to Diogenes the Cynic (Diogenes Laertius 6.24) and his disciple, Crates (*Gnomologium Vaticanum* 386).

61. For the complexities of Chrysippus's views, see further Rist, *Stoic Philosophy*, pp. 239–42.

62. Diogenes Laertius 7.28.

63. A. Bonhoeffer, *Die Ethik des Stoikers Epictet* (Stuttgart: Enke, 1894), pp. 38–39. This was already recognized by John Donne, *Biathanatos* 1.2.3.

64. Rist, *Stoic Philosophy*, p. 243.

65. So again Rist, *Stoic Philosophy*, p. 243.

66. Diogenes Laertius 7.176.

67. We owe this observation to Rist, *Stoic Philosophy*, p. 243.

68. Cicero, *Tusculan Disputations* 1.74. According to Plutarch, Cato himself was inspired by the example of Socrates and read the *Phaedo* the night before he fell on his sword (*Cato Minor* 67–68).

69. Cicero, *Tusculan Disputations* 1.118.

70. Cicero, *On the Republic* 6.15–16.

71. Cicero, *On Duties* 1.112.

72. On this, see Rist, *Stoic Philosophy*, p. 245.

73. A complete collection of the relevant primary sources, including passages in the tragedies, is provided by N. Tadic-Guilloteaux, "Sénèque face au suicide," *L'antiquité classique* 32 (1963): 541–51.

74. See Rist, *Stoic Philosophy*, pp. 246–50. Cf. M. T. Griffin, *Seneca: A Philosopher in Politics* (Oxford: Clarendon Press, 1976), pp. 367–88, who is critical of Rist's interpretation. She maintains (incorrectly, in our view) that Seneca adhered to the "orthodox" Stoic position on voluntary death.

75. Seneca, *On Anger* 3.15.3–4. Cf. *Epistles* 12.10; 26.10; 66.13; 70.5, 12, 16, 23–24; 77.15. These passages overstate the importance of voluntary death in a way that would have been unacceptable to earlier Stoics (*pace* Griffin).

76. Cato stabbed himself, but accomplished his death by tearing open the wound his physician had attempted to bind up (see Plutarch, *Cato Minor* 70).

77. Seneca, *On Providence* 2.9–12. Cf. *Epistles* 13.14; 24.6–8; 71.8–17.

78. Rist, *Stoic Philosophy*, p. 248.

79. Seneca, *Epistle* 26.10.

80. Seneca, *Epistle* 12.10.

81. Seneca, *Epistle* 70.4–5; cf. 17.9; 77.5–20.

82. Seneca, *Epistle* 70.14–15.

83. Seneca, *On Providence* 6.7.

84. See J. N. Sevenster, *Paul and Seneca*, SNT 4 (Leiden: Brill, 1961), p. 58.

85. Rist, *Stoic Philosophy*, p. 249. The reference to an "ostentatious death" occurs in Tacitus, *Agricola* 42.

86. For example, family and friends (*Epistle* 104.3–4). Seneca is also sharply critical of what he calls a "lust for death" (*libido moriendi*) among weak men (*Epistle*

24.25), and he condemns those who take their lives for mere *frivolae causae* (*Epistles* 4.4; 24.22; *On the Tranquility of the Soul* 2.15).

87. Nevertheless, Seneca's death is still in the tradition of Socrates. Although condemned by the state, Seneca was still free before God. The deaths of Seneca and his wife are reported in great detail by Tacitus, *Annals* 15.60–64; cf. Cassius Dio, *Roman History* 62.25.

88. Tacitus, *Annals* 11.3. We owe this reference to Rist, *Stoic Philosophy*, p. 248.

89. Nock, *Conversion*, p. 198.

90. Epictetus 1.9.13–15.

91. These are, *mutatis mutandis*, the reasons why the apostle Paul contemplated taking his own life. See our discussion in chap. 5.

92. Epictetus 1.9.16.

93. Epictetus 1.9.22–26. Epictetus was a student of the Stoic philosopher Musonius Rufus. Our knowledge of Epictetus's teachings derives from his disciple, Flavius Arrianus, who collected his lectures (or diatribes) and later composed a summary of his philosophy, the *Encheiridion* (or manual). Both were published posthumously and had a significant influence on the emperor Marcus Aurelius.

94. Epictetus 2.19.13.

95. Epictetus 2.1.17. Cf. 2.5.14; 3.22.33; 3.26.4; and the discussion in Bonhoeffer, *Die Ethik des Stoikers Epictet*, pp. 29–39.

96. Epictetus 2.1.15 (referring to Plato, *Phaedo* 77e).

97. Epictetus 1.29.29; cf. 1.9.16. For the influence of Socrates on Epictetus in this regard, see K. Dörrie, *Exemplum Socratis: Studien zur Sokratesnachwirkung in der kynisch-stoischen Philosophie der frühen Kaiserzeit und ihm frühen Christentum*, Hermes Einzelschriften 42 (Wiesbaden: Steiner, 1979), pp. 52–54.

98. Epictetus 4.10.27; cf. 1.25.18–20.

99. Epictetus 4.7.30–31.

100. Epictetus 3.24.96–102; cf. 2.6.20–22. Epictetus's views are in line with those of his teacher, Musonius Rufus, who said, "One who by living is of use to many has not the right to die, unless by dying he may be of use to more" (see C. E. Lutz, "Musonius Rufus: 'The Roman Socrates,'" *Yale Classical Studies* 10 [1947]: 132–33).

101. Marcus Aurelius, *Meditations* 5.29; cf. Epictetus 1.25.18; 4.10.27.

102. Marcus Aurelius, *Meditations* 7.33, 64.

103. Marcus Aurelius, *Meditations* 10.32.

104. Marcus Aurelius, *Meditations* 3.1.

105. Marcus Aurelius, *Meditations* 11.3; cf. 8.47; 10.8. The reference to Christians in 11.3 is possibly a later gloss.

106. For an excellent introduction to the life and philosophy of Plotinus, see J. M. Rist, *Plotinus: The Road to Reality* (Cambridge: Cambridge Univ. Press, 1967).

107. That is, the five reasons that the Stoics argued were justifiable (i.e., rational) pretexts for voluntary death. See n. 57 above.

108. The fragment from Elias can be found after *Ennead* 1.9 in the Loeb edition of Plotinus translated by A. H. Armstrong. See further Rist, *Plotinus*, pp. 175–76; 262 n.18; and the literature there cited.

109. Rist, *Plotinus*, p. 176. Cf. *Ennead* 4.4.44.23: "It seems reasonable (*eulogon*) not to withdraw from life because of the difficulties of acclimating oneself to living."

110. Porphyry, *Life of Plotinus* 11. On this episode, see F. Cumont, "Comment Plotin détourna Porphyre du suicide," *Revue des études grecques* 32 (1919): 113–20.

111. *Ennead* 1.4.7.31–32; cf. 1.4.7.44–45.

112. *Ennead* 2.9.9.17; cf. 2.9.8.43.

113. Rist, *Plotinus*, p. 175.

114. See, in particular, *Ennead* 1.8.6.9–13.

115. This is Rist's point; *contra* Cumont, "Comment Plotin," p. 115 and n. 3; and W. R. Inge, *The Philosophy of Plotinus*, 3rd ed. (London: Longmans, Green, 1929), vol. 2, p. 173.

116. See A. Cameron, "The Date and Identity of Macrobius," *Journal of Roman Studies* 56 (1966): 25–38. Some have maintained that Macrobius was a Christian, but there is no evidence for this.

117. We have used W. H. Stahl's translation, *Macrobius: Commentary on the Dream of Scipio* (New York: Columbia Univ. Press, 1952).

118. There has been much debate about the sources Macrobius used in this chapter. It is possible to take Macrobius at his word, that he read Plato and Plotinus, but it seems more likely that his knowledge of Plato and Plotinus was derived from Porphyry's *On the Return of the Soul*. See the discussion in Stahl, *Macrobius*, pp. 26, 31, and 139, n. 10.

119. Note the reference in 1.13.2 to Scipio's desire for death: "He began to wish for death that he might really live."

120. We shall return to Macrobius in the chapter on Augustine, his contemporary, to see what they have in common and where they differ on the problem of voluntary death.

121. Of course, some Neoplatonists, such as Macrobius and (perhaps) Plotinus, did grant to the individual the right to take his own life if done so at the command of God.

122. For Stoic ideas of the afterlife, see Cicero, *Tusculan Disputations* 1.117–19; and Seneca, *Epistle* 71.16.

123. As we shall see, Augustine's case against voluntary death will be based, *mutatis mutandis*, upon the first and third arguments, and to the exclusion of the second and fourth.

◆

CHAPTER 3

A Time to Die

The Old Testament, or Hebrew Bible, records six specific cases of voluntary death, and there are that many more in the Apocrypha.[1] Although these biblical accounts are largely anecdotal, without any detailed analysis, they become important to subsequent Jewish and Christian discussions. In this chapter we examine these cases, with other relevant texts in the Hebrew Bible and Apocrypha, to uncover the ancient Hebrew and early Jewish attitudes toward voluntary death. We begin with the six accounts in the Hebrew Bible.

ABIMELECH

The story of the death of the ruthless mass murderer Abimelech, son of Gideon, is found in Judges 9:50–57. Abimelech led his forces in an attempt to capture the city of Thebez. The citizens fortified themselves in a tower in the city, and Abimelech, below, attempted to burn it down. A woman on the roof threw down a millstone, which struck Abimelech on the head, crushing his skull. With no hope of recovery, Abimelech called his armor-bearer and demanded, "Draw your sword and kill me, lest men say of me, 'a woman killed him' " (v. 54). The servant accordingly slew Abimelech.

This account touches on the complicated issue of culpability, which we encounter frequently in our discussion. Strictly speaking, Abimelech's death comes not by his *own hand*, since his armor-bearer actually carries out the deed. Whether his wounded condition rendered him incapable of the act, or such a request for assistance was customary in that time (cf. Saul in 1 Sam. 31), nonetheless, his death was by his own choice. And yet, since he was mortally wounded *by another*, his choice of death was not absolutely his own. Finally, the text ends with the comment: "Thus *God requited the crime of Abimelech*, which he committed against his father in killing his seventy brothers" (v. 56). So, at least according to the author, God is also involved, as an additional party. Indeed, God providentially "causes" these events to unfold in the interest of justice.[2]

As with all six accounts of voluntary death in the Hebrew Bible, this one is recorded without censure or condemnation, which is all the more surprising since Abimelech is not a positive figure. The author has no quarrel with the *manner* of his death. The point of the story is that God saw that justice was done. It is death by the hand of a woman that brings shame, not the act of voluntary death per se.

SAUL AND HIS ARMOR-BEARER

The next case, that of Saul, demonstrates that a voluntary death, given the appropriate circumstances, was seen as an *honorable* act. Saul's death, along with that of his armor-bearer, is recorded in 1 Samuel 31. In a battle with the Philistines Saul was badly wounded by archers. Like Abimelech, Saul commanded his armor-bearer to kill him with a sword, "lest these uncircumcised come and thrust me through, and make sport of me" (v. 4). The armor-bearer was afraid and refused to kill the king. Saul then took his own sword and fell upon it. When the armor-bearer saw that his master was dead, he too fell upon his sword and died.[3]

Both men take their own lives *by their own hands*. The circumstances are crucial. Saul would have been killed anyway by his enemies, but unlike Abimelech, he is strong enough to fall on his own sword. He fears the dishonor and shame of falling into enemy hands and being humiliated. The way in which the battle's death toll is summarized is significant: "Thus Saul died, his three sons, his armor-bearer, and all his men, on the same day together" (31:6). The author makes no distinction between those slain in battle and Saul and his armor-bearer, who take their own lives. He and his sons are subsequently mourned by David and given a proper burial, which was a sign of honor in Hebrew culture (1 Sam. 31:13; 2 Sam. 21:12–14).[4] This account, from the "early source," in 1 Samuel, presents Saul's death as tragic but wholly noble.[5]

There are two additional versions of this story in the Hebrew Bible. In 2 Samuel 1:1–16, which comes from a later tradition, an otherwise unknown Amalekite told David how *he* took Saul's life at Saul's request. The armor-bearer is not mentioned. The Amalekite reports it as a "mercy killing," justifying his action to David with the claim "I was sure he could not live after he had fallen" (v. 10). David was enraged that this foreigner would dare to take a hand in the death of "Yahweh's anointed" and had him slain for his deed.[6]

In the later, postexilic account of Saul's death the chronicler follows 1 Samuel almost word for word (1 Chron. 10:1–7). But, like the portions of Samuel dependent on the "late source," the author presents Saul as an utterly unworthy character and thus entirely deserving of death. His dislike of Saul is so intense that he apparently brings him into the story only to contrast him with David, his unabashed hero. Following the account he adds a theological interpretation characteristic of his "history": "So Saul died for his unfaithfulness; he was unfaithful to Yahweh in that he did not keep the command of Yahweh, and also consulted a medium, seeking guidance, and did not seek guidance from Yahweh. Therefore *Yahweh slew him*, and turned the kingdom over to David the son of Jesse" (vv. 13–14).

Like the Deuteronomic interpretation of the Abimelech story, the chronicler has Yahweh *directly* responsible for Saul's death, even though, strictly speaking, it came *by Saul's own hand*. This theological overlay illustrates how the issue of culpability, in tales like this, can be multilayered.[7]

SAMSON

There is yet another account of voluntary death in the book of Judges, the well-known tale of Samson pulling down the temple of the Philistines (Judg. 16:23–31). As with Abimelech and Saul, this story is fraught with ambiguities. The scene is a dramatic one. Samson, now blind and without his supernatural strength, was a prisoner of the Philistines at Gaza. At a sacrificial festival to their god Dagon, with thousands gathered inside the palace and on the roof, the Philistines brought Samson out to mock him. He stood between the two foundation pillars of the house and begged Yahweh for strength, "only this once . . . that I may be avenged upon the Philistines for one of my two eyes" (v. 28). Samson specifically prayed, "Let me die with the Philistines" (v. 29). He then bowed with all his might and pulled down the whole structure, taking his own life and those of the crowd.

Unlike the previous cases, Samson is not mortally wounded, though he certainly finds himself in a hopeless and desperate situation. At the moment of his death he is facing *humiliation*, which was also a strong factor in the two previous accounts. God is directly involved in his death in that he must *grant* Samson the supernatural strength for this last feat. In other words, God must approve it. Samson makes his choice, God concurs, and it is done. Again, as with the previous cases, the text gives no indication whatsoever that Samson's choice to take his own life was viewed with disapproval. On the contrary, the author relates the story with fascination and sympathy, commenting, "So the dead whom he slew at his death were more than those whom he had slain during his life" (v. 30). This positive evaluation of Samson's act is further indicated by the report that he is given an *honorable burial* by his family (v. 31).

These two cases from the book of Judges present an interesting contrast. Abimelech is a despicable character and deserves his death. Samson is a tragic figure but ends his life well. One is disliked, the other admired. But in neither case is the fact of *voluntary death* the issue, or even *an* issue.[8]

AHITHOPHEL

The next case, that of Ahithophel, the esteemed adviser of David and Absalom, illustrates what might well be called the "routinization" of voluntary death. Ahithophel had a brilliant career. The narrator tells us that in former times "the counsel which Ahithophel gave was as if one consulted the oracle of God; so was all the counsel of Ahithophel esteemed, both by David and by Absalom" (2 Sam. 16:23). This is important to the unfolding drama. Ahithophel sided with David's son Absalom in a revolt to seize the throne. David was clearly disappointed, and when he heard the bad news he uttered a prayer: "O Yahweh, I pray thee, turn the counsel of Ahithophel into foolishness" (2 Sam. 15:31). Ahithophel was vital to Absalom; he was the real power behind the scene. It was at Ahithophel's advice that Absalom pitched a tent on the roof of the palace and publicly had sex with the women of David's harem (2 Sam. 16:20–22). Later, when Ahithophel's plan for attacking David's forces was rejected in favor of an alternative strategy, he was humiliated and crushed. His death by his own hand is reported in a matter-of-fact manner: "When Ahithophel saw that his counsel was not followed, he saddled his ass, and went off home to his own city. And he set his house in order, and hanged himself; and he died, and was buried in the tomb of his father" (2 Sam. 17:23). As with the previous cases, God is seen at work in bringing about this turn of events. David, God's beloved and the tragic hero in the story, had prayed that Ahithophel's career would fail. When Absalom rejected Ahithophel's advice, the text notes, "For Yahweh had ordained to defeat the good counsel of Ahithophel, so that Yahweh might bring evil upon Absalom" (2 Sam. 17:14b). So, according to this story, the circumstances that led to Ahithophel's choice of death were *determined* by God.

This story of Ahithophel is part of a special section of the book of 2 Samuel, chapters 9–20, sometimes referred to as "The Court History of David."[9] It is characterized by strikingly vivid, brilliant storytelling, with strong personal interest. The author seems to be following a well-informed source, and the material is not heavily edited by later writers. A good case can be made, based on this text, and on the account of Saul's death in 1 Samuel 31, that within Israelite society, as early as the period of the united monarchy, voluntary death, given the proper circumstances, was understood as honorable and even routine. The matter-of-fact way in which these events are recorded supports such a conclusion.

ZIMRI

The sixth and final case of voluntary death in the Hebrew Bible is that of Zimri, the short-lived king of northern Israel during the divided monarchy (c. 880 B.C.). He lived during a time of upheaval and civil war. He had been a top military commander under the previous king, Elah, whom Zimri assassinated in a palace revolt. Upon seizing the throne, he killed all the male kinsmen of Baasha (the father of Elah) in an attempt to solidify his power and begin a new dynasty. Omri, a commander of the army, opposed him and marched against Tirzah, where Zimri had fortified himself. The text records Zimri's drastic end, followed by the characteristically negative evaluation that the Deuteronomic editor provides for all the kings of Israel during this period: "And when Zimri saw that the city was taken, he went into the citadel of the king's house, and burned the king's house over him with fire, and died, because of his sins which he committed, doing evil in the sight of Yahweh, walking in the way of Jeroboam, and for his sin which he committed, making Israel to sin" (1 Kings 16:18–19).

Apparently Zimri "reigned" for only seven days. Earlier, in recording how Zimri murdered all the relatives of Baasha, the narrator comments that this was "according to the word of Yahweh, which he spoke against Baasha by Jehu the prophet" (1 Kings 16:12). Here Zimri is seen in positive terms, as a punitive agent of God. In fact, none of the evils of his reign are specified. Since the formulaic condemnation is simply tacked on to the account, it should not be read as a condemnation of Zimri's *act* of taking his own life. It is reported in the same matter-of-fact manner that characterizes the other accounts we have surveyed. Apparently, Zimri's act *did* become legendary, and his name a byword—*not* his act of voluntary death but rather his murder of his master, King Elah. In the famous and macabre death scene of the despised Jezebel, she confronted her murderer Jehu with the exclamation: "Is it peace, *you Zimri,* murderer of your master?" (2 Kings 9:31). Zimri was remembered in popular imagination not for taking his own life but for being a traitor.

These six cases are our only *direct* material on voluntary death in the Hebrew Bible. This material, which lacks any theoretical or philosophical discussion, reminds one of the type of anecdotal stories in Greek and Roman literature. Indeed, this type of story is common throughout Mediterranean antiquity. We have scores of examples of the same types of motives and justifications for voluntary death: to preserve honor, express patriotism, avoid ignomiy, show bereavement, avoid capture or persecution, and so forth. There is no particular or distinguishing "biblical" or "Jewish" approach to voluntary death in the ancient Israelite period. Such tales are international. The ways in which they are told are strikingly similar across time and culture.

One might question whether these diverse texts should be considered as a group. For example, Joseph Blenkinsopp has argued that Samson should not be counted as a "suicide" because he did not intend his own death. He further excludes the cases of Abimelech, Saul (and his armor-bearer), and Zimri as occurring "in battle" and thus not properly suicides. This leaves the unique instance of Ahithophel, a contemptible traitor and, according to Blenkinsopp, the only "suicide" in the Hebrew Bible.[10]

In our treatment we have purposely avoided such terminology and classifications. David Daube has made a careful study of what he aptly calls "the linguistics of suicide."[11] There is no single verb, or set of verbs, in the Hebrew Bible to describe the generic act of voluntary death, irrespective of method or motivation. In each case the action is described, e.g., "Saul took his own sword and fell upon it," Ahithophel "set his house in order and hanged himself," and Zimri "burned the king's house over him with fire, and died." Indeed, there is no such verbal expression for the act in the Hebrew language until Talmudic times. Further, and perhaps of more significance, there is no noun corresponding to anything like "suicide" in any Hebrew texts until the nineteenth century, and then only under influence of English and European usage. As Daube demonstrates, it is always the *verb* that develops first, then the *noun*. A fundamental error of historians, as he points out, is to attribute the noun to pronouncements of an epoch as yet satisfied with the verb.[12]

Even more erroneous is to assume a standard *verbal* expression when there is none. Accordingly, the accounts in the Hebrew Bible are twice removed from the later conceptualization of the general act of "suicide." It is, therefore, inexcusably anachronistic and misleading to dispute whether or not Ahithophel, or any of these other cases, "committed suicide." As explained in the introductory chapter, we prefer the more neutral and descriptive term *voluntary death* for these very reasons. Therefore, given our definition of voluntary death (i.e., taking one's life or requesting or allowing it to be taken), we consider all six of these cases together, excluding none on the basis of later categories.

It is common in discussing these texts to speak of the "silence" of the Hebrew Bible regarding the matter of "suicide." For example, the note in the *Oxford Annotated Bible* on 1 Samuel 31:5 says simply, "Biblical suicides are rare: compare 2 Sam. 17:23; 1 Kg. 16:18; Mt. 27:5."[13] G. Margoliouth accounts for "only a very few cases . . . recorded in the O.T." with the explanation that the "ancient Hebrews were, on the whole, a naive people, joyously fond of life, and not given to tampering with the natural instinct of self-preservation."[14] But this is seriously to misinterpret the texts we have considered. This so-called silence is truly deafening in its significance. As we will see below, the rabbis and Christian theologians were hard pressed to locate *any* biblical texts that prohibit or speak negatively about voluntary death. Both Jews and Christians constructed their worlds from the closed canons of "sacred texts." The power of a single text can hardly be overemphasized in such a dogmatic enterprise. A single line or reference of censure to some practice or event, however insignificant in context, could have enormous and lasting impact. Consider the notorious case of Onan, who "spills his semen on the ground" (Gen. 38:9). The author's brief comment that "what he did was displeasing in the sight of Yahweh and he slew him" (v. 10) gave rise to centuries of discussion regarding masturbation, birth control, and related matters, while rating Onan an entry in our modern dictionaries (s.v. "Onanism"). The context is ignored, but the fragmented quote lives on. Other such examples abound: e.g., the guilt of the Jews in the murder of Christ based on Matthew 27:25, or the divine right of the state based on Romans 13:1–2. Texts such as these have exerted extraordinary influence. If any of these six accounts of voluntary death contained the slightest editorial comment, say, "and this deed was displeasing in the eyes of Yahweh," the issue of voluntary death would have been settled among Jews and Christians long before the fourth century A.D.

Further, we question the very assertion of "rarity" in the first place. There are only a very few accounts of voluntary death in Homer (Epikaste, Aias, Iokaste, Antikleia), and a half dozen or so in all of Herodotus. Anecdotal reports in ancient Near Eastern materials other than the Hebrew Bible are indeed rare. There is the case of the Assyrian Shamashshumukin, brother of Ashurbanipal, who took his life by jumping into a burning pit to escape humiliation and probable death.[15] We are told of a conspiracy during the reign of Ramses III (c. 1220 B.C.) involving a plot to kill the pharaoh. Trials were held, and we are told that when the accused were found guilty, "they took their own lives, no penalty was carried out against them."[16] Yet, these are the only two references we find in the standard collections of translated ancient Near Eastern literature. In contrast, the evidence from the Hebrew Bible is actually rather full. But numbers are not our point. It is the *way* in which these cases are reported that is significant. In all six cases the act of voluntary death itself draws no special comment. At least three of them are definitely seen in a positive light (Saul and his armor-bearer in the early source, and Samson). The other three are viewed negatively by the editors, and their downfall is said to be determined by God. But in no case is any point made about the individuals' taking their own lives or, in the case of Abimelech, demanding that his life be taken. If the act *itself* was despicable in ancient Israelite culture, the editors would not have resisted adding this to their litany of misdeeds. This point cannot be overemphasized. In fact, in the cases of Saul and his armor-bearer, Samson, and Ahithophel, an honorable burial is specifically mentioned, clearly indicating that the *manner* of death was not culturally proscribed.

Finally, as few as these texts may be, they come from a relatively wide range of periods. They allow us to conclude that from earliest times, down through the postexilic chroniclers, and into Second Temple times, acts of voluntary death were reported as acceptable and, in certain circumstances, noble.

Too often, in discussions of the so-called biblical attitude toward suicide, these examples are simply lumped together with materials from the rabbinic or patristic periods and discussed in the light of later Talmudic or Christian dogmatic interests.[17] Yet, as we have seen, the way these stories are reported indicates that their authors and editors shared no such concerns.[18]

JONAH

The postexilic tale of the prophet Jonah is seldom included in the list of examples of voluntary death in the Hebrew Bible. We believe it merits attention in our discussion.[19] According to this story, Jonah fled from Yahweh, unwilling to carry out his prophetic commission to warn the city of Nineveh to repent or perish. He took a ship bound for Tarshish in southern Spain, and a violent storm, sent by Yahweh, ensued. The crew feared the ship would sink. By casting lots they determined that Jonah was to blame. He admitted he was a Hebrew, fleeing from his God, so they asked Jonah what to do. He replied, "Take me up and *throw me into the sea*; then the sea will quiet down for you; for I know it is because of me that this great tempest has come upon you" (Jon. 1:12). The crew was reluctant to sacrifice Jonah, knowing it would mean certain death for him. They attempted to row on, but the storm only increased. Finally, in desperation, they cried to the Hebrew God, "We beseech thee, O Yahweh, let us not perish for this man's life, and lay not on us innocent blood" (1:14). Then they cast Jonah into the sea as he had requested.

Jonah's voluntary choice of death is a form of self-inflicted *capital punishment* for his rebellion against God. Both he and the ship's crew expected his certain death. Subsequently Jonah is swallowed by a fish and spends three days and three nights in its belly. He is then vomited out upon the dry land and carries out his mission to Nineveh. In view of this ending, one might maintain that this is merely an "attempted" act of voluntary death. But it is not clear from the text whether the author intends to report Jonah's *actual death* and resuscitation or his bare escape from death. The language used in Jonah's prayer from the belly of the fish might indicate that Jonah actually died and was then revived. He says, "I went down to the land whose bars closed upon me for ever; yet thou didst bring up my life *from the Pit*" (2:6).[20] As Jonah's soul fainted within him, he cried to Yahweh. This reminds one of the language of the Psalms, in which similar experiences of death, or "near death," are reported.[21]

Whether Jonah actually died in this story is a moot point. What is relevant to our discussion is Jonah's *choice* of death. Later, at the end of the story, on two separate occasions he prays not for deliverance but *for death:* "Therefore now, O Yahweh, *take my life from me,* I beseech thee, for it is better for me to die than to live" (4:3); "It is *better for me to die than to live* . . . I do well to be angry, angry enough to die" (4:8–9).[22]

Jonah's choice of death, as well as his requests to die, combine a number of important motifs encountered often in this study. We have the notion of a self-imposed death sentence, whether performed willingly or under compulsion, in response to human or divine decree. Jonah's willingness to be thrown off the ship raises the issue of heroic self-sacrifice, since his voluntary submission to death results in saving others. This is in contrast to Samson, whose death, though seen as heroic by the author, results in thousands of enemies slain. Jonah's pleading for death reminds one of the material from Job and is parallel to accounts of Moses and Elijah, as we will see.

THE "DEPARTURES" OF ELIJAH, AARON, AND MOSES

Closely related to the phenomenon of voluntary death in the Hebrew Bible are stories of unusual deaths or "departures" of important figures in Israelite history. The cases of Enoch and Elijah are well known, difficult to interpret, and the subject of unending speculation in subsequent Jewish and Christian literature.[23] Strictly speaking, it is unclear from the texts themselves whether either case is reported as a *death.* Genesis 5:24 simply reports that "Enoch walked with God; and he was not, *for God took him.*" Presumably, from the context, Enoch escaped death in some way. Elijah's case is more apropos. He told his designated successor, Elisha, as they were walking along, that he was to be "taken away" from him. A chariot and horses of fire appeared and separated them, and the text simply reports, "And Elijah went up by a whirlwind into heaven . . . and he saw him no more" (2 Kings 2:9–12).[24]

Whether this disappearance is Elijah's "death" or his removal or retirement from the scene is not clear from the text.[25] Previously Elijah had pleaded with Yahweh *that he might die.* In deep discouragement he prayed, "It is enough; now, O Yahweh, *take away my life;* for I am no better than my fathers." He then lay down to sleep under a tree (1 Kings 19:4–5). It is on that occasion, when Elijah had declared his choice of death, that God told him to go and anoint Elisha "to be prophet in your place" (1 Kings 19:16). This is the first indication that Elijah's time of departure had come, and it is, according to the narrative, the *end* of his prophetic ministry. This sequence appears significant: Elijah asked God to *take his life;* in response Elijah is told that his time is over and he is to anoint his successor. The next time Elijah is mentioned, he is taken away from the earthly scene. Though no act of self-destruction is involved, we might term this a "voluntary departure" or perhaps even a "voluntary death." We will encounter this phenomenon again in chapter five, when we discuss the deaths of Jesus and Paul. Both speak of "departing" to be with the deity at the end of their careers.

The departures or "disappearances through death" of Moses and Aaron have similar features. Both are "submissively voluntary"; that is, they are carried out at God's command. Like the "weary prophets" Elijah and Jonah, Moses pleaded, on two separate occasions, that God would take his life.[26] Following the golden calf incident Moses prayed for the forgiveness of the people of Israel. He tells Yahweh that if he will not turn away his wrath, "blot me, I pray thee, out of thy book" (Exod. 32:32).[27] Later, when the people become a burden to him with their constant complaints, he cries out, "I am not able to carry all this people alone, the burden is too heavy for me. If thou wilt deal thus with me, *kill me at once*, if I find favor in thy sight, that I may not see my wretchedness" (Num. 11:14–15). When the time came for them to depart, God told Moses and Aaron before they crossed into Canaan, "Aaron shall be gathered to his people: for he shall not enter the land which I have given to the people of Israel, *because you rebelled against my command* at the waters of Meribah. Take Aaron and Eleazar his son, and bring them up to Mount Hor; and strip Aaron of his garments, and put them upon Eleazar his son; and Aaron shall be gathered to his people, and *shall die there*" (Num. 20:24–26).

The account of this failure on the part of Moses and Aaron is given a few verses earlier in the same chapter (Num. 20:10–13). Aaron's death is the result of his "rebellion" and can properly be seen as a form of "capital punishment," imposed by God's decree. Like Elijah in the story above, Aaron passes on his office to a successor. The text reports that Moses followed the instructions, and "Aaron died there on the top of the mountain" (v. 28). Moses and Eleazar then came down the mountain, and when all the congregation "saw that Aaron was dead," they wept for him thirty days (v. 29). There is no indication that Aaron was ill or near death. The exact manner of his death is not reported. However, his death is voluntary in the sense that he submitted to God's decision. It was *time* for him to die; he accepted his (capital) punishment and died (cf. Num. 33:38).

The case of Moses is more to the point. In Numbers 27:12–13 Moses is told that he will ascend a mountain and look over the land but not enter it: "You also will be gathered to your people, as your brother Aaron was gathered, *because you rebelled against my word.*" As with Aaron, this decree of death is a punishment for sin. When the time comes, Moses' departure, like that of Aaron and Elijah, is connected to succession. He is told, "Behold, the days approach when *you must die*; call Joshua, and present yourselves in the tent of meeting, that I may commission him" (Deut. 31:14). Later the language is even more direct: "*Ascend* this mountain . . . and *view* the land of Canaan . . . and *die* on the mountain which you ascend, and be gathered to your people" (Deut. 32:49–50). The series of imperative verbs here is striking: ascend! view! and die! Nothing is said about the way Moses is to die, but his willingness to submit is apparent. The actual account of Moses' death, given two chapters later, adds a further note of mystery. The text merely reports that "Moses the servant of Yahweh, *died* there . . . according to the word of Yahweh, and he [i.e., Yahweh!] buried him in the valley . . . but no man knows the place of his burial to this day" (Deut. 34:5). Again, the manner of Moses' death is not specified, but the author stresses that Moses, though 120 years old, is healthy, and even sexually active, until the day of his death (v. 7)! Whether Moses himself took a hand in his own death or not is left unclear, though it might well be implied.

We can classify all three of these cases as "forced retirements" or departures. Since Moses and Aaron clearly die, one could speak of God taking or, better, *requiring* their lives as a punishment for their failures. However, they willingly submit, even if they have little choice. This idea of God sending death, or determining the moment of death, is a common theme throughout the Hebrew Bible, as we have noted in the cases surveyed above. With the exception of the "early source" for Saul's death in 1 Samuel, the deaths of Abimelech, Samson, Saul, Ahithophel, Zimri, and Jonah are all reported as being either willed, determined, or directly caused by God. The point we want to emphasize here is that the distinctions tend to be blurred between a request that God take one's life, God's determining the time of death, and one's taking a hand to carry out such a choice or decision. One is reminded here of the Socratic tradition of receiving the divine "sign," or "necessity," indicating that death is to be one's lot or fate, regardless of the precise way in which that death comes about. In the previous chapter we saw how this motif influenced the Greco-Roman discussion of the proper time for choosing death. These accounts of the deaths of Moses and Aaron reflect a similar idea. Yahweh gives his "bidding" that the time for their departure has arrived, and they willingly comply.

There are two elements that bring all these cases loosely together. First, each individual either wills to die or voluntarily cooperates in his own death. Second, each of the deaths is ultimately brought about by God. How they are viewed beyond that—whether as heroic sacrifice, cooperative capital punishment, or noble exit from life—is left open to interpretation. Certainly Moses and Aaron, despite their failures, are seen by the authors as heroic and noble, in death as well as in life. This also appears to be the case with Samson, Saul and his armor-bearer (at least in the early source), and Jonah.

JOB AND ECCLESIASTES

Beyond these individual cases of voluntary death, there are a handful of minor texts that are relevant to our discussion.[28] In addition, Job and Ecclesiastes contain reflective material on the value of life in the face of acute suffering, tragedy, and despair. Although these texts do not report instances of individuals who actually took their lives, the broader philosophical discussion they reflect is related to our topic.

We begin with Job.[29] To simplify this discussion we will deal only with the central "dialogue" of the book (chaps. 3–31), assuming, with most critics, a relatively late date—well into the Second Temple period.[30] The final edited version of the biblical text of Job has a resolved, even "happy," ending. But in the older "dialogue," even though there is no indication that Job actually took his life, he does *long for death*. He stoutly maintains throughout that, given the injustice he experiences and sees about him, death is to be preferred to life.

The dialogue opens with Job cursing the day of his birth: "Why did I not die at birth, come forth from the womb and expire?" he cries (3.11). He imagines and longs for the peace of the grave, where all the dead lie at rest:

> There the wicked cease from troubling,
> and the weary are at rest.
> There the prisoners are at ease together; they hear not the
> voice of the taskmaster.
> The small and the great are there, and the slave is free
> from his master (3:17–19).

Death is understood here to be a journey "down to Sheol," with no hope of return. It is a final escape from both men and God. Job reminds God of this at one point:

> As the cloud fades and vanishes, so he who goes down to Sheol
> *does not come up*; he returns no more to his house, nor does
> his place know him any more. . . .
> For now I shall lie in the earth; thou wilt seek me, but I shall
> not be (7:9–10, 21b).

Job's view of Sheol is vividly expressed further on, as he tells his friends:

> Let me alone, that I may find a little comfort before I go whence
> I shall not return, to the land of gloom and deep darkness,
> the land of gloom and chaos, where light is as darkness (10:20–22).

At one point Job contrasts his own mortal nature with that of a tree, which, though cut down, can live again:

> For there is hope for a tree, if it be cut down, that it will
>   sprout again, and that its shoots will not cease. . . .
> But man dies, and is laid low; man breathes his last, and
>   where is he?
> As the waters fail from a lake, and a river wastes away and
>   dries up, so man lies down and rises not again; till the
>   heavens be no more he will not awake, or be roused
>   out of his sleep (14:7–12).

Throughout the dialogue Job accepts death as the final end. His friends hold the same view but argue that although God's ways are often mysterious, there is justice here and now in this world. Job stubbornly maintains the opposite: that he has done nothing to deserve his terrible suffering (chap. 13) and, further, that more often than not the wicked prosper while the innocent suffer (chaps. 21 and 24). He cries out:

> I am blameless; I regard not myself; I loathe my life.
> It is all one; therefore I say, he destroys both the blameless
>   and the wicked.
> When disaster brings sudden death, he mocks at the calamity of
>   the innocent.
> The earth is given into the hand of the wicked; he covers the
>   face of its judges—if it is not he, who then is it? (9:21—24).

Given such injustice and his view of Sheol as the final resting place of all humans, Job expresses his longing for, but never his faith in, some postmortem vindication.[31] He has already said that it would have been *better* never to have survived birth. He now asks God to take his life:

> O that I might have my request, and that God would grant my
>   desire; that it would please God to crush me, that he would
>   let loose his hand and *cut me off!*
> This would be my consolation; I would even exult in pain
>   unsparing; for I have not denied the words of the Holy One.
> What is my strength, that I should wait?
> And what is my end, that I should be patient?
> Is my strength the strength of stones, or is my flesh bronze?
> In truth I have no help in me, and any resource is driven from me (6:8–13).

Job has given up and is ready to die. Like other ancient Hebrews, he believes his life and circumstances are in God's hands, and that death is something that God sends.[32] Nonetheless, Job does not kill himself. But he refers directly to the idea of taking his own life further on in the same speech:

> When I say, "My bed will comfort me, my couch will ease my
>   complaint,"
> then thou dost scare me with dreams and terrify me with visions,
> so that I would *choose strangling and death* rather than my bones
>   [my wasted frame].
> I loathe my life; I would not live forever.
> Let me alone, for my days are a breath (7:13–16).

The text makes clear his reason for choosing to live on. Job feels that if he were not to do so, his "hope" or cause, which he has so vehemently maintained, would be lost. He states this point explicitly:

> If I look for Sheol as my house, if I spread my couch in
>   darkness, if I say to the pit, "You are my father," and to
>   the worm, "My mother," or "My sister," where then is my
>   hope? Who will see my hope?
> Will it go down to the bars of Sheol?
> Shall we descend together into the dust? (17:13–16).

As long as Job is alive, he believes there is hope that he can somehow be vindicated. Nonetheless he loathes his life and longs for death. The core of the book, chapters 3–31, supports this interpretation. The later prologue (1:1–2:13), perhaps in reaction to this sharp language expressing a preference for death, adds Job's pious response to his wife when she tells him to curse God and die: "You speak as one of the foolish women would speak. Shall we receive good at the hand of God, and shall we not receive evil?" (2:9–10).

Job's view of Sheol as the shadowy underworld of the dead, a "land of no return," is characteristic of most Mediterranean cultures in the archaic period.[33] Generally life was affirmed, and the earth was seen as the proper human place. Other texts in the Hebrew Bible, in which individuals find themselves in severe and threatening circumstances somewhat similar to those of Job, likewise view Sheol as a place where one is cut off from God and remembered no more.[34] Psalm 115:16–18 is an epitome of this cosmology common to the Hebrew Bible:

> The heavens are Yahweh's heavens, but the earth he has given to
>   the sons of men.
> The dead do not praise Yahweh, nor do any that go down into
>   silence.

But we will bless Yahweh from this time forth and for
evermore.

Nowhere in the Hebrew Bible is death seen as a departure to a better life in
a world beyond.[35] From Abraham, to Moses, to any common Israelite, all
depart to Sheol. Salvation is spoken of in many texts, but it always refers to rescue or deliverance in *this life* from such evils as illness, enemies, and exile.[36]

Given this context, Job raises an important issue for our discussion: that of
vindication. In these ancient materials, death might offer relief, but it never
offers justice or vindication. That Job longs for death and asks God to take his
life shows how desperate he has become. In later times, as we will see below,
Job's dilemma is addressed quite differently. Death itself becomes a way of
obtaining such vindication. But in Job's case, without such hope, his vivid language expressing his preference and desire for death becomes all the more
striking.

It is sometimes maintained that since Job did not take his life, despite his
strong longing for death, the author indicates that such an action would be
morally wrong.[37] Although this is possible, it seems to go beyond the evidence.
The *reason* Job determines to live on is made clear in the text—his insistence
on vindication, here and now, in this life. Further, the request that *God* take
one's life does not preclude one taking one's own life or allowing it to be taken
(e.g., Jonah), with the understanding that such is God's will and action. As we
have already noted, such acts of *self-destruction* were often seen as *acts of
Yahweh* as well, with a resulting ambiguity over who ultimately brings about
death. There is no reason to attribute to Job any other attitude toward voluntary death than that we have found to be common in these other texts in the
Hebrew Bible.

Ecclesiastes is one of the latest books of the Hebrew canon, dating perhaps
from the third century B.C.[38] The author, whom scholars refer to as *Qoheleth*
("the preacher"), begins to reflect philosophically upon the common Hebrew
evaluation of life and death. He soberly declares,

> For the fate of the sons of men and the fate of beasts is the same; as one dies, so
> dies the other. They all have the same breath, and man has no advantage over
> the beasts; for all is vanity. All go to one place; all are from the dust, and all turn
> to dust again (3:19–20).

The preacher goes on to ask skeptically, "Who knows whether the spirit of
man goes upward and the spirit of the beast goes down to the earth?" (v. 21).
But it is clear that the author puts no stock in such ideas, which may have
begun to circulate in Jewish circles. He holds to the "old view" and warns his
readers,

But he who is joined with all the living has hope, for a living dog is better than a dead lion. For the living know that they will die, but the dead know nothing, and they have no more reward; but the memory of them is lost. Their love and their hate and their envy have already perished, and they have no more for ever any share in all that is done under the sun (9:4–6).

In the face of the stark reality of death, the author does offer some positive counsel, quite the opposite of any admonition to choose death:

Enjoy life with the wife whom you love, all the days of your vain life which he has given you under the sun, because that is your portion in life and in your toil at which you toil under the sun. Whatever your hand finds to do, do it with your might; for there is no work or thought or knowledge or wisdom in Sheol, to which you are going (9:9–10).

But such "cheerful" advice should not be misunderstood. It is not a simple repetition of the common Hebrew affirmation of life over death. The text reflects a serious debate in this regard. Life is not easily affirmed. On the whole the core of Ecclesiastes is profoundly pessimistic.[39] All is vanity and a "striving after wind" (chaps. 1–2). There is no justice; one must not even expect such. At one point, reflecting upon these realities, the author concludes, "So I *hated life*, because what is done under the sun was grievous to me" (2:17). And further on, after reflecting upon all the "oppressions practiced under the sun," the author goes further in his verdict of despair: "And I thought the dead who are already dead more fortunate than the living who are still alive; but better than both is he who has not yet been" (4:2–4). This is the closest he comes to *longing* for death, to the point of even regretting his birth.[40] This closely parallels Job's laments, as we have seen (Job 3:11–19; 10:18–22). But in Job's case we have the suffering of an individual, while here the author clearly intends to extend this preference for death (or "nonbirth") to all humankind, whether rich and powerful, or poor and oppressed.[41] His attitude is one of resignation. He accepts the human lot. Several times he repeats his basic advice: "There is nothing better for a man than that he should eat and drink, and find enjoyment in his toil" (2:24).[42]

Our point here is not that Ecclesiastes supports the notion of voluntary death. It does not. Though profoundly pessimistic, the text advocates the choice of life. However, what we begin to see, in both Job and Ecclesiastes, is a critical discussion of the value and meaning of life, when it is primarily characterized by suffering, injustice, and, finally, death. The questions and issues raised in these texts do not disappear but become central to the developing understanding of voluntary death among various Jewish groups in the Hellenistic period.

Ecclesiastes speaks of "a time to be born and a *time to die*" (3:2).[43] These texts from the Hebrew Bible are aptly represented by this phrase. They all deal with the circumstances in which the proper "time to die" has come and is accordingly chosen.

THE TRANSCENDENCE OF DEATH

In the Hellenistic period (from around 300 B.C.), strikingly different responses to these fundamental problems were formulated in Jewish circles. The finality of death was reversed or transcended through schemes of apocalyptic eschatology, which offered "resurrection from the dead," or the promise of immortality of the soul.[44] When death came to be seen as an entry into immortality, or as reversible through a resurrection to heavenly glory, then the notion of *voluntary death* in the face of the injustices of life underwent a profound transformation.

It is during this period, beginning in the second century B.C., that we encounter stories of Jews who choose death rather than submit to a violation or prohibition of religious faith or practice.[45] Such accounts often express belief in these emerging ideas of immortality of the soul or resurrection from the dead.

The idea of voluntary death as a religiously motivated self-sacrifice occurs already in late portions of the Hebrew Bible. The so-called suffering servant texts in Second Isaiah (40–55) speak of a "servant of Yahweh," who willingly gives his life "like a lamb led to the slaughter" (53:7). He "makes himself an offering for sin" by "pouring out his soul to death" (53:10, 12).[46] It is common to interpret this language about the suffering servant of Isaiah 53 against the background of temple cult and sacrifice.[47] Though such allusions are possibly present, the primary context is that of divine vindication for the righteous sufferer, who *chooses death* in the face of persecution and evil. The image of the "lamb led to the slaughter" is one of persecution and oppression, not cultic atonement (see Ps. 44:9–12; and especially Jer. 11:18–20). As a result of his voluntary death, the "servant" receives some type of vindication or resurrection (53:10–12). This is made explicit in the Dead Sea Scroll text of Isaiah, which says, "He will see the light of life and be satisfied" (v. 11). It is not clear whether the author has in mind an individual or some collective portion of the nation of Israel itself.[48] The latter sections of Isaiah refer to a minority group, viewed by the authors as persecuted but faithful to Yahweh. They are directly addressed and promised vindication:

> Hearken to me, you who know righteousness,
> the people in whose heart is my Torah;

fear not the reproach of men,
and be not dismayed at their reviling (51:7).

In a later section we read:

Hear the word of Yahweh, you who tremble at his word:
"Your brethren who hate you and cast you out for my name's
sake, have said 'Let Yahweh be glorified,
that we may see your joy';
but it is they who shall be put to shame" (66:5).

This section of Isaiah seems closely related to the so-called Isaiah Apocalypse (chaps. 24–27).[49] There the faithful, addressed as "my people" (26:20), are promised protection and exaltation as God's apocalyptic wrath is poured out on the wicked of the world (26:20–21). Indeed, "their dead" are promised life:

Thy dead shall live, their bodies shall rise
O dwellers in the dust, awake and sing for joy!
For thy dew is a dew of light,
and on the land of the shades thou will let it fall (26:19).

This is in contrast to the enemies of God, now slain, who will never rise (26:14).

What emerges in these diverse sections of Isaiah is a fundamental pattern of "cosmic reversal" that is the heart of apocalyptic eschatology. The suffering of the righteous minority will be vindicated in a sudden and total overthrow of the forces of evil that hold sway in human history:

Therefore thus says the Lord Yahweh:
Behold my servants shall eat,
but you will be hungry;
behold my servants shall drink,
but you shall be thirsty;
behold my servants shall rejoice,
but you shall be put to shame (65:13).

Such a reversal brings together the whole complex of ideas associated with Jewish apocalypticism, e.g., resurrection of the dead and/or heavenly immortality, punishment of the wicked, and a new transformed age to come. So, though not explicitly apocalyptic in language, the "suffering servant" material in Isaiah fits best into the general context of these hopes for *reversal* and *vindication* that permeate the later Hebrew prophets. It is in that light that the servant's voluntary death can be properly understood. Here we have the beginnings of the influential idea that death is not simply an end or exit from life but rather a step toward redemption and salvation—for oneself, or others, or both.

Daniel, which is probably the latest document in the Hebrew Bible, reflects a further development of these same themes.[50] Daniel focuses on a time when a contemptible, blasphemous, Gentile ruler will come to Jerusalem and profane the temple, forcing Jews to violate the covenant (Dan. 11:21, 29–32). During this time faithful Jews "shall fall by sword and flame, by captivity and plunder, for some days" in order to "refine and cleanse them" (vv. 33–35). This terrible time of trouble will mark the end of the age and lead to the resurrection of the dead and a final judgment (Dan. 12:1–3).

Critical scholars are agreed that these thinly veiled references are to the Syrian successor of Alexander, Antiochus IV (Epiphanes), who in 167 B.C., according to Jewish legend, entered the Jerusalem temple, instituted certain rites of idolatrous worship, and attempted to stamp out basic observances of Judaism. Interpretations of his motives and what actually transpired are disputed. The popular legendary account is given in 1 and 2 Maccabees, though scholars question the historical accuracy of these texts.[51]

The author of Daniel sets his stories and visions in a much earlier time, during the sixth-century B.C. Judean captivity by the Babylonians and their successors, the Persians. His well-known story of the three Hebrew youths Shadrach, Meshach, and Abednego, who were thrown into a fiery furnace for their refusal to worship an image of gold, captures the essential spirit of an oft-repeated scenario (Dan. 3). They reply boldly to the Babylonian king Nebuchadnezzar: "If it be so, our God whom we serve is able to deliver us from the burning fiery furnace; and he will deliver us out of your hand, O King. But if not, be it known to you, O king, that *we will not serve your gods or worship the golden image* which you have set up" (Dan. 3:17–18).

The key element here is the absolute and stubborn refusal to compromise, even when threatened with death. In this story, which was obviously written to build faith and encourage such willingness to die, the youths are delivered, and the king himself becomes a convert to Yahweh.

Yet Daniel apparently addresses a community that had experienced death rather than any such dramatic supernatural rescue. Instead of immediate deliverance, Daniel holds out the imminence of the end of the age and a final cosmic judgment as comfort and incentive to those who choose to die rather than compromise their religion. His message is clear: a heavenly reward is certain, and the oppressors will soon be everlastingly punished (12:1–3). These ideas of final judgment, resurrection of *both* the righteous and wicked dead, and eternal life, or everlasting punishment, occur only here in the Hebrew Bible. Yet in the

Hellenistic period they are found throughout our Jewish sources and become prime factors in the discussion of voluntary death. Precisely how and why such ideas come to predominate subsequent Jewish materials is disputed, but this development is closely related to the penetrating issue of the vindication of the righteous sufferer.[52] The issue becomes sharply focused: when one chooses to die in order to remain faithful to the commandments of God, what is to be said for justice in this world?

In most of the biblical texts from this period on, beginning with Daniel, new answers are given to this question. Complete vindication is promised, especially for those who choose to die, but only at the final judgment. According to Daniel, these terrible times come upon the people of Israel in order to "refine and cleanse" them before the end. As with Isaiah, one finds throughout these texts the idea of a faithful persecuted remnant, an "elect" group, who endure to the point of death and are assured their eventual heavenly reward.

As one would expect, we find a parallel development in noncanonical Jewish texts from this period. For example, in the *Testament of Moses*, chapters eight through ten also deal with the period under Antiochus IV.[53] Chapter eight describes the various tortures to be inflicted on Jews who will not give up their faith. In chapter nine a Levite named Taxo exhorts his seven sons:[54]

> Now, therefore, sons, heed me. If you investigate, you will surely know that never did our fathers nor their ancestors tempt God by transgressing his commandments. Yea, you will surely know that this is our strength. Here is what we shall do. We shall fast for a three-day period and on the fourth day we shall go into a cave, which is in the open country. There *let us die rather than transgress the commandments* of the lord of lords, the God of our fathers. For if we do this, and do die, our blood will be avenged before the Lord (9:4–7).

This is an extraordinary text. It advocates a withdrawal from the world through fasting and retreat, ending in death (perhaps through fasting?). This sacrificial death will bring about the intervention of God and the manifestation of the kingdom, which is described in chapter ten.[55] As in Isaiah 53, these Jews viewed the voluntary deaths of the righteous in terms related to redemptive atonement.[56]

The books of the Apocrypha contain many such stories, often rivaling one another in their lurid accounts of heroism in the face of torture.[57] First Maccabees reports that in the early stages of the Maccabean revolt the Jewish rebels refused to fight on the Sabbath day, even if attacked. They chose to die rather than violate this commandment of God. They exhorted one another: "*Let us all die* in our innocence; heaven and earth testify for us that you are killing us unjustly" (1 Macc. 2:37). On one occasion a thousand people, including women and children, chose to die in this manner.[58]

One of the earlier stories in 1 Maccabees concerns a certain Eleazar, who fought against the Syrians under Antiochus V. The Syrians were using elephants in the battle. Eleazar, thinking that Antiochus himself was riding one particular beast, threw himself under the elephant, stabbed it from beneath, but was crushed to death when the animal fell. What might be seen as the foolish miscalculation of a would-be hero is transformed by the author into an act of salvific self-sacrifice. He comments, "So he *gave his life to save his people* and to win for himself an everlasting name" (1 Macc. 6:44).

Second Maccabees, an epitome of a five-volume history by Jason of Cyrene, offers an extreme and exaggerated version of the revolt, roughly paralleling 1 Maccabees 1:10–7:50 (180 to 161 B.C.). Jason appears to be the first writer to celebrate the glorious deeds of those heroes willing to die for the faith. He fully accepts the developing idea of resurrection of the dead and final judgment, and even endorses the notion of prayer and sacrifice on behalf of the dead (2 Macc. 12:39–45). According to this author the offenses of Antiochus were unconscionable. Antiochus dedicated the temple of Yahweh to Zeus, filled it with harlots and merchandise, and offered pigs and other abominable animals on the altar. Jews were forbidden to circumcise their children and to practice the Torah and were compelled to participate in the pagan sacrifices (2 Macc. 6:1–7). The author tells of two women who had dared to circumcise their children being paraded about the city "with their babies hung at their breasts, then hurled . . . down headlong from the wall" (2 Macc. 6:10). Another group were burned alive when they gathered secretly to observe the Sabbath day (6:11). All this came about "not to destroy but to discipline our people," he declares (6:12).

He recounts the dramatic story of another hero, also named Eleazar:

> Eleazar, one of the scribes in high position, a man now advanced in age and of noble presence, was being forced to open his mouth to eat swine's flesh. But he, *welcoming death with honor* rather than life with pollution, *went up to the rack of his own accord*, spitting out the flesh, as men ought to go who have the courage to refuse things that it is not right to taste, even for the natural love of life (2 Macc. 6:18–20).

The author concludes the story noting that Eleazar's death left "an example of nobility and a memorial of courage" (v. 31).[59] Two major themes in this account occur repeatedly in subsequent stories: the *willingness* of the individual to die and the *nobility* that voluntary death exemplifies.

Second Maccabees also relates the infamous story of the martyrdom of the mother and her seven sons. When the king tried to force them one by one to

eat swine's flesh, he fell into a rage as each in turn refused. Echoing the deter-
mination of Daniel's three companions, they declared, "We are ready to die
rather than transgress the laws of our fathers" (2 Macc. 7:2). They were subjected to gruesome torture: scalping; amputation of hands, feet, and tongue; and
being fried in a pan until dead. Each breathed his last with declarations of faith
in the resurrection of the dead and warnings of future judgment for the
torturers. Their assurance of justice and vindication in the afterlife (i.e., resurrection) is a dominant element of this story and is repeated eight times.

Finally, there is the gruesome account of Razis, an elder of Jerusalem in
Maccabean times. His tale represents still another level of ambiguity in these
accounts, for though under threat, he clearly *takes his own life*. He was
denounced to Nicanor, the Syrian governor of Judea, as a strong and stubborn
advocate of the Jewish faith. Nicanor sent five hundred soldiers to arrest Razis.
He took refuge in a tower, and, as the soldiers were about to break in, he fell
upon his own sword, *"preferring to die nobly* rather than fall into the hands of
sinners and suffer outrages unworthy of his noble birth" (2 Macc. 14:42). He
only wounded himself, and, as the crowd burst through the door, he ran upon
the outside wall and jumped down into a courtyard below. The story ends with
the grisly account of his death:

> Still alive and aflame with anger, he rose, and though his blood gushed forth
> and his wounds were severe he ran through the crowd; and standing upon a
> steep rock, with his blood now completely drained from him, he tore out his
> entrails, took them with both hands and hurled them at the crowd, calling upon
> the Lord of life and spirit to give them back to him again. Such was the manner
> of his death (2 Macc. 14:45–46).

Fourth Maccabees is an expansion of 2 Maccabees 6:12–7:42. It retells the
stories of the old man Eleazar, and of the mother and her seven sons.[60] In this
elaborated account Eleazar taunts his torturers: "I will not transgress the
sacred oaths of my ancestors concerning the keeping of the law, not even if
you gouge out my eyes and burn my entrails . . . get your wheels ready and fan
the fire more vehemently!" (4 Macc. 5:29–32). In the account of the seven
brothers and their mother, a new element is introduced. After denouncing his
attackers, the youngest brother *"flung himself* into the braziers and so ended
his life" (4 Macc. 12:19). Similarly, his mother, "when she, too, was about to
be seized and put to death, *she threw herself into the fire so that no one would
touch her body"* (4 Macc. 17:1). Here we move from being willing to die to
directly killing oneself.

Fourth Maccabees also advocates the striking idea that these deaths bring
vicarious atonement for the sins of the nation. The language used in this regard
is of particular note. They become a "ransom for sin," and "through the blood

of those devout ones and their death as an expiation" Israel is preserved (17:21–22). Here, as in the Isaiah materials, we see the way in which the language of sacrifice and atonement can be combined with that of voluntary death and self-sacrifice.

Taking these accounts in the Apocrypha together, we observe a number of common elements. First, they reflect situations of opposition and persecution. Second, the choice to die, which these individuals make, is viewed by the authors as necessary, noble, and heroic. Third, these individuals are often eager to die; indeed, in several cases they end up directly *killing themselves*. Fourth, there is often the idea of vicarious benefit resulting from their suffering and death. And finally, the expectation of vindication and reward beyond death, more often than not, is a prime motivation for their choice of death. As we will see, all of these elements are important in New Testament materials, as well as in subsequent "martyrologies," both Jewish and Christian.

The belief in an afterlife, whether immortality of the soul or resurrection of the dead, is a view that faced opposition and competition in this period, as 2 Maccabees 12:44–45 shows. The debate is clearly reflected in the Wisdom materials as well.[61] The older Hebrew view of no vital afterlife is put in the mouth of the *wicked* in Wisdom 2, only to be forcefully rejected in 3:1–4:

> But the souls of the righteous are in the hand of God, and no torment will ever touch them. In the eyes of the foolish they seemed to have died, and their departure was thought to be an affliction . . . for *though in the sight of men they were punished, their hope is full of immortality.*

This is a critical passage that illustrates the transition of thought at this time. Things are not as they appear. As we argued above, this is the heart and core of apocalyptic thinking. Many texts of this period, whether explicitly apocalyptic or not, reflect these characteristic elements of cosmic reversal, divine vindication, and the transcendence of death. The new case for resurrection of the dead, or immortality of the soul, has to be made against the background of the Hebrew Bible, in which no such hope is dominant. This is the great divide between Job and Ecclesiastes, on the one hand, and these Jewish materials from Greek and Roman times, on the other. This is also the difference between all the cases of voluntary death in the Hebrew Bible and these later tales in the books of the Apocrypha. Ecclesiastes reflects on the meaning of *this life only*. Job contemplates death; he even longs for it, but not in order to receive a better life or a reward but as a bare escape from his suffering. He determines to live on in order to find vindication. In his view, if he chooses to take his life, he will lose any chance to challenge God. Once this Hebrew view of Sheol, which is parallel to the archaic Greek notion of Hades, begins to shift toward the hope of resurrection of the dead, or immortality in a life beyond death, the basic questions related to voluntary death are posed in sharply different ways. We see the beginnings of this development in Daniel and the texts from the Apocrypha. Increasingly, death is understood as a *way to obtain* eternal life, and, as our next chapter shows, "even in a single moment."

NOTES

1. The six are Abimelech (Judg. 9:50–57), Saul and his armor-bearer (1 Sam. 31:1–13), Samson (Judg. 16:28–31), Ahithophel (2 Sam. 17:23), and Zimri (1 Kings 16:15–20). There are a number of other examples that are less direct, but worth consideration: Jonah, who is thrown overboard at sea at his request and subsequently asks to die (Jon. 1:12; 4:3, 8); Moses and Elijah, who pray for death in times of discouragement (Exod. 32:32; Num. 11:15; 1 Kings 19:4); David, whose servants fear he might take his life when in deep depression (2 Sam. 12:18); and Zebah and Zalmun'na, who insist that Gideon slay them (Judg. 8:18–21). We will discuss several of these below. We use "Hebrew Bible" to refer to the books of the Jewish canon of scripture, called by Protestants the Old Testament. The Apocrypha refers to the additional books used as scripture, or "for edification," by various branches of the Eastern and Western churches from ancient times. See *The New Oxford Annotated Bible with the Apocrypha: Expanded Edition*, edited by Herbert G. May and Bruce M. Metzger (New York: Oxford Univ. Press, 1977), for a full collection of these texts. In this chapter we have used the Revised Standard Version. Emphases within quotes are ours. We have substituted the divine name "Yahweh" for the RSV rendering "LORD."

2. As we saw in the previous chapter, the avoidance of shame is a common justification for voluntary death in antiquity. This specific motif of a wounded military leader choosing to die is likewise widespread in the ancient world. See the examples in H. J. Rose et al., "Suicide," *Encyclopaedia of Religion and Ethics*, vol. 12 (1922), pp. 21–40. This phenomenon is international, as this survey article of eight ancient cultures shows.

3. The linking of the voluntary death of a servant to the choice of his master is a commonly reported phenomenon in Mediterranean antiquity. For example, Xenophon reports that at the death of Cyrus, his chief of staff, Artapates, and others took their lives (*Anabasis* 1.18). For further examples see A. W. Mair, "Suicide (Greek and Roman)," *Encyclopaedia of Religion and Ethics*, vol. 12, pp. 26–33.

4. It was a sign of special shame in Hebrew culture when burial was neglected or made impossible (see 1 Kings 14:10–13; 16:1–4; 21:23–24; 2 Kings 9:30–37). Much later, in a passage we will discuss in the following chapter, Josephus says that the Jews have a custom of exposing unburied until sunset the body of one who takes his own life. We have no evidence of such a law or practice among ancient Israelites, but if such was the case, these ancient examples of normal burial become all the more indicative of an attitude of tolerance, respect, and honor.

5. See P. Kyle McCarter, Jr., *I Samuel*, The Anchor Bible (Garden City, NY: Doubleday, 1980), pp. 21–22. McCarter finds no signs of reworking of early sources in 1 Sam. 16–31 (other than in 19:18–21; 25:1; and 28:3–25). He dates this material around the eighth century B.C.

6. The account is noteworthy as an example of someone assisting another to die when it appears that death is certain to come shortly anyway.

7. It is a truism throughout the Hebrew Bible that God is ultimately responsible for (or even *causes*) everything (see Isa. 45:7). We will return to this point below in considering the "disappearances" of Elijah, Aaron, and Moses, each at Yahweh's bidding.

8. There is an interesting similarity in the two cases. Abimelech must get another, his armor-bearer, to aid him in his death, while God must grant Samson his supernatural strength. In both cases a second party must concur and act as an aid.

9. See P. Kyle McCarter, Jr., *II Samuel*, The Anchor Bible (Garden City, NY: Doubleday, 1984), pp. 9–10, who holds that 2 Sam. 9–20 was part of an old narrative from a supporter of King Solomon.

10. See his letter to the editor (*Bible Review*, June 1990, p. 7) in response to Arthur Droge's article, "Did Paul Commit Suicide?" (*Bible Review*, Dec. 1989, pp. 14–21).

11. See David Daube, "The Linguistics of Suicide," *Philosophy and Public Affairs* 1 (1972): 387–437.

12. Daube, "Linguistics of Suicide," pp. 394–406.

13. *Oxford Annotated Bible*, p. 373 (note by William F. Stinespring). The same point is made in the standard reference articles: see G. Margoliouth, "Suicide (Jewish)," *The Encyclopaedia of Religion and Ethics*, vol. 12 (1922), pp. 37–38; and F. W. Young, "Suicide," *The Interpreter's Dictionary of the Bible*, vol. 4 (1962), pp. 453–54.

14. Margoliouth, "Suicide, (Jewish)," p. 37.

15. See the Rassam Cylinder of Ashurbanipal's reign in D. D. Luckenbill, ed., *Ancient Records of Assyria and Babylonia*, 2 vols. (Chicago: Univ. of Chicago Press, 1927; reprint, New York: Greenwood Press, 1968), vol. 2, pp. 302–4. We are indebted to Joseph Blenkinsopp for this reference.

16. See James Pritchard, ed., *Ancient Near Eastern Texts*, 3d ed. (Princeton, NJ: Princeton Univ. Press, 1969), p. 215.

17. See for example, the survey articles: Margoliouth, "Suicide (Jewish)"; L. I. Rabinowitz and H. H. Cohn, "Suicide," *Encyclopaedia Judaica*, vol. 15, pp. 489–91; T. C. Kane, "Suicide," *The New Catholic Encyclopaedia*, vol. 13, pp. 781–83; Paul M. Bretscher, "Suicide and the Church," *Encyclopaedia of the Lutheran Church*, vol. 3, pp. 2275–77; Young, "Suicide"; and Marilyn J. Harran, "Suicide," *The Encyclopedia of Religion*, vol. 14 (1987), pp. 125–31. Harran's treatment is better than most, though she begins her discussion of the Jewish materials with the assertion: "Whereas suicide was at the very least tolerated, and often applauded, among the ancient Greeks and Romans, the Hebrew people disapproved of it" (p. 126). Specific scholarly treatments of the question are little

better; see for example, Fred Rosner, "Suicide in Biblical, Talmudic, and
Rabbinic Writings," *Tradition* 11 (1970): 25–40. Rosner merely cites the texts,
then goes to later Jewish "commentators" for his interpretations, all in the service
of his dogmatic conclusion that "Judaism" strictly forbids "suicide." This is unfortunately true even of the recent study by Sidney Goldstein, *Suicide in Rabbinic
Literature* (Hoboken, NJ: KTAV, 1989), pp. 3–12. Voluntary death is obviously a
highly sensitive subject for most writers. For a treatment of these biblical materials that is free from such assertions, see David Daube, "Death as a Release in the
Bible," *Novum Testamentum* 5 (1962): 82–104. Also, more recently, James T.
Clemons, *What Does the Bible Say About Suicide?* (Minneapolis, MN: Fortress
Press, 1990), offers a more evenhanded treatment.

18. It should also be added that these texts from the Hebrew Bible know nothing of
the later Jewish ideas of resurrection of the dead or of eternal life in "the world to
come." And none of them can properly be seen as "martyrdom" accounts either.
The idea of giving up one's life as a religious testimony, or for religious principles,
comes later. For these reasons one must avoid pulling them indiscriminately into
subsequent discussions of voluntary death.

19. Jonah is included in the recent discussion by Clemons, *What Does the Bible Say?*
pp. 22–23. There is a prophet Jonah, son of Amittai, mentioned in 2 Kings 14:25
who was active in the time of Jeroboam II (786–746 B.C.). Few, if any, critical
scholars connect the book of Jonah with this figure. The reference in Jon. 1:1
appears to be a case of pseudonymous attribution, a technique quite common in
the Second Temple period. The book of Jonah likely comes from the fifth century B.C. or later. See Julius A. Brewer, *A Critical and Exegetical Commentary on
Haggai, Zechariah, Malachi and Jonah*, The International Critical Commentary
(New York: Scribner's, 1912), p. 13, who places it between 400 and 200 B.C.;
Michael Fishbane, "Jonah," *The Encyclopedia of Religion*, vol. 8 (1987), p. 115,
who puts it around the fourth century B.C.; and D. W. Watts, "The Books of Joel,
Obadiah, Jonah, Nahum, Habakkuk and Zephaniah," *The Cambridge Bible
Commentary* (Cambridge: Cambridge Univ. Press, 1975), p. 74, who dates it
between 537 B.C. and the end of the fifth century.

20. The word translated "Pit" (*sahat*) is used regularly for the realm of death, the
grave, or destruction. See Job 9:31; 33:18–30; Pss. 16:10; 49:9–12.

21. The most vivid examples are Pss. 16:9–11; 22; and 88. Compare also Isa. 53:8–12,
where the suffering servant apparently dies, but is then revived to receive vindication. Early Christians subsequently made use of these texts, as well as the story of
Jonah's "death," as prophetic precursors of Jesus' *voluntary death* and resurrection.

22. This expression translated "therefore now, O Yahweh, take my life" is identical to
the one used by Elijah in 1 Kings 19:4. For other related texts in the Hebrew
Bible see our discussion of Moses below.

23. Enoch and Elijah, by virtue of their "translations," are often paired together as
heavenly figures, usually with an eschatological mission, though Elijah is often
mentioned alone. Some of the more important references to these figures are the
following: Mal. 4:5 (an enormously influential text); Wisd. of Sol. 4:13, 16; *Jub.*

4:16–26; 4 Ezra 6:26; *Adam and Eve* 51:9; *T. Benj.* 10:6; *T. Sim.* 5:4; *1 Enoch*; *2 Enoch*; *Apoc. Zephaniah* 9:4–6; *Greek Apoc. Ezra* 5:20–22; 6:5–7; *Apoc. Dan.* 14:1–3; *Sibylline Oracles* 2:187–95; 8:169–70; Mark 9:11–13; Heb. 11:5; Irenaeus, *Against Heresies* 5.5.1; and *3 Enoch*. On the Elijah cycle of materials, preserved in fragments in various languages, see J. H. Charlesworth, *The Pseudepigrapha in Modern Research with a Supplement*, Septuagint and Cognate Studies, no. 7S (Missoula, MT: Scholars Press, 1981), pp. 95–98; 277–78; and M. E. Stone and J. Strugnell, *The Books of Elijah: Parts 1–2*, Texts and Translations, no. 18, PS8 (Missoula, MT: Scholars Press, 1979). For a general discussion of these traditions, see James D. Tabor, "Returning to the Divinity: Josephus's Portrayal of the Disappearances of Enoch, Elijah, and Moses," *Journal of Biblical Literature* 108 (1989): 225–38.

24. The chronicler apparently takes this to be not Elijah's death, but merely his removal to some remote area. Years later he has the prophet write a letter rebuking Jehoram, king of Israel, and predicting his agonizing death (2 Chron. 21:11–15). Most scholars take this to be a fanciful creation of the chronicler, who wanted to make use of the reputation of Elijah. See further Jacob M. Myers, *II Chronicles*, The Anchor Bible (Garden City, NY: Doubleday, 1965), pp. 121–22.

25. It is anachronistic to read this account as an ascent to heavenly enthronement. The idea of ascent to heavenly glory develops much later; see James D. Tabor, *Things Unutterable: Paul's Ascent to Paradise in Its Greco-Roman, Judaic, and Early Christian Contexts*, Studies in Judaism (Lanham, MD: Univ. Press of America, 1986), pp. 57–111, for bibliography and a discussion of the historical development of this idea.

26. Compare Jeremiah, who at several points cursed the day of his birth (Jer. 15:10; 20:14–16).

27. On these passages see Daube, "Death as Release," pp. 91–93. Daube collects a number of other similar texts throughout the Bible. See the loosely related language in the cases of Rebekah (Gen. 27:46), Rachel (Gen. 30:1), the people of Israel (Ex. 16:3), Delilah (Judg. 16:16), and David (2 Sam. 18:33). The reference to being blotted out of the "book" is a standard Hebrew expression for the "book of the living" and clearly means Moses is asking to die; see Ps. 69:28; Isa. 4:3.

28. In addition to those listed in the previous note, there is the account of David's grief and depression over the illness of his infant son, born of his adulterous union with Bathsheba. At one point his servants fear that "he may do himself harm" (2 Sam. 12:18). This indicates that such a possibility, in the face of terrible grief, would be understandable in that culture. Finally, there is also the story of Zebah and Zalmun'na, who demand that Gideon slay them (Judg. 8:18–21).

29. The dating and literary strata of the book of Job are problematic. See the discussion by Marvin H. Pope, *Job*, The Anchor Bible (Garden City, NY: Doubleday, 1973), pp. xxiii–xlvii; and Robert Gordis, *The Book of God and Man: A Study of Job* (Chicago: Univ. of Chicago Press, 1965), pp. 216ff.

30. Pope, *Job*, pp. xxiii–xl, arguing on the basis of parallel Mesopotamian texts, places the "Dialogue" in the seventh century B.C. This is too early. His argument that

the "level" of discussion regarding theodicy in Job is found in early Babylonian materials is not a conclusive one. In Babylonian wisdom literature there is a text from the first millennium B.C. that is usually titled "The Babylonian Theodicy." Robert Pfeiffer has dubbed it the "Babylonian Ecclesiastes," though it also has strong parallels with Job; see Pritchard, ed., *Ancient Near Eastern Texts*, pp. 438–40. One should compare the poem of the righteous sufferer, *Ludlul bel memeqi*, which has sometimes been called the "Babylonian Job." The author, like his Hebrew counterpart, is abandoned by his god and finds his afflictions unjustified and unbearable. The doubting "sufferer" cites all his calamities, while a friend upholds the "orthodox" notion that despite all appearances, justice is found in this world. At one point the friend of the sufferer says, "People in fact give up and go the way of death; it is an old saying that they cross the river Hubur." The meaning is obscure, but it appears that the "sufferer" has suggested death as a way out of his plight. His friend seems to counsel otherwise. For translation and notes see W. G. Lambert, ed., *The Babylonian Wisdom Literature* (Oxford: Clarendon Press, 1960), pp. 21–62. See Jacobsen's discussion of this text in Henri Frankfort, H. Frankfort, John A. Wilson, and Thorkild Jacobsen, eds., *Before Philosophy: The Intellectual Adventure of Ancient Man* (Baltimore, MD: Penguin Books, 1949), pp. 227–31.

31. See 14:13–15; 19:23–29. The interpretations and translations of both these passages (especially of 19:23–29) are problematic. Most scholars doubt that Job expresses belief in life after death. The English translations, particularly those in the King James tradition, are characterized more by later Christian piety than by accuracy. See the *Tanak* (Philadelphia: Jewish Publication Society, 1985) for an accurate translation; also the notes in Pope, *Job*, pp. 108–9, 143–48. We have no evidence that the debate over resurrection of the dead or immortality of the soul existed in *Jewish* circles until well into Second Temple times. On this development, see R. H. Charles, *Eschatology: The Doctrine of a Future Life in Israel, Judaism, and Christianity, A Critical History* (New York: Schocken Books, 1963, reprint of 1913 ed.), which is still valuable, particularly for primary sources. Among recent studies, see W. E. Nickelsburg, Jr., *Resurrection, Immortality, and Eternal Life in Intertestamental Judaism* (Cambridge, MA: Harvard Univ. Press, 1972), and H. C. C. Cavallin, *Life After Death: Paul's Argument for the Resurrection of the Dead in I Cor. 15: Part I: An Enquiry into the Jewish Background* (Lund: GWK Gleerup, 1974).

32. Compare Ps. 104:29; and the pleas of Elijah and Jonah (1 Kings 19:4; Jon. 4:3).

33. See the essay by Thorkild Jacobsen, "Mesopotamia," in Frankfort et al., *Before Philosophy*, pp. 103–33, and Morton Smith, "The Common Theology of the Ancient Near East," *Journal of Biblical Literature* 71 (1952): 135–47. For the Greeks, see Homer, *Odyssey* 11, and the summary article by Werner Jaeger, "The Greek Ideas of Immortality," in *Immortality and Resurrection: Death in the Western World*, ed. Krister Stendahl (New York: Macmillan, 1965), pp. 97–114. Egyptian views of death develop along somewhat different lines; see the survey essay by John A. Wilson, "Egypt," in Frankfort et al., *Before Philosophy*, pp. 39–133.

34. See Pss. 6:4–6; 88:1–12. This is the general view. In a rare text such as Ps. 139:8, poetically at least, God penetrates even that dark realm. Compare Isa. 26:19, apparently a late addition to Isaiah, where "light" is spoken of as falling on the land of the shades below. For the subsequent development of the Hebrew concepts of afterlife, see the survey chapter by S. G. F. Brandon, *The Judgment of the Dead* (New York: Scribner's, 1967), pp. 56–75, and the literature cited above, n. 31. See T. H. Gaster, "Cosmology," *Interpreter's Dictionary of the Bible*, vol. 1, pp. 702–9, for discussion, further bibliography, and a pictorial sketch of this ancient Hebrew conception of the universe.

35. The earliest unambiguous reference to resurrection of the dead in the Hebrew Bible is in Dan. 12:2–3, which comes from the second century B.C. We will discuss this development below.

36. The author of 1 Kings, in describing the ideal reign of Solomon, offers a short but telling summary of this ancient Hebrew view of the good life: "Judah and Israel were as many as the sand by the sea; they ate and drank and were happy (4:20)."

37. Blenkinsopp makes this very point in his letter mentioned above: "Job prays ardently for death but never contemplates suicide" (*Bible Review*, June 1990, p. 7). See the brief discussion in Clemons, *What Does the Bible Say?* pp. 33–34, 44.

38. For an introductory discussion of dating, see R. B. Y. Scott, *Proverbs-Ecclesiastes*, The Anchor Bible (Garden City, NY: Doubleday, 1965), pp. 196–201. In general, see the excellent study by Robert Gordis, *Koheleth, the Man and His World*, 3d ed. (New York: Schocken Books, 1968).

39. The somewhat "optimistic" ending of 12:13–14 was probably added by a later editor, who was concerned that the force of the book might lead one to turn from God. See Scott, *Proverbs-Ecclesiastes*, p. 199.

40. Compare 6:3, where he argues that given life's injustices, "an untimely birth," that is, a miscarriage, would be better than life.

41. There is a Babylonian text, titled "The Dialogue of Pessimism," which is much clearer on this point. It discusses whether taking one's life makes sense, given the futility of the human condition, and apparently concludes that death is the better choice. It is a dialogue between a master and his servant. The master bids the servant repeatedly to do this or that; the servant agrees, commending the master for his choice. The master then changes his mind, convinced of the ultimate futility of any action, whereupon the servant agrees; nothing really matters. The actions range from the mundane to the weighty, reflecting all the typical duties of a Mesopotamian nobleman:

    "Slave, listen to me."

    "Here I am, sir, here [I am]."

    "I am going to love a woman."

    "So love, sir, love. The man who loves a woman forgets sorrow and fear."

    "No, slave, I will by no means love a woman."

    "[Do not] love, sir, do not love. Woman is a pitfall—a pitfall, a hole, a ditch; woman is a sharp iron dagger that cuts a man's throat" (lines 46–52).

    The pessimism builds with each exchange until the final lines, when death itself becomes the subject. The master asks the servant what is good, suggesting that "to break my neck, your neck, throw both into the river—that is good." The servant answers by quoting a proverb, expressing resignation in the face of human insignificance. The master, changing his mind as always, then suggests, "No, servant, I shall kill you and send you ahead of me," to which the servant wisely replies, "[Then] would my lord [wish to] live even three days after me?" (lines 80–86). The servant has the last word, and the point of the whole seems to be, why continue, for even a short time, a life so devoid of meaning? See Pritchard, ed., *Ancient Near Eastern Texts*, pp. 337–38; compare Lambert, ed., *Babylonian Wisdom Literature*, p. 149. See the comments and discussion of Jacobsen, in Frankfort et al., *Before Philosophy*, pp. 231–34.

42. The author of the "Song of the Harper," like his Hebrew counterpart *Qoheleth*, advocates hedonism in the face of the transitory nature of life; see the translation of John Wilson, in Pritchard, ed., *Ancient Near Eastern Texts*, p. 467.

43. Note that other contrasts in this poem (such as "a time to plant, and a time to pluck" or "a time to kill, and a time to heal," vv. 2–3) have to do with direct human choice and activity. It is possible that the phrase "a time to die" could refer to voluntary death.

44. John J. Collins traces these developments in two important articles: "Apocalyptic Eschatology as the Transcendence of Death," *Catholic Biblical Quarterly* 36 (1974): 21–43; and "The Root of Immortality: Death in the Context of Jewish Wisdom," *Harvard Theological Review* 71 (1978): 177–92. For a general survey of these shifts and changes, see James D. Tabor, "The Future," in *What the Bible Really Says*, edited by Morton Smith and R. Joseph Hoffmann (Buffalo, NY: Prometheus Books, 1989), pp. 33–51.

45. As we explained in our introductory chapter, we generally avoid the use of the terms *martyrdom* and *suicide*. Either expression prejudges the important issues related to voluntary death. On the problem of categories and definitions, see the survey articles by Harran, "Suicide"; and Samuel Z. Klausner, "Martyrdom," in *The Encyclopedia of Religion*, vol. 9, pp. 230–38. Both cite important secondary literature.

46. John L. McKenzie, *Second Isaiah*, The Anchor Bible (Garden City, NY: Doubleday, 1968), dates this material to 537–445 B.C. (p. xix).

47. See the discussion of Sam K. Williams, *Jesus' Death as Saving Event: The Background and Origin of a Concept*, Harvard Dissertations in Religion, no. 2 (Missoula, MT: Scholars Press, 1975); and David Seeley, *The Noble Death: Greco-Roman Martyrology and Paul's Concept of Salvation*, JSNT Supplement Series, no. 28 (Sheffield: JSOT, 1990), pp. 39–58.

48. The nation as "Yahweh's servant" seems more likely given references such as Isa. 41:8; 43:10; 44:1–2; and 45:4. However, some passages seem to speak of an idealized individual, otherwise unknown to us. See, for example, 42:1–4; 49:1–6; 50:4–11; 52:11–53:12. For a discussion of the identity of the servant, see McKenzie, *Second Isaiah*, pp. xliii–lv.

49. The date of this diverse material in Isaiah is impossible to determine with precision. It is certainly postexilic and usually put in the fifth century B.C. However,

judging from the apocalyptic themes and patterns, it could well come from the Hellenistic period.

50. In the Hebrew canon Daniel is not included in the division of the prophets, but is placed in the last section, "Writings," with other materials from the late Persian and early Hellenistic periods.

51. For critical discussion, see Elias Bickerman, *Der Gott der Makkabäer* (Berlin: Schocken Verlag, 1937), pp. 80–86; Victor Tcherikover, *Hellenistic Civilization and the Jews* (Philadelphia: Magnes Press, 1959), pp. 175–203; and Martin Hengel, *Judaism and Hellenism* (Philadelphia: Fortress Press, 1974), vol. 1, pp. 267–309.

52. See Nickelsburg, *Resurrection, Immortality, and Eternal Life,* for a general discussion of these developments in Second Temple times, but, more particularly, note the argument of Collins, "Apocalyptic Eschatology as the Transcendence of Death."

53. The dating of this composite document is disputed. The persecution it describes has been variously identified as that of 587 B.C., that of Antiochus IV, the capture of Jerusalem by Pompey in 63 B.C., the Jewish revolt of A.D. 66–70, and the Bar Kosiba war of A.D. 132–135. See James H. Charlesworth, ed., *The Old Testament Pseudepigrapha,* 2 vols. (Garden City, NY: Doubleday, 1983–85), vol. 1, pp. 918–26, for discussion and bibliography.

54. This Taxo is otherwise unknown. The motif of "seven sons" reminds one of the stories of the mother with seven sons in the Maccabean materials we will discuss below. Some have seen him as a "suffering servant" or messianic figure. See Charlesworth, *Old Testament Pseudepigrapha,* vol. 1, pp. 922–23.

55. Morton Smith has suggested, on the basis of an earlier passage in 5:4–5, that the group behind this document, like other Jewish sectarians such as those at Qumran, rejected the sacrifices of the Jerusalem temple as impure (*Palestinian Parties and Politics That Shaped the Old Testament,* 2d ed. [London: SCM Press, 1987], p. 120).

56. As we will see in chap. 5, the Gospel traditions on the voluntary death of Jesus, as well as Paul's own language about choosing death, draw upon this language of sacrifice.

57. See Seeley, *Noble Death,* esp. chap. 5, for a recent evaluation of this developing idea of "martyrdom." Also see the papers edited by J. W. van Henten, *Die Entstehung der jüdischen Martyrologie,* Studia Post-Biblica, no. 38 (Leiden: Brill, 1989).

58. According to 1 Macc. 2:39–41, this decision was reversed by Mattathias and his men once they realized what a disaster the policy had brought. This discussion, of when one is required or allowed to give up or take one's life rather than violate a commandment of God, persisted in Jewish circles. We will discuss the rabbinic resolution of the problem in the following chapter.

59. It is worth noting that the author of 2 Maccabees relates that Ptolemy Macron, who "took the lead in showing justice to the Jews," took poison and "ended his life" (2 Macc. 10:10–13). He acted under pressure from Antiochus V Eupator, son

of Antiochus IV Epiphanes. References of this type are common in classical authors. Although Jason records it in passing, he places it in a favorable light. Ptolemy is hardly a "martyr," but he does show favor to the Jews and suffers accordingly. Indeed, Ptolemy's act of self-destruction could be seen as an expression of repentance.

60. Though never formally canonized, this book was treasured in the Eastern churches. See *Oxford Annotated Bible*, pp. ix–xxii.

61. See Collins, "The Root of Immortality," for an important evaluation of this key development. We agree with Collins that there is no critical difference between the "Hebrew" notion of "resurrection of the dead" and the "Greek" idea of "immortality of the soul." There is a merger of terms and concepts, and both reflect the same essential shift in thought—from the view that death is the end, to the idea that death can be transcended. See James D. Tabor, "Resurrection and Immortality: Paul and Poimandres," in *Christian Teaching: Studies in Honor of LeMoine G. Lewis*, edited by Everett Ferguson (Abilene, TX: Abilene Christian Univ. Press, 1981), pp. 72–91.

CHAPTER 4

❧

Acquiring Life in a
Single Moment

In the previous chapter we noted the important shift in the way voluntary death was perceived by Jews in the Hellenistic period. We encountered cases in which the choice of death was seen not only as noble, heroic, or necessary to avoid shame or suffering but also as a *way to acquire life* in the world to come.[1]

Such an understanding of voluntary death among Jews in this period is related to a broader phenomenon: a *dualistic* understanding of the universe and of the human person, in which this material world was devalued over against a spiritual existence beyond. Death was seen, paradoxically, as life.[2]

In the ancient Mediterranean world the origins of this dualistic understanding of reality are particularly associated with Pythagorean, Orphic, and Platonic philosophical traditions from the fifth and fourth centuries B.C.[3] However, such a perspective was broadly influential in a variety of contexts in later Hellenistic times. Cicero aptly captures the popular literary development of this Platonic dualism in his account of the "Dream of Scipio." In this dream Scipio the Younger travels to the spiritual world beyond, encountering his deceased father Paulus and his grandfather, Scipio the Elder, whom he questions about the nature of death: "I nevertheless asked whether he himself and my father Paulus and the others whom we thought of as dead were still alive. 'Those are indeed alive,' he said, 'who have escaped from the bondage of the body as from a prison; what you call life is in reality death.' "[4]

This dualism of body and soul is closely related to a dualistic understanding of the cosmos itself, in which the lower material earth is seen in contrast to the spiritual or heavenly world above.[5] Such a "transvaluation of reality," as Werner Jaeger aptly terms it, in which life in this world is "death," while death is an exit, or escape, to heavenly life, becomes a critical element in the development of attitudes toward voluntary death among both Jews and Christians in the Greco-Roman period. When the body is seen as a "prison" of the immortal soul, and the soul is understood to *belong*, fundamentally, in the heavenly world beyond, questions of how and when the "release" is to come rise to the fore. In this chapter we will examine texts from Josephus, Philo, and the rabbis of the Mishnah, Midrashim, and Talmuds, tracing out the development of Jewish attitudes toward voluntary death into the post-Talmudic period.

JOSEPHUS

The writings of Josephus are replete with references to voluntary death. In his *Jewish Antiquities*, which covers Jewish history from Adam and Eve to the emperor Nero, he includes his own interpretation of the six standard examples of voluntary death in the Hebrew Bible. He also provides accounts of the Jews who chose to die around the time of the Maccabean revolt. Further, in the *Antiquities* and the *Jewish War* he reports as many as two dozen separate incidents of voluntary death, from the period of Roman occupation (63 B.C.), down through the Jewish revolt (A.D. 66–73). Indeed, he is the first writer in antiquity to use a Greek *noun*, rather than a verbal phrase, to describe the act of voluntary death.[6] He tells of his own narrow escape from a "death pact" at Jotapata while serving as commanding officer of the Galilean rebel forces during the Jewish revolt. He is our main source for the infamous case of Masada, where, according to Josephus, 960 men, women, and children took their own lives rather than face Roman capture. In the incidents at Jotapata and Masada he also provides us with extensive philosophical discussion of the general problem of voluntary death.

Unfortunately the evidence is as problematic as it is full. Josephus wrote his two great histories, the *Jewish War* (c. A.D. 75) and the *Jewish Antiquities* (c. A.D. 93), while living in Rome in a former palace of the emperor Vespasian, supported by an imperial pension.[7] He is at one and the same time an apologist for his own Jewish people, with whom Rome had fought a protracted and frustrating war, and a client of the Flavians. He writes decades after the revolt, dominated by the interests of his contemporary situation. He covers the entire history of the Hebrew Bible up through his own time. As we read his works, we are hearing some combination of Josephus the devout Jewish Pharisee, the Roman citizen and friend of the imperial family, the former commander of a group of Jewish rebels, the Greco-Roman historian, and the professional Jewish apologist. So, despite the rather abundant materials Josephus offers us on voluntary death, it is sometimes difficult or impossible to know to what degree his opinions and evaluations might represent Jewish thinking more generally.

We begin with Josephus's versions of the voluntary deaths of Abimelech, Samson, Saul and his armor-bearer, Ahithophel, and Zimri, as he works his way through the narrative of the Hebrew Bible. Josephus often edits his biblical material quite freely, adding and cutting at will. It is noteworthy that he includes *all six* of these accounts.[8] The way in which he treats them gives an indication of his general attitude toward voluntary death.

Josephus reports Abimelech's death in a matter-of-fact way. Though he is negative regarding Abimelech as a character, nonetheless he does not find Abimelech's manner of death any cause for special comment (*Ant.* 5.251–53). Like the biblical text, Josephus reports that Abimelech got what he deserved as an evildoer, having brutally murdered the Shechemites.

In contrast, Josephus is most positive about Samson. He considerably elaborates the biblical text with terms of praise and admiration. He writes,

> And it is but right to admire the man for his valour, his strength, and *the grandeur of his end*, as also for the wrath which he cherished to the last against his enemies. That he let himself be ensnared by a woman must be imputed to human nature which succumbs to sins; but testimony is due to him for *his surpassing excellence in all the rest*. His kinsfolk then took up his body and buried him at Sarasa, his native place, with his forefathers *(Ant.* 5.317).[9]

This text offers clear evidence that Josephus considered voluntary death, given the proper circumstances, as noble and heroic. He even notes that Samson was given an honorable burial. This is no insignificant detail but a further indication of Josephus's approval of Samson's choice. At Jotapata, when Josephus tries to dissuade his troops from taking their lives, he refers approvingly to the custom of *forbidding* honorable burial to "those who have laid mad hands upon themselves" (*JW* 3.375). Obviously, he does not classify all acts of self-destruction as resulting from "mad hands."

In the cases of Saul and his armor-bearer, Josephus combines the basic account of 1 Samuel 31, where Saul falls on his own sword, with the alternative story of 2 Samuel 1, where an Amalekite claims responsibility for Saul's death (*Ant.* 6.370–73). According to Josephus's composite version, Saul *tries to kill himself* by falling on his sword but is too weak to do so. He then asks the help of an Amalekite, who forces the sword in. At that point the armor-bearer, who had earlier refused Saul's request to assist him to die, takes his own life. So, according to Josephus, Saul did not *directly* take his own life. Still, there is no reason to think that Josephus alters the story to remove the reference to Saul's direct act of self-destruction. Josephus's interest here is harmonization. He wants to smooth out the contradiction between the two biblical accounts. Josephus has little praise for Saul, noting that his defeat came because he disobeyed God. If he understood the *manner* of Saul's death in the account of 1 Samuel 31 negatively, he would not have hesitated to make such a point. He reports the self-inflicted death of the armor-bearer without comment, knowing his readers will view it as a common and justifiable action in such circumstances.

Josephus's positive attitude toward voluntary death, given justifiable circumstances, is further indicated in his account of Ahithophel, who hanged himself. Josephus *adds* his own positive interpretation to the biblical text: "Therefore, he [Ahithophel] said, it would be better for him to *remove himself from the world in a free and noble spirit* than surrender himself to David to be punished for having in all ways helped Absalom against him" (*Ant.* 7.229).

The biblical text does not attribute any such motive to Ahithophel (2 Sam. 17:23). There he faces humiliation and chooses death. There is no indication that his life is in any immediate danger. Josephus recasts the text in this way, because, in his view, the *ultimate justification* for voluntary death is that it provides a noble escape from intolerable circumstances.[10] As we will see, in case after case throughout his writings, he recounts similar scenes with approval. He reflects the general consensus we saw among many Greek and Roman writers in chapter two.

The final biblical case of voluntary death, that of Zimri, Josephus reports in the most straightforward manner. He says Zimri set the palace on fire and "allowed himself to be consumed with it after a reign of only seven days" (*Ant.* 8.311). His phrasing makes it clear, perhaps a bit more so than the biblical text, that Zimri *intended* his own death; it was no accident (cf. 1 Kings 16:18). Otherwise Josephus reports it without comment.

To summarize, in none of these six cases does Josephus appear to be negative about the act of voluntary death itself. In two of the cases, Samson and Ahithophel, Josephus goes *beyond* his biblical source to stress that the choice to die was a noble one. In the four cases where the biblical text reports the *honorable burial* of the deceased (Samson, Saul and his armor-bearer, and Ahithophel), Josephus includes the information, thus indicating his general approval.

In recounting the period of the Maccabean revolt, Josephus generally follows the story as it is told in 1 Maccabees. There, Antiochus IV tries to force the Jews to give up their religious practices. Josephus says those "of *noble soul* disregarded him," choosing to die rather than submit: "Indeed, they were whipped, their bodies were mutilated, and while still alive and breathing, they were crucified, while their wives and sons whom they had circumcised in despite of the king's wishes were strangled, the children being made to hang from the necks of their crucified parents" (*Ant.* 12.256).

Josephus relates how the Jewish rebels, in the early stages of the conflict, would refuse to fight on the Sabbath and were willing to give up their lives passively rather than violate this commandment of God (*Ant.* 12.274; cf. 1 Macc. 2:32–38). Josephus obviously sees this as a noble decision and seems to expect that his readers will admire the courage displayed. In both his histories he recounts, with obvious admiration, the heroic tale of Eleazar and the elephant attack (*Ant.* 12.373; *JW* 1.41–44).

Josephus reports the charge of the dying Jewish rebel commander Mattathias to his sons:

I wish you to remain constant as such and to be superior to all force and compulsion, *being so prepared in spirit as to die for the laws*, if need be, and bearing
this in mind, that when the Deity sees you so disposed, He will not forget you,
but in *admiration of your heroism* will give them back to you again. . . . For
though our bodies are mortal and subject to death, we can through the memory
of our deeds, attain the heights of immortality (*Ant.* 12.281–82).

Josephus composes these scenes of courage in the face of compulsion with
obvious pride. He specifically praises and defends such willingness to die for
one's convictions in his work *Against Apion*. There he asks if anyone has ever
heard of a case of the Jewish people "proving traitors to their laws or afraid of
death." He says he is thinking here not of death on the battlefield but of choosing death, even when accompanied by physical torture, rather than violating
ancestral laws. He claims the Jewish people are particularly noted for this kind
of heroism:

To such a death we are, in my belief, exposed by some of our conquerors, not
from hatred of those at their mercy, but from a curiosity to witness the astonishing spectacle of men who believe that the only evil which can befall them is
to be compelled to do any act or utter any word contrary to their laws. There
should be nothing astonishing in our facing death on behalf of our laws with a
courage which no other nation can equal (*AgAp.* 2.233–34).

Josephus obviously expects his Greek and Roman readers to understand
and admire such acts of courage. Here he echoes popular Cynic-Stoic arguments for the essential inviolacy of the self over against any outside opposition.[11]

Josephus's many postbiblical accounts of voluntary death often echo this
commonplace Cynic-Stoic theme. There are nine such reports in the *Antiquities*,
with another dozen or so in the *War*.[12] Raymond Newell has shown that these
reports generally follow a set pattern with three elements: (1) a description of
the hopeless predicament leading to the choice of death; (2) the reason for the
death; and (3) a description of the act itself.[13]

For example, at the accession of Antiochus Epiphanes to the throne,
Josephus relates that Hyrcanus, "fearing his great power, and expecting to be
captured and punished for what he had done to the Arabs, ended his life by his
own hand" (*Ant.* 12.236). Sometimes, in reporting the justification for the
choice of death, Josephus will state or imply his own attitude.

The most common justification given in these incidents is that death will
guarantee freedom from slavery and torture. For example, around 100 B.C. there
was a fierce Jewish attack upon Gaza. Josephus tells us that many of the

Gazaeans, knowing they faced certain defeat, "with their own hands made away with their children and wives, this being the means by which they were compelled to *deliver them from slavery to their foes*" (*Ant.* 13.364). Josephus relates many similar accounts, often with vivid and touching details. In 38 B.C. Herod was on a campaign against Jewish "bandits," who were hidden in the caves of Arbela. They were protected by the sheer cliffs surrounding them. Herod was slowly able to ferret them out by lowering men with ropes to the mouths of the caves and throwing in firebrands. He offered asylum to those who would surrender. Josephus says, "Not one of them voluntarily surrendered, and of those taken by force *many preferred death to captivity*" (*JW* 1.311). He concentrates his story on one particular family:

> It was then that one old man, the father of seven children, being asked by them and their mother permission to leave under Herod's pledge, killed them in the following manner. Ordering them to come forward one by one, he stood at the entrance and slew each son as he advanced. Herod, watching this spectacle . . . was profoundly affected and, extending his hand to the old man, implored him to spare his children; but he, unmoved by any word of Herod and even upbraiding him as a low-born upstart, followed up the slaughter of his sons by that of his wife, and having flung their corpses down the precipice, finally threw himself over after them (*JW* 1.312–13).[14]

Josephus similarly recounts the brutal self-inflicted death of Phasael, brother of Herod and tetrarch of Judea. The Parthians had invaded around 40 B.C. and had even taken Jerusalem. They had installed Antigonus as king. Phasael, though fettered and thus deprived of the use of his hands, was determined to take his life. He dashed his head upon a rock and died (*JW* 1.271).[15] Josephus offers a positive evaluation of Phasael's action in his later account in the *Antiquities*:

> As for Phasael, one must *admire his courage*, for though he knew that he was marked for slaughter, he did *not look upon the death as terrible in itself* but believed that it was a most bitter and shameful thing to suffer at the hands of a foe . . . which he thought was the best thing to do in view of his helpless position, and thus he deprived the enemy of the power of killing him as they pleased (*Ant.* 14.368).

Though Josephus is no friend of the Herodian family, he makes the same points repeatedly, whether in behalf of Jew or Roman, friend or foe: voluntary death brings freedom; when chosen in the face of hopeless circumstances, it is justified and admirable.[16]

In at least one case Josephus praises such a choice of death as loyalty to God. When the Roman general Pompey besieged the temple at Jerusalem in

63 B.C., Josephus says Pompey slaughtered twelve thousand Jews. Finally, the temple itself was taken:

> Then it was that many of the priests, seeing the enemy advancing sword in hand, calmly continued their sacred ministrations, and were butchered in the act of pouring libations and burning incense; *putting the worship of the Deity above their own preservation* . . . countless numbers flung themselves over the precipices; some, driven mad by their hopeless plight, set fire to the buildings around the wall and were consumed in the flames (*JW* 1.150–51).

In a few cases, however, Josephus interprets the act of voluntary death more negatively, either as a type of self-inflicted punishment or as rash and unnecessary. His account of one Simon, a Jew of Scythopolis (Bethshan), one of the cities of the Decapolis, is a case in point. The Jews of Scythopolis supported the city in its opposition to the revolt and found themselves fighting their own countrymen. Josephus notes that Simon was especially valiant and had slain large numbers of the Jewish attackers. The citizens of Scythopolis, however, did not trust their Jewish population and forced them into a grove near the city. There they slaughtered them all, thirteen thousand in number. When Simon saw his Jewish brethren falling, he drew his sword, but instead of fighting the attackers he cried out, "Justly am I *punished for my crimes*, men of Scythopolis, I and all who by such a slaughter of our kinsmen have sealed our loyalty to you . . . *let us, I say, die, as cursed wretches, by our own hands*; for we are not meet to die at the hands of the enemy" (*JW* 2.472–73). Simon then rushed over to his own family, killing first his gray-headed father and mother with his sword, then his wife and children. Josephus says they offered no resistance, each almost "rushing upon the blade, in haste to anticipate the enemy" (*JW* 2.475).[17] Then Simon plunged the sword to the hilt into his own throat.

There was a somewhat similar incident at Gadara. In 20 B.C. the inhabitants of Gadara denounced Herod as too severe in his rule. When they saw that Caesar was likely to take the side of Herod, "they were afraid of being maltreated, and so some of them cut their own throats during the night, while others threw themselves down from high places or *willfully destroyed themselves* by jumping into the river" (*Ant.* 15.358–59). Josephus says these actions were regarded as "self-condemnation of their rashness and guilt," so Caesar promptly acquitted Herod of the charges. Josephus does not report these deaths as heroic, since he does not seem to agree that their condition was hopeless. He sees their action as premature, a miscalculation. He implies that Caesar might well have ruled in their favor had they not been so hasty.

This question of the proper circumstances under which voluntary death is justified is more systematically addressed by Josephus when he recounts his own situation at Jotapata and in his treatment of the Masada incident. During the Jewish revolt Josephus was commander of the rebel forces in Galilee and present at the siege of Jotapata, which lasted forty-seven days. When the Romans finally took the city, they began to massacre the population. Josephus reports there were forty thousand dead with only twelve hundred prisoners. He writes, "The situation even drove many of Josephus's picked men to suicide [*autocheiria*]; seeing themselves powerless to kill a single Roman, they could at least forestall death at Roman hands, and, retiring in a body to the outskirts of the town, they there put an end to themselves" (JW 3.331).[18]

Josephus and forty other survivors hid in a cave. They determined to take their own lives rather than surrender. Josephus claims that he argued against this decision, urging surrender to the Romans. He preserved a full account of his speech, which we will analyze below. His comrades overrode his appeal, and in desperation he suggested that they draw lots to see the order in which they would kill themselves. They began to do so, one by one, until, by the providence of God, Josephus claims, only he and one other were left. He then persuaded this final survivor to surrender with him. He was subsequently brought before Vespasian and gained his support and favor by prophesying that the Roman general would soon become emperor.

Of all these accounts of voluntary death, it is the tale of Masada that most interests and occupies Josephus.[19] The bare facts, according to Josephus, are the following. Masada was the last fortress to be conquered by the Romans. It was occupied by the Sicarii, led by one Eleazar, a descendant of the infamous rebel Judas the Galilean.[20] On May 1, A.D. 73, the day before the Romans were expected to finally storm the fortress, Eleazar delivered a long speech urging the Jews to take their own lives rather than submit to capture. They chose ten of their number by lot, who then killed all the others. Finally those ten killed themselves. Josephus says their total number was 960. An old woman, and one other survivor who was a relative of Eleazar, along with five children, hid in the subterranean aqueducts and escaped death. The next day the Romans broke through the wall without resistance and found the bodies. They learned what had happened from these survivors. Josephus says that the Romans refused to exult over their capture but "admired the nobility of their resolve and the contempt of death displayed by so many" (JW 7.406).

Despite its length, the basic elements and framework of the Masada account are strikingly similar to Josephus's other narratives on voluntary death that we have just surveyed. Josephus introduces Eleazar's protracted speech with a standard set of justifying circumstances that we have encountered several times previously: "Seeing the wall consuming in the flames, unable to devise any further means of deliverance or gallant endeavor, and setting before his eyes what the Romans, if victorious, would inflict on them, their children and their wives, he [Eleazar] deliberated on the death of all" (JW 7.321).

The problem comes with the speech itself. Why does Josephus go to such length to record Eleazar's arguments *for voluntary death*, while at the same time he records his own arguments at Jotapata *against* the action? One obvious point that should not be overlooked is that at Jotapata Josephus's *own life* is at stake. Since he reports, throughout his works, that so many during his time had freely offered their lives rather than surrender to the Romans, how can he justify his own actions? But the issues are more complicated than this. Why should Josephus even include this lengthy account of Masada? And more important, why does he present the details of Eleazar's argument with such obvious sympathy? Does he intend to present these rebels, who took their own lives, as unqualified heroes? Finally, how is the Masada account related to the other episodes of voluntary death Josephus reports in his works, especially those he presents with sympathy and even praise? All of these questions must be addressed.[21]

Clearly the two speeches, that of Eleazar at Masada and that of Josephus at Jotapata, are *purposely* antithetical. Both rely directly on arguments from Plato's *Phaedo*, and, as we will see, this is the key to understanding the whole problem. Also, both echo many of the themes and evaluations Josephus presents in his many accounts of voluntary death in both the *Antiquities* and the *War*. In both works, but especially in these two speeches, Josephus has his Greco-Roman audience, both Jewish and non-Jewish, clearly in mind.

The Eleazar speech, *defending* voluntary death, falls into three sections with overlapping points. In the first section Josephus makes three main arguments. (1) Since the rebels have determined to serve God alone, and not the Romans, God has now granted through his providence the opportunity to *die nobly and in freedom*. They have "the free choice of a noble death." (2) God has doomed the Jewish nation by all evidence. To choose to die will actually be carrying out a self-inflicted, *just penalty for crimes* paid to God, not to the Romans. (3) Death is the only way to *escape the dishonor and slavery* that will come upon wives and children (JW 7.323–36).

In the second section, Eleazar begins to reason philosophically with the people, drawing upon various Greek sources, particularly Plato's *Phaedo* (JW 7.341–57).[22] What we have here is commonplace Hellenistic dualism reinforced with two examples, one from nature and the other from ethnography. Life, not death, is the human misfortune, asserts Eleazar. Death gives *liberty to the immortal soul, imprisoned in the body*, so it can depart to its proper and pure abode. Therefore death is pleasant and should be welcomed like sleep. Finally, Eleazar cites the noble example of the Indians who *hasten* to release their souls from their bodies.

In the third and final section of his speech, Eleazar reverses himself, returning to his earlier approach (JW 7.358–88). He says that even if one formerly held the opposite doctrine, that *life* is the highest blessing and *death* is a calamity, the present crisis calls upon one to turn to death.[23] Again, he makes three points, related to his earlier arguments in the first section: (1) God wills that the rebels die; the Jewish cause is doomed. It is not the Romans who have brought defeat, but God. (2) No one sensitive to the tragedies that have come upon the Jewish nation would want to go on living. (3) The wrath of the Romans will be great once they capture the fortress; death is thus the only way of escape, a way of making the Romans react with admiration to the fortitude of the rebels.

These points strikingly parallel the evaluations Josephus has given in his various accounts of voluntary death that we have just surveyed. Josephus repeatedly stresses that, given the right circumstances, the choice to die is a noble act of freedom. He also reports many cases where the decision to kill oneself is justified by the dire situation one faces. Finally, he maintains that the choice to die can be understood as a self-inflicted death penalty for crimes, and even as a just retribution from God. It is certainly no accident that through Eleazar's speech Josephus rehearses each of these three points, effectively highlighting his own views on the subject.

Josephus's argument *against* voluntary death in his Jotapata speech is based almost entirely on Plato's discussion in the *Phaedo* of the crucial question: *when ought one to choose death?* He says, "It is equally cowardly not to wish to die when one *ought to do so*, and to wish to die when one *ought not*" (JW 3.365). As we saw in chapter two, this is the essential point in the debate over voluntary death that runs through the Greco-Roman sources. Josephus maintains that taking one's life is permitted, given the proper *necessity*, or "signal" from God. Otherwise "suicide" or "ownhandedness" (*autocheiria*) is an act of impiety. He specifically says of God, "For it is from Him that we have received our being, and it is to Him that we should leave the decision to take it away" (JW 3.371). Josephus warns that those who disregard this principle, laying "mad hands upon themselves," will descend to the darker regions of Hades (JW 3.375). His argument is a simple one: the Romans have offered to spare them; accordingly, there is *no necessity* or proper justification for choosing death. He is making a conditional, not an absolute, argument against voluntary death. Lest anyone charge that he only opposes death when his own life is involved, he boldly declares, "Were I now flinching from the sword of the Romans, I should assuredly *deserve to perish by my own sword* and my own hand; but if they are moved to spare an enemy, how much stronger reason have we to spare ourselves" (JW 3.364).[24]

It should be pointed out here that Josephus views himself as a "prophet," with a divinely guided destiny involving none other than the future emperor Vespasian. He has had dreams as to the outcome of the Jewish revolt. In his view, it was clearly *not* his time to die (JW 3.351–52). He reports his escape from the "death pact" his troops made, in spite of his ineffective pleading in this speech, as a providential act of God (JW 3.387–91). In his case, there has been no divine "signal" that he is to leave the body. Quite the opposite, he has a mission for God to fulfill.

The two speeches, of Eleazar and Josephus, though arguing opposite points, are both nonetheless rooted in Plato and strangely complement one another. Plato presents arguments *both for* and *against* voluntary death in the *Phaedo*, as we saw in chapter two. Without actually quoting Plato as a source in either speech, Josephus presents us with his own versions of the commonplace debates over the key issue of "necessity."

Several important questions remain. Why does Josephus recount the Masada story at all? Does he present the victims as heroes? Josephus is no advocate or defender of the rebels. What is often overlooked in the Eleazar speech is that the choice of death is presented as a self-imposed *punishment* for the crime of the revolt. Further, as Ladouceur has shown, Thackeray's translation in the Loeb edition is not without serious flaws at this point. It puts a more positive light on the event than the Greek text merits.[25] We must not forget that we are reading Josephus's account of Eleazar's arguments, which are supposed to be convincing to his hearers but do not represent the whole debate. According to the story, at the end of Eleazar's speech they rush to follow his bidding. Therefore, Josephus has Eleazar make good use of the Socratic argument that voluntary death is justified when God has given the signal and that proper necessity is present. For Josephus these unfortunate victims of the revolt are *not* the popular martyrs of subsequent imagination, whether popular or scholarly.[26]

We make one additional point: Josephus's tendency to be ambiguous about controversial issues. As a patron of the Flavian emperors but one who also desires to place his nation in the best possible light, he is ever the apologist. It has been shown that in his speech at Jotapata he skillfully uses stock language about the "immortality of the soul," but in ways that can also be understood, at the same time, to support the Jewish doctrine of resurrection from the dead.[27] Elsewhere he describes the three Jewish sects of his day as Greek philosophical "schools," paralleling the Stoics (Pharisees), Epicureans (Sadducees), and Pythagoreans (Essenes).[28] It should not surprise us, then, to find that he treats the subject of voluntary death, especially in the cases at Jotapata and Masada, in ways that can be read from several angles. He wants to present his Jewish characters, even the rebel Eleazar, and certainly himself, as somewhat sophisticated and "philosophically" astute. Though Jews, they both use Plato to support their positions. At the same time he wants to present the Jewish revolt as a misguided venture, doomed by God himself. But overall, regarding the history of his people, he must present a story that is admirable and noble by the common standards of his time. His skill in combining these concerns is considerable.

Josephus represents for us the beginning of the philosophical discussion of voluntary death in the Jewish sources. He is not particularly original, given his dependence on Plato, but all in all he is fairly consistent. As we have seen, he coins a noun (*ownhandedness*) for the act of voluntary death. For him, this term is a neutral one. It has no pejorative or disparaging connotations. There is a type of voluntary death that he proscribes: "laying mad hands upon oneself" or "rashly" taking one's life when no necessity is present. But he has no special term for such an act, and he shows little interest in detailed classification in this regard.

Finally, Josephus subscribes to a general and popular form of Hellenistic dualism. The Jewish sects of which he approves, the Pharisees and Essenes, he describes as mainstream proponents of the doctrines of the immortality of the soul, rewards and punishments in the afterlife, and the ascetic ideal.[29]

These views form an important context for understanding the texts of Josephus related to voluntary death. As Eleazar forcefully argues, and Josephus obviously agrees, the mortal body is a prison, from which the soul seeks release. Ultimately, death is a form of true life, and death by choice, given the proper circumstances, is a way to obtain that life.

PHILO

Philo (30 B.C.–A.D. 45) is our other important prerabbinic source for Judaism in this period. He touches on the subject of voluntary death a few times, but since he is not presenting us with historical narrative, he lacks the anecdotal richness of Josephus. The most important passage is in his work *Embassy to Gaius*. In A.D. 41 the emperor Gaius Caligula had threatened the Jewish temple rites and demanded that his own statue be erected in Jerusalem. Philo reports the dramatic address of a Jewish delegation before Petronius, the Roman officer who is to carry out the emperor's orders. They declare their willingness to face death to forestall this plan:

> One thing only we ask in return for all, that no violent changes should be made in this temple and that it be kept as we received it from our grandparents and ancestors. But if we cannot persuade you, *we give ourselves for destruction* that we may not live to see a calamity worse than death. . . . We gladly put our throats at your disposal. Let them slaughter, butcher, carve our flesh without a blow struck or blood drawn by us and do all the deeds that conquerors commit.

But what need of an army! *We ourselves will conduct the sacrifices*, priests of a noble order; wives will be brought to the altar by wife-slayers, brothers and sisters by fratricides, boys and girls in the innocence of their years by child-murders. . . . Then standing in the midst of our kinsfolk after bathing ourselves in their blood, the right bathing *for those who would go to Hades clean*, we will mingle our blood with theirs by the crowning slaughter of ourselves. . . . And this aim will be accomplished if we take our departure *in contempt of the life which is no life* (233–36).[30]

This is an extraordinary text, in which Philo skillfully combines most of the stock motifs related to voluntary death that we have just seen in Josephus. Indeed, the scene Philo imagines reminds one of Masada. The Jews will take the lives of their own families, then of themselves, in contempt of life itself under such conditions.[31] But such a self-slaughter is interpreted as a sacrifice, allowing one to enter the world beyond in a *purified* condition. Josephus reports that a similar scene actually occurred in the reign of the procurator Pontius Pilate. Pilate had brought into the city Roman standards that contained ornamentation considered idolatrous and offensive to the stricter Jews. A crowd of protesting Jews were surrounded and threatened with death if they did not disperse. According to Josephus, they all cast themselves to the ground and bared their throats, declaring that "they had *gladly welcomed death* rather than make bold to transgress the wise provisions of the laws" (*Ant.* 18.59; cf. JW 2.169–74).

As one might expect, Philo echoes other common themes from Hellenistic philosophy as well. He asserts that "the wise would most gladly choose death rather than slavery" (*Every Good Man Is Free* 135). He echoes the Stoic-Cynic indifference to threats of death from tyrants: "I will fear none of the tyrant's menaces, even though he threaten me with death, for death is less evil than dissimulation" (*On Joseph* 68–69). His account of the death of Moses, whom he sees as the perfect God-king and savior, the ruler of the cosmos, goes far beyond his biblical text. It reminds one of the portrayal of Jesus in the Gospel of John, which we will examine in chapter five. Moses' "death" is hardly death; it is a glorious "departure to the colony of heaven," called at the proper time by the Father.[32] Moses receives the "signal" from God and "abandons his mortal life." Again, with Philo, we encounter the legacy of Socrates.

RABBINIC MATERIALS

We conclude with a survey of the ways in which voluntary death is treated in rabbinic literature, namely, in the Mishnah, Talmud, and Midrash. It is only in recent times that these vast collections of texts, with their complex history of traditions spanning several centuries, have been subjected to social and scientific analysis, using the standard methods of historical criticism.[33] The evidence is at once fascinating, complicated, and contradictory, resisting easy systematization. Unfortunately, such simplification, in the interest of dogmatic theological and moral concerns, has often controlled the secondary studies of this material.[34]

For example, *The Encyclopedia of Judaism* states that "Judaism regards all life as given by God . . . and suicide is considered as murder."[35] Technically, as we will see, this came to be the case, but the assertion ignores five hundred years of Jewish discussion of this difficult issue. C. W. Reines, while admitting that "actual cases of suicide were not unknown," asserts that "Judaism expressed a general and absolute condemnation of suicide."[36] Fred Rosner asserts much the same: "Judaism regards suicide as a criminal act and strictly forbidden by Jewish law. The cases of suicide in the Bible as well as from the Apocrypha, Talmud and Midrash took place under unusual and extenuating conditions."[37]

Such approaches imply that "Judaism," even in antiquity, existed as a monolithic entity and spoke with a single voice that corresponded to later *halachic* rulings. Louis Rabinowitz is a bit more candid, beginning his article with the admission that "suicide" is "nowhere explicitly forbidden in the Talmud," though it came to regarded as a "most heinous sin, even worse than murder," by post-Talmudic authorities.[38] Most of these studies also sharply distinguish between the categories of "suicide" and "martyrdom," with the latter given the highest approval. Sidney Goldstein, for example, states in his conclusions, "The only time that Judaism ever viewed suicide affirmatively was when it was committed as an act of martyrdom. Otherwise it was *never* sanctioned. It may have been considered inculpable due to various exonerating circumstances, but it was never an approved act."[39]

As we have pointed out previously in this study, questions of definition and categorization are the very issues in dispute within the texts themselves. There is no noun in the Talmud for "suicide," though in post-Talmudic tractates the *verbal* phrase "to destroy oneself wittingly" appears.[40] Daube's evidence simply invalidates any discussion that begins with the term "suicide" and proceeds to apply it to these ancient materials.

The rabbinic materials on voluntary death are more often anecdotal, though we do have some systematic, legal discussion along the way. Sometimes the two are mixed.

We begin with an obvious problem. As we have seen, there is no biblical prohibition against taking one's life, neither in legal materials nor in attitudes reflected by the various accounts of self-killing in the Hebrew Bible. This meant, as is often the case in rabbinic texts, that anyone who wished to argue against such action had to construct his points indirectly. We see a good illustration of this problem in instances when the rabbis mention some of the biblical characters who did take their own lives.

The case of Ahithophel is instructive. In the Mishnah we read: "Three kings and four commoners have no share in the world to come. . . . The four commoners are Balaam and Doeg and Ahithophel and Gehazi" (m. Sanhedrin 10.2).[41]

Why is Ahithophel condemned here? We must not assume it was because of his act of self-destruction. In the subsequent discussion in the same Talmudic tractate we learn that some interpreters maintained the opposite: that Ahithophel would enter the world to come (b. Sanhedrin 104b–5a).[42] Ahithophel also comes up in a separate discussion in the Talmud where a completely different explanation than that in the Bible is given for his choice to take his life (b. Makkoth 11a). The rabbis are discussing a precept of Rab, that "the curse of a Sage, though uttered without cause, takes effect." As evidence that such is the case, we are told that when David, who is the "sage" in this story, was once digging out the temple foundation the deep came surging up, threatening to flood the world. David inquired as to what the Torah would say about writing the divine name on a shard and throwing it into the deep to make it subside. He declared, "Whoever knows anything on this topic and would not tell, may he be suffocated!" Ahithophel reasoned in his own mind that such an action would be permissible. The story concludes:

> "Yes, it is allowed!" [exclaimed Ahithophel]. The Divine Name was thereupon inscribed on a shard and thrown in the Deep; it subsided and abode in its own region. Nevertheless it is recorded, and when Ahithophel saw that his counsel was not followed, he saddled his ass and arose and went home to his house, to his city and put his household in order, and hanged himself and died.[43]

As it stands, the text appears contradictory. Ahithophel does speak out, and his advice is followed by David. Why then should he fall under David's "curse" and inevitably end up "suffocating" himself by hanging? Perhaps the rabbis have in mind David's earlier prayer (curse?) against Ahithophel recorded in 2 Samuel 15:31. If so, the point here would be that even this later "good" advice would not save him from his fated destiny. But that still does not seem to fit the story here in Makkoth. The Epstein translation may be incorrect to add in brackets "exclaimed Ahithophel." Perhaps the idea is that he did remain silent and was thus cursed, even though he did not deserve it.

This story is instructive either way. Here we encounter the same idea we have seen repeatedly: that voluntary death carries out some type of predetermined fate or punishment. Here the "sage" stands in the place of God. Although Ahithophel's death is determined by David's "curse," the act of self-destruction itself is not condemned. Indeed, his example is given as one who is cursed "without cause." The irony here is that he "suffocated," not by another's hand but of his own choice.

Samson is another important case the rabbis discuss. In general he is lauded and praised for his legendary feats. The Talmud says that God answered his prayer and allowed him the strength to *destroy his own life* and the lives of the Philistines because of his egalitarian style of rule as judge of Israel (*b. Sotah* 10a). The Targum stresses that he *prayed* for strength and this prayer was answered, resulting in his self-destruction.[44] There is no condemnation of his act; indeed, the trend in later Jewish interpretation is to understand his choice as a redemptive act of self-sacrifice.[45]

It is Saul who receives uniform praise by the rabbis. They are sometimes troubled by the account of his death in 1 Samuel 31, since he clearly takes his own life. Some prefer the alternative version of his death in 2 Samuel 1, where an Amalekite actually carries out the deed at Saul's request.[46] In an important Midrashic discussion of Genesis 9:5, which some rabbis took to be the single biblical text condemning the shedding of one's own blood, Saul is specifically *excepted* and put with the "martyrs" Hananiah, Mishael, and Azariah (*Genesis Rabbah* 34:13). In a later Midrash collection Saul is told by Samuel that he is to fall by the sword, and heeding this instruction would allow his death to bring atonement, and he would dwell in Paradise![47] As Goldstein concludes:

> The rabbinic sources are not concerned with the suicidal aspects of the final moments of Saul's life. The texts deal with his death as an act of atonement which came about through his acceding to Samuel's authority. They also praise his gracious acceptance of the terrible decree. Samuel's prophecy was fulfilled with gruesome effectiveness.[48]

In the absence of any biblical prohibition against voluntary death, the Tannaim differed as to whether, and under what circumstances, one was allowed to "injure oneself." Rabbi Eleazar maintained that voluntary death was forbidden. He turned to a single phrase found in Genesis 9:5: "For *your lifeblood* [lit., your blood of your lives] I will surely require a reckoning." He interpreted this to mean "I will require your blood if shed by the hands of yourselves" (*b. Baba Kamma* 91b). This interpretation is repeated in *Genesis Rabbah* 34:13, where we read that the phrase "your blood of your lives" from Genesis 9:5 "includes one who strangles himself." However, as mentioned above, this very text goes on to make Saul an *exception*. So, clearly, there were exceptions, even among those who understood this ruling as binding. Notably, the Targumim do not make use of Rabbi Eleazar's interpretation when they explain Genesis 9:5, so it does not seem to have received general acceptance until much later.[49]

Obviously, with no clear injunction against voluntary death in the Hebrew Bible, and given the ambiguous but generally positive evaluation of the actions of Samson and Saul (and even Ahithophel in certain cases), those rabbis who wished to proscribe certain types of self-inflicted death had to go elsewhere than the biblical texts to establish their case.

One somewhat obscure text in *Aboth* was understood by some as forbidding voluntary death:[50]

> And let not your [evil] inclination assure you that the grave is a place of refuge for you; for without your will you were fashioned, without your will you were born, without your will you live, *without your will you die*, and without your will are you of a certainty to give an account and reckoning before the King of the Kings of Kings, blessed be He (4.22).

Though the language about not seeing the "grave as a place of refuge" and the phrase "without your will you die" might conceivably apply to one taking one's life, this text was apparently not interpreted that way by many rabbis. It seems more likely from the context that it is a polemic against those who deny the afterlife, thinking that death is the end. The overall point appears to be that final judgment is as *inevitable* as birth, life, or death.

The rabbis also discuss when, and under what conditions, one might endanger one's life or allow one's life to be taken. The general principle that one should not unnecessarily injure oneself or put one's life in danger is discussed in numerous texts in the Talmud.[51] When David pours out the water that some of his men had *risked their lives* to bring to him from his well at his home in Bethlehem, he was seen to be honoring this principle (2 Sam. 23:16–17). In this connection a rule is quoted: "No *halachic* matter may be quoted in the name of one who surrenders himself to meet death for words of the Torah" (*b. Baba Kamma* 61a). But again, there are many exceptions, and obviously this rule was seldom followed.

The account of the death of Rabbi Hanina ben Teradion, who lived during the time of Hadrian, brings together some of the major interpretive difficulties (*b. Abodah Zarah* 18ab).[52] He is taken by the Romans and burnt at the stake with a Torah scroll wrapped around him. At one point, seeking to lessen his suffering by hastening his death, his disciples cry out to him, "Open your mouth so that the fire enters into you." Hanina replies, "Let Him who gave me [my soul] take it away, but *no one should injure himself.*" The text continues:

> The Executioner then said to him, "Rabbi, if I raise the flame and take away the tufts of wool from over your heart, will you cause me to enter into the life to come?" "Yes," he replied. "Then swear to me" [he urged]. He swore to him. He thereupon raised the flame and removed the tufts of wool from over his heart, and his soul departed speedily. The Executioner then jumped and *threw himself*

into the fire. And a *bat-qol* exclaimed: R. Hanina b. Teradion and the Executioner have been assigned to the world to come. When Rabbi heard it he wept and said: *One may acquire eternal life in a single hour,* another after many years.

Hanina's basic position is that one must not take a hand in even *hastening* one's death; God is the one who must take away life. Such a position might have been based on texts of the Bible (Job 1:21; 2:9–10; Eccles. 3:2), or even the quotation from *Aboth* 4.22 above: *"without your will* you will die." In content it is reminiscent of the statements in Plato and Cicero that we examined in chapter two: one is not to depart this life except at the bidding of the gods. It also closely parallels the argument of Josephus at Jotapata, as we have seen. But in this story, Hanina nonetheless agrees to have someone else, namely, the executioner, *act in his behalf,* immediately bringing about his death. Presumably this means he is not directly responsible. Yet *he* makes the choice and accordingly has an indirect part in the action. It is not clear in this story whether Hanina expects the executioner to jump in the fire with him, when he promises him eternal life for his assistance. Regardless, the act of the executioner receives the highest approval, the voice from heaven declaring that he has obtained eternal life. If one can obtain life by a deliberate act of self-destruction, what happens to Hanina's original statement that one must not even hasten death, much less directly destroy oneself?

The text leaves all these elements in unresolved tension. The final declaration that "one may acquire eternal life in a single hour" is indeed a radical one. Here we have an outsider, a Roman official at that, who receives eternal life instantly through voluntary death. We find a similar motif in the case of Saul referred to above. The prophet Samuel, brought forth in a seance, tells Saul that if he accepts his sentence of death, which is to be self-executed, he can join Samuel in his heavenly rank in the world beyond (*Leviticus Rabbah* 26:7).

The complexities of Hanina b. Teradion's death do not end here. Why was he arrested and executed by the Romans in the first place? One version has it that he insisted, against Roman proscription, on "occupying himself with Torah." But we are also told that "the punishment of being burnt came upon him because he pronounced the Name in its full spelling," and, according to this text, his wife was also slain and his daughter consigned to a brothel because of her immodest behavior before the Romans (*Abodah Zarah* (17b–18a). But even with such charges the whole family is pronounced blessed because they "submitted to [the divine] righteous judgment," facing their punishments without complaint. Is Hanina's death, like that of Saul, both a punishment and a way of atonement? Notably, he, along with Akiba, is included in the standard lists of the ten great rabbis who suffered death in the Hadrianic persecution.[53]

These ten, along with the two brothers Julianus and Papus of Lydda, who had also died in the "great persecution" in the time of Hadrian, were said to occupy the highest places in Paradise, so exalted none could compare with them.[54] The Midrash Rabbah contains many passages extolling the virtues of those who withstood Roman persecution and were willing to die during this time. In one text the persecutors pose questions, followed by the response of the faithful: "*What is the reason* that you go forth to be stoned? Because I circumcised my son. *What is the reason* that you go forth to be burned? Because I have kept the Sabbath. *What is the reason* that you go forth to be killed? Because I have eaten unleavened bread" (*Leviticus Rabbah* 32.1).[55]

Such questions as these get at the heart of the matter. For what reasons should one, or must one, voluntarily face death in a time of persecution? These issues are most fully formulated in *b. Sanhedrin* (74a–75a), possibly in response to the Hadrianic persecutions following the failure of Bar Kochba's revolt. The discussion centers on the following declaration: "By a majority vote, it was resolved . . . that in every [other] law of the Torah, if a man is commanded: 'Transgress and suffer not death,' he may transgress and not suffer death, excepting idolatry, incest, [which includes adultery] and murder." A stricter party insisted that this ruling only applied when "there is no royal decree," that is, when one faced opposition from individuals. When there is a "royal decree," that is, when the opposition is public and backed by the government, "one must be martyred even for a minor precept rather than violate it."[56]

Alongside these *halachic* discussions there are dozens of anecdotal reports of voluntary death that run through the rabbinic materials. As with the story of Hanina above, though they resist simple classification and systematization, they indirectly relate to some of the fundamental issues of our study.

In *b. Gittin* 57b we find a series of fascinating stories of voluntary death. On one occasion four hundred boys and girls were carried off by sea to be sold as slaves in brothels. They declared to one another, "If we drown in the sea *we shall attain the life of the future world.*" First the girls leaped overboard. The boys then reasoned that if the girls, for whom sexual penetration is a *natural* act, were willing to die, then certainly they should join them, since it is *unnatural* for them. They also jumped into the sea and drowned.[57] A story of a woman and her seven sons follows, somewhat loosely related to the tale in 2 Maccabees. Each son dies in turn, courageously quoting scriptures to his persecutors. The mother encourages them, telling them that they will immediately see Abraham in the world beyond. She then goes up on a roof and throws herself down and is killed. A voice comes from heaven quoting Psalm 113:9: "A joyful mother of children." The irony is that this text blesses the "barren woman" by making her the mother of children. Here the woman, having lost her sons, is barren, but gains them back in death. This is a good example of the "death as life" and "life as death" reversal we introduced at the beginning of the chapter. Further, as in 4 Maccabees, this woman *takes her own life*, and, in this case, in her own way, rather than dying at the hand of the enemy.[58] The text continues quoting Rabbi Simeon b. Lakish, who declared, "The words of the Torah abide only with one who *kills himself for them.*"

We also find many stories in which voluntary death becomes an expression of extreme shame, humiliation, or repentance. For example, we are told of a certain student who once left his *tefillin* on a shelf outside a bathroom while he went in to relieve himself. A harlot passed by and stole them. Later she showed up at the house of study and said, "See what this student has paid me for my hire." When the student heard it, he went to the top of a roof, jumped off, and killed himself (*b. Berakoth* 23a).[59] There is an account of a man who hanged himself when he was embarrassed at not having the proper food to set before guests. Another follows about a man and his wife who jumped off the roof after the father struck his child and killed him for eating the last three eggs available for guests (*b. Hullin* 94a).

Several accounts directly connect the choice of death with retribution for sins. Hiyya b. Abba, an ascetic who even avoided his own wife sexually, is tempted to lust after her when she disguises herself as a harlot to get his affections. Even after she reveals herself, he climbs into the oven to take his life, declaring that, regardless of the outcome, his intention was evil and he deserved to die (*b. Kiddushin* 81b). Jakum of Zeroroth is perhaps the most vivid example of this "repentance unto death." He had taunted R. Jose, who was to be hanged, expressing his doubts that serving God brings blessings. Later he bitterly repents. He determines that he deserves to die by all four modes of execution: stoning, burning, decapitation, and strangulation:

> He got a beam and drove it into the ground. To the beam, he firmly tied a rope. He placed sticks of wood in a row and built a wall of stones over them. Then he piled up fuel in front of the beam and put a sword, pointing upward, in the midst of the fuel. After lighting a fire under the sticks of wood beneath the stones, he hanged himself from the beam and thus strangled himself. The rope broke, and he fell into the fire, the sword met him, and the wall of stones tumbled upon him (*Genesis Rabbah* 65.22).

His soul departs, and because of his repentance he enters Paradise. R. Jose, having almost expired from hanging, declares, "This man by a brief hour precedes me into the Garden of Eden."[60]

Here, as in several of these tales, voluntary death actually *brings eternal life.* Perhaps the most striking of such tales is the account of the death of the great Rabbi Judah:

> On the day the Rabbi died a *bat-qol* went forth and announced: Whosoever has been present at the death of Rabbi is destined to enjoy the life of the world to come. A certain fuller, who used to come to him every day, failed to call on that day; and, as soon as he heard this, went up on a roof, fell down to the ground

and died. A *bat-qol* came forth and announced: That fuller also is destined to enjoy the life of the world to come (*b. Kethuboth* 103b).[61]

A somewhat similar story is told about a Roman officer who decreed the arrest of Rabbi Gamaliel. The officer approached him secretly and said, "If I save you will you bring me into the world to come?" Gamaliel swore that he would. The officer went up on a roof and threw himself off and died. There was a tradition among the Romans that a decree would be broken by death, so Gamaliel was freed by the soldier's death. A voice was then heard from heaven declaring that the Roman was destined to enter the world to come (*b. Taanith* 29a).

These rabbinic accounts take us back full circle, to the death of Hanina b. Teradion and the instantaneous salvation of his executioner. What overall conclusions can we draw regarding these materials?

Most of the motifs we encounter in these texts we also noted in Josephus and Philo: choosing death over humiliation or to avoid torture, taking one's life as a self-inflicted punishment for crimes, and dying to gain eternal life. There is an extraordinary focus on the "world to come." What one assumes might lie behind some of Josephus's reports, given his endorsement of dualism here and there in his works, comes to dominate these materials. It is simply assumed throughout that obtaining "eternal life" beyond this world is the human goal. Such an orientation will of necessity involve a devaluation of this present life and a revaluation of death as the way to Paradise. Given this perspective, the issues of when one can properly choose to depart become unavoidable.

One might wish that some of the *halachic* discussions would focus on this particular question, yielding some systematic treatment of how such acts were understood to bring salvation. The opposite is the case. Instead we get story after story where individuals and groups are commended, even by the voice of heaven, for their decisions to take their own lives and enter the world to come. One of the only qualifications given is the standard one, in the mouth of Hanina b. Teradion, that one must not go unless God wills. Yet in that very story R. Hanina himself allows his death to be hastened, and his executioner is directly rewarded with eternal life when he jumps into the fire and kills himself. In the other accounts, no such point regarding waiting for the divine bidding is even made. The explicit idea of the proper "necessity" is largely missing, but presumably implied by the way in which the stories are reported. The few attempts to proscribe voluntary death, such as Eleazar's interpretation of Genesis 9:5, seem to have no decisive influence, either in these early rabbinic legal discussions or in the ways these stories of voluntary death are related.

Instead of a focus on when one is *allowed* to choose death, the most systematic discussion in these materials, that of *b. Sanhedrin* (74a–75a) deals with the opposite problem: when is one *required* to choose death rather than violate the commandments of God? The standards are fairly strict; consequently those who have chosen death in the face of persecution are exalted and said to occupy the highest and best places in the world beyond. There are no firm distinctions made between taking one's life, having it taken, and offering it up freely.

It is only in the relatively late, post-Talmudic tractate *Semahot* that specific laws regarding "suicide" are formulated.[62] The text declares, "For a suicide [*sic*] no rites whatsoever should be observed" (2:1).[63] But the crucial question of how to determine a culpable "suicide" remains. The text says,

> Not one who climbs to the top of a tree or to the top of a roof, and falls to his death. Rather, it is one who says, "Behold, I am going to climb to the top of the tree, or to the top of the roof, and then throw myself down to my death," and thereupon others see him climb to the top of the tree, or to the top of the roof, and fall to his death (2:2)

What must be established is *sane and deliberate* intent. Thus the self-inflicted death of a minor was not regarded as a culpable suicide. One had to establish clear and undisputed evidence of intent. The slightest indication was enough to establish an "unsound mind." Rabbi Ishmael is quoted in *Semahot*: "Woe, he has taken his life, he may be lamented: Alas! misguided fool!" Rabbi Akiba is cited in disagreement: "Leave him in silence, neither honor him nor curse him" (2:1). In practice, so many qualifications and extenuating circumstances could be raised that as often as not burial and mourning rites were observed.

Nonetheless, the uncompromising *halachic* position came to be that "suicide" was murder. Only to avoid idolatry, murder, or sexual immorality would one be required to die voluntarily. All too often the Talmudic material we have surveyed is read "backward" from this finalized dogmatic perspective.[64] Yet the texts themselves resist such attempts. Indeed, they declare quite the opposite: that voluntary death, given the proper circumstances, not only is noble but also can lead to life in the world to come.

Baruch Brody asks in a provocative article that surveys these rabbinic materials "whether traditional Judaism is committed to the doctrine of the sanctity of human life." Surprisingly, his answer is *no*—certainly not in strict or absolute terms. He argues that no doctrine of the sanctity of human life could justify "penitential acts of suicide . . . killing oneself to avoid sinning under coercion . . . killing oneself to avoid a mocking and cruel death," and so forth. He concludes that Judaism tries to balance the value of preserving life, particularly the life of the innocent, with a complex variety of other values.[65] We would add that one of these values, and hardly a minor one in these classic rabbinic texts, is a desire to enter the world to come. The choice of death, however motivated or prompted, is understood to be an entry into eternal life.

NOTES

1. Our earliest biblical text reflecting this shift is Dan. 12:2–3. The "many" who are to awake from death and receive everlasting life are those who died faithful to the covenant; see 11:32–35. The tale of the mother and her seven sons, from 2 Macc. 7 (cf. 4 Macc. 5), is perhaps the most dramatic illustration of this shift. They each breathe their last with obstinate declarations of faith in the sure rewards of the afterlife.

2. Werner Jaeger describes this phenomenon as "a radical transvaluation of reality" and considers it "the greatest revolution in [Western] human thought that had ever occurred," in his 1958 Ingersoll lecture, "The Greek Ideas of Immortality," conveniently available in K. Stendahl, ed., *Immortality and Resurrection: Death in the Western World* (New York: Macmillan, 1965), pp. 97–114.

3. For a recent scholarly assessment of these developments, see Walter Burkert, *Greek Religion*, trans. by John Raffan (Cambridge, MA: Harvard Univ. Press, 1985), pp. 293–300, 317–29.

4. Cicero, *Republic* 6.14. Translation from the Loeb Classical Library edition. Cicero's dependence on Plato's *Phaedo* is obvious here.

5. On this "new cosmology," and the shifts in religious and philosophical perspectives related thereto, especially the collection of essays by Jonathan Z. Smith in *Map Is Not Territory*, Studies in Judaism in Late Antiquity, no. 23 (Leiden: Brill, 1978).

6. See Daube, "The Linguistics of Suicide," *Philosophy and Public Affairs* 1 (1972): 399, 409–11. The Loeb Classical Library translators render such nouns in Josephus as "suicide," which is quite misleading. The use of a noun, rather than a verb, is indeed significant, but our English word *suicide*, as we discussed in chap. 1, carries with it proscriptive and pejorative connotations that Josephus certainly did not share.

7. The best and most comprehensive discussion of Josephus and his works is by Louis Feldman, "Flavius Josephus Revisited: The Man, His Writings, and His Significance," in *Aufstieg und Niedergang der römischen Welt*, ed. Wolfgang Haase (Berlin: Walter de Gruyter, 1984), II.21.2, pp. 763–862.

8. On Josephus's strategies in interpreting the biblical text, see Feldman, "Flavius Josephus Revisited," pp. 788–804.

9. We are using the translations of the Loeb Classical Library for Josephus; emphasis within quotations and bracketed comments are ours unless otherwise indicated.

10. It is noteworthy that Josephus elsewhere tells us of an Egyptian seer, Amenophis, who kills himself after foretelling misfortune (AgAp. 1.232–59). In this case, in contrast to Ahithophel, Josephus seems to be critical not of the act itself so much as its lack of necessity. We will return to this point below, since Josephus does on occasion argue *against* certain acts of voluntary death.

11. See Epictetus's famous description of the divine mission of the "Cynic scout" who fears nothing external, scoffing at exile and even death (3.21.1–19).

12. Four of the accounts in the *Antiquities* he related previously in the *War*. Accordingly, this material offers us an opportunity to note how Josephus retells

such stories in subsequent works, recasting them, or shifting his evaluations with his changing interests. For a general discussion, see L. D. Hankoff, "The Theme of Suicide in the Works of Flavius Josephus," *Clio Medica* 2 (1976): 15–24.

13. Raymond R. Newell, "The Suicide Accounts in Josephus: A Form Critical Study," in *Society of Biblical Literature Seminar Papers* (Missoula, MT: Scholars Press, 1982), pp. 351–69. Newell concentrates on the literary pattern Josephus used when describing "suicides" and compares it with such reports in contemporary authors. Sometimes (1) is missing or merged with (2). As Newell points out, two of the cases where the description of the hopeless situation is missing are Josephus's reports of the death of the Roman emperor Otho, and that of Sabinus, one of Caligula's assassins (*JW* 4.547–548; *Ant.* 19.273).

14. When Josephus retells the same story in the *Antiquities*, he specifically justifies the old man's actions as "submitting to death rather than to slavery," but he adds the claim that *many surrendered* (*Ant.* 14.427–30). This directly contradicts his earlier claim that no one surrendered voluntarily; all chose death. This ambiguity may well have to do with Josephus's own situation at Jotapata, which we will discuss below.

15. Josephus notes an alternative version of this story that has it that Phasael recovered from this self-inflicted blow but was subsequently poisoned by a physician sent to him by Antigonus (*JW* 1.272).

16. There are many similar stories. On Pentecost in 4 B.C. the Romans set fire to the porticoes of the Jerusalem temple. Josephus comments, "Many, in despair of being saved and *in dismay at the awful fate that confronted them*, either threw themselves into the fire or escaped it only by turning their swords on themselves" (*Ant.* 17.263). Josephus tells of several other cases during the first revolt when masses of people took their lives in desperation. The people of Joppa fled in ships and got caught in a storm. Many, "regarding the sword as a lighter evil than the sea, anticipated drowning by suicide" (*JW* 3.425). At Gamala he tells of five thousand Jews, who, when trapped by the Romans, "plunged headlong with their wives and children into the ravine which had been excavated to a vast depth beneath the citadel" (*JW* 4.78–80). After the capture of Jericho great numbers fled to the Jordan River area. Josephus reports that fifteen thousand were killed by the Romans, "while the number of those who were driven to fling themselves of their own accord into the Jordan was incalculable" (*JW* 4.435–36). He also singles out a number of heroic individuals who took their lives in extreme circumstances. Eleazar, a hotheaded rebel, attacked the Herodium and got trapped. He jumped off the ramparts, killing himself instantly (*JW* 4.519–20). Longus, a young Roman soldier, when trapped by fire during the siege of Jerusalem, killed himself with his sword rather than surrender. Josephus says he "*shed lustre on the whole tragedy*" and proved himself the bravest of them all (*JW* 6.187–88). He praises two others, Meirus and Josephus, son of Dalaeus, men of distinction, he says, who, when the Jerusalem temple was finally taken, "having the choice of saving their lives by going over to the Romans or of holding out and sharing the fortune of the rest, plunged into the fire and were consumed with the temple"

(*JW* 6.280). He records with favor the general statement of Joshua ben Gamala, who declared that once committed to the revolt, he would choose a noble death before Roman captivity (*JW* 4.249–50).

17. Josephus reports that Simon bar Giora was such a powerful and feared leader that his followers would gladly have killed themselves at his bidding (*JW* 5.309).

18. This is the first use in Greek literature of a noun for the act of voluntary death, lit. "own-handedness." See Daube, "Linguistics of Suicide," pp. 409–11, for a discussion of this important development. As noted previously, the word *suicide*, in this translation by Thackeray, is inappropriate.

19. His lengthy account is found in *JW* 7.252–406. Unfortunately, he is our only clear source for the incident, and historians have raised many questions regarding the accuracy of Josephus's story. Indeed, some scholars have contended that the entire Masada episode is a conscious fabrication by Josephus. The archeological findings of Yadin are not conclusive. The literature on this problem is exhaustive; see Louis Feldman, *Josephus and Modern Scholarship (1937–1980)* (Berlin: Walter de Gruyter, 1984), pp. 772–89, for a bibliographical survey and critical discussion of the issues. A version of the story is found in Josippon, a tenth-century Hebrew narrative of the Second Temple period.

20. See *JW* 2.118 on Judas. Earlier Josephus reported that a certain Menahem, son of Judas the Galilean, occupied Masada, took arms from the store there, and marched on Jerusalem. He was subsequently killed (*JW* 2.433–48). Two other descendants of Judas, his sons James and Simon, were crucified under Tiberius Alexander (46–48 A.D.), presumably because of their family connections with rebel causes (*Ant.* 20.102).

21. See the essential analysis by David Ladouceur, "Josephus and Masada," in L. Feldman and G. Hata, eds., *Josephus, Judaism, and Christianity* (Detroit, MI: Wayne State Univ. Press, 1987), pp. 95–113, on these central problems.

22. For references and detailed discussion, see Ladouceur, "Josephus and Masada."

23. Compare Josephus's language in reporting Herod's defeat of the Arab tribes in 31 B.C. He says they "reckoned it a gain if they died, a misfortune to live" (*Ant.* 15.158).

24. In *Life* 137–38, the subject of Josephus's willingness to die also comes up. His bodyguard, Simon, advises him to kill himself "like a general," before his enemies kill him themselves. Josephus says he will commit his fate to God.

25. Ladouceur, "Josephus and Masada," pp. 104–6. For example, where Thackeray has "filled with delight at the thought of a death so noble," a more literal rendering would be "filled with pleasure supposing such a death to be noble" (7.337). Ladouceur has also argued that we should read the story in the context of the Flavian political environment in Rome in the seventies A.D. ("Josephus and Masada," pp. 99–101).

26. Modern Jewish theological discussions of Masada too often begin with the assumption that Josephus and everyone else have the highest praise for these "martyrs." The problem is to show that they somehow died "for the faith" in accordance with late Jewish tradition. See the bibliography and discussion in

Feldman, *Josephus and Modern Scholarship*, pp. 799–89. The debate has been sharp among orthodox Jewish scholars; see, for example, Sidney Hoenig, "The Sicarii in Masada—Glory or Infamy?" *Tradition* 11 (1970): 5–30; and Shubert Spero, "In Defense of the Defenders of Masada," *Tradition* 11 (1970): 31–43.

27. See Tabor, "Returning to the Divinity." In general see Feldman, "Flavius Josephus Revisited," pp. 838–58.

28. *Ant.* 13.171–73; *JW* 2.119–66; *Life* 10.

29. He reports such views with pride, implying his strong agreement. For the texts and a brief discussion, see Tabor, "Returning to the Divinity," pp. 231–33.

30. We are using the translation of the Loeb Classical Library; emphases are ours.

31. Given Philo's radical dualism it might well be that his phrase "in contempt of the life which is no life" might admit a double meaning. On the one hand, it certainly applies to the circumstances under Gaius. On the other hand, any life, lived in the prison of the body, is actually "no life" in contrast to the heavenly world.

32. See *Life of Moses* 2.288, and the interpretation of E. R. Goodenough, *By Light, Light: The Mystic Gospel of Hellenistic Judaism* (1935; reprint Amsterdam: Philo Press, 1969), pp. 223–29.

33. Particularly, we refer to the pioneering work of Jacob Neusner and his students. For a summary of important results, see Jacob Neusner, *Judaism: The Evidence of the Mishnah*, 2d ed. (Atlanta, GA: Scholars Press, 1987); and *Judaism: The Classical Statement: The Evidence of Bavli* (Chicago: Univ. of Chicago Press, 1986), as well as the various volumes by Neusner and others dealing with "Method" in the Brown Judaic Studies series published by Scholars Press.

34. Some of the more important studies are G. Margoliouth, "Suicide (Jewish)," *The Encyclopaedia of Religion and Ethics*, vol. 12, pp. 37–38; A. Perls, "Der Selbstmord nach der Halacha," *Monatsschrift für Geschichte und Wissenschaft des Judentums* 55 (1911): 287–95; C. W. Reines, "The Jewish View of Suicide," *Judaism* 10 (1961): 160–70; Fred Rosner, "Suicide in Biblical, Talmudic, and Rabbinic Writings," *Tradition* 11 (1970): 25–40; L. I. Rabinowitz and H. H. Cohn, "Suicide," *Encyclopaedia Judaica*, vol. 15, pp. 489–91; and, most recently, S. Goldstein, *Suicide in Rabbinic Literature*.

35. *The Encyclopedia of Judaism*, s. v. "Suicide," p. 670.

36. Reines, "Jewish View of Suicide," pp. 165–66.

37. Rosner, "Suicide in Biblical, Talmudic, and Rabbinic Writings," pp. 38–39.

38. Rabinowitz and Cohn, "Suicide," p. 489.

39. Goldstein, *Suicide in Rabbinic Literature*, p. 56; emphasis is his. We are indebted to Goldstein for a full and helpful discussion of the relevant sources. His study is the best recent topical survey of the rabbinic materials.

40. See Daube, "Linguistics of Suicide," pp. 396–99, for the significance of this point. On the later discussion see *Semahot* 2:1–5 and the discussion of Perls, "Der Selbstmord," p. 288, and the *halachic* summary of Cohn, "Suicide," cols. 490–91.

41. For quotations from the Mishnah we are using the translation of Herbert Danby, *The Mishnah* (Oxford: Oxford Univ. Press, 1933). A similar negative evaluation of Ahithophel is found in *Aboth de-Rabbi Nathan* 36 and 41.

42. *Numbers Rabbah* 14:1 says the same.

43. Quotations of the Babylonian Talmud are from *The Babylonian Talmud*, edited by Isaac Epstein (London: Soncino Press, 1948), with minor modifications of archaic expressions. Brackets within quotations are those of the Epstein edition; emphases are ours. Translations of the Midrash Rabbah are from *Midrash Rabbah*, translated and edited by H. Freedman and Maurice Simon (London: Soncino Press, 1939).

44. See Targum Jonathan, Judg. 16:28.

45. See the notes and discussion in Goldstein, *Suicide in Rabbinic Literature*, p. 8.

46. See the discussion in Goldstein, *Suicide in Rabbinic Literature*, pp. 8–9.

47. *Pirkei de-Rabbi Eliezer* 33; compare *Leviticus Rabbah* 26:7. We are indebted to Goldstein for these references.

48. Goldstein, *Suicide in Rabbinic Literature*, pp. 8–9. Goldstein isolates a number of important issues related to the case of Saul. If the deaths of Saul and others in the Hebrew Bible who take their lives are supernaturally foreordained, what of the principle of inevitability? Does "suicide" in such cases become a mere carrying out of the divine "sentence"? What if one's physical condition is such that one has no chance to live on anyway? What of the factors of duress in the case of Saul? What dire circumstances can justify such action?

49. Later Jewish commentators are divided as to whether or not to accept Eleazar's opinion on this verse; see Goldstein, *Suicide in Rabbinic Literature*, pp. 52, 104.

50. See the notes in Epstein, *The Soncino Talmud. Nezikin*, pp. 56–57.

51. See *Berakhot* 3a, 8b; *Shabbath* 32a; *Pesahim* 112a; *Taanit* 5b.

52. On these reports of Roman persecution, see Gerald J. Blidstein, "Rabbis, Romans, and Martyrdom—Three Views," *Tradition* 21 (1984): 54–62. Blidstein discusses the accounts of R. Hanina b. Teradion's death.

53. The list includes Ishmael, Gamaliel, Yeshebab, Judah b. Baba, Huzapith, Judah the Baker, Akiba, Ben Azzai, and Tarfon. Some accounts exclude Tarfon for Eleazar b. Harsum. See *Lamentations Rabbah* 2.2.

54. See *b. Pesahim* 50a; *Ecclesiastes Rabbah* 9.10.

55. See *Genesis Rabbah* 82.8; *Exodus Rabbah* 15:7; *Song of Songs Rabbah* 2.7.1; and the multiple tales in *Lamentations Rabbah* 1.16.43–51.

56. The text goes on to make further distinctions: "How minor is minor? One must even resist changing one's shoe strap": that is, even minor matters of custom. Jews wore white shoe latchets, while Romans wore black. "What constitutes a public persecution, how many opponents must there be?—As few as ten." Obviously this represents a minority opinion of extreme rigor.

57. There is a related story in *Lamentations Rabbah* 1.16, set in the time of Vespasian. Three ships of Jewish men, being taken to Rome for the brothels, determine to jump overboard, knowing they will enter life in the world to come.

58. Compare the story of Miriam and her seven sons in *Lamentations Rabbah* 1.16.50. There the mother became "demented and fell from a roof and died."

59. This story comes up in a perfectly serious discussion of what to do with *tefillin* when one needs to relieve oneself. The example of this student's experience led

to the ruling that one should hold them tightly in hand and take them in. The fear was they might be dropped or contaminated.

60. Compare the similar account in *Midrash on Psa.* 11.

61. *P. Ketuboth* 12.3 also discusses this incident.

62. *Semahot*, also known as *Evel Rabbati*, is a minor tractate appended to *Nezikin*. Some would try to place it in the Tannaitic period, but this seems unlikely given the Talmudic materials we have just surveyed. See Dov Zlotnick, ed., *Semahot: Tractate "Mourning,"* Yale Judaica Series, no. 17 (New Haven, CT: Yale Univ. Press, 1966).

63. Note how the use of the English noun *suicide*, rather than a verbal phrase, gives the text a more stringent cast than would otherwise be the case.

64. For example, Joseph Blenkinsopp maintains that these rabbinic texts we have cited demonstrate only "that one might merit a place in the world to come *in spite of* suicide" (*Bible Review*, June 1990, p. 7). His position assumes a pejorative formulation of some act termed "suicide." This is wholly lacking in these materials. See Daube, "Linguistics of Suicide," p. 397. It also seems to ignore the positive force of such tales and the corresponding lack of prohibition in Tannaitic materials, whether *halachic* or *haggadic*.

65. Baruch A. Brody, "Jewish Casuistry on Suicide and Euthanasia," in *Suicide and Euthanasia: Historical and Contemporary Themes*, edited by Baruch A. Brody (Dordrecht, Boston, and London: Kluwer Academic Publishers, 1989), pp. 39–75, quotation from pp. 74–75.

❦

CHAPTER 5

To Die Is Gain

One of the difficulties Augustine and later theologians had in defending their condemnation of voluntary death is that the Bible never explicitly prohibits the act. In chapter three we saw that none of the individuals who were reported to have killed themselves in the Hebrew Bible received censure. Their acts of self-destruction were scarcely commented on, leading one to conclude that voluntary death was regarded as something acceptable and, in certain circumstances, noble. In the New Testament there is only one indisputable case of an individual taking his own life: Judas Iscariot, the betrayer of Jesus. Like the examples of voluntary death in the Hebrew Bible, Judas's act of self-killing is not condemned.

The details of Judas's death are obscure. Two accounts of it have been preserved in the New Testament (Matt. 27:3–10; Acts 1:16–20), each connecting his death with the fulfillment of prophecy and the existence of a cemetery for foreigners in Jerusalem.[1] But the accounts disagree about the means of death. In Acts Judas dies as the result of a violent fall,[2] whereas in Matthew he hangs himself. The Matthean version of the story bears closer examination.

> When Judas, his betrayer, saw that he was condemned, he *repented* and brought back the thirty pieces of silver to the chief priests and the elders, saying, "I have sinned in betraying innocent blood." They said, "What is that to us? That is your affair." And throwing down the pieces of silver in the temple, he departed; and he went and *hanged himself* (Matt. 27:3–5).[3]

What is of note in the Matthean account is the reference to Judas's repentance for the sin of betraying an innocent man. It is clear that Judas did not act under any external threat; indeed, his self-accusation was contemptuously rejected by the Jewish authorities. Judas was his own judge *and* executioner. Matthew shows no trace of disapproving of the means of death as such. On the contrary, the implication is that Judas's act of self-destruction was a result of his remorse and not an additional crime.[4] It was only much later that Christian theologians overturned the implicit judgment of Matthew and argued that

Judas was more damned by his act of self-destruction than by his betrayal of Jesus. "When Judas killed himself," Augustine wrote, "he killed a criminal, and yet he ended his life guilty not only of Christ's death, but also of his own. One crime led to another."[5] Augustine's condemnation cannot be sustained on the basis of the text. If the Matthean or Lukan account of the death of Judas had contained even the slightest comment, say, that "Judas's act was displeasing to God" or that "his death brought shame upon him," then Augustine would have had a case. But the texts do *not* say this. According to Matthew, Judas's act of self-destruction was the measure of his repentance.[6]

Neither is there any condemnation of the would-be suicide of Paul's Philippian jailer in Acts 16:25–34.[7] When an earthquake broke open the prison doors for Paul and his fellow prisoners at Philippi, the jailer, waking up and fearing that the prisoners had escaped, drew his sword to kill himself. He felt that it was better to take one's life than suffer humiliation and punishment from one's superiors for having been asleep on the job.[8] Seeing what he was about to do, Paul immediately cried out that all were present and accounted for, and so the jailer's death was prevented. There is no indication in the text that Paul kept the jailer from killing himself because he thought that such an act was a sin. Rather, he kept him from his deed in order to convert him to Christianity.[9]

In considering what the New Testament may have to say about voluntary death, our attention is drawn to the two figures who dominate its pages: Jesus and Paul. Jesus is known to us only from his earliest biographers, the authors of the four Gospels; Paul, from his own letters.

The death of Jesus is ambiguous. Was it the legal execution of a criminal, an example of heroic martyrdom, or a case of suicide? (As we saw in chapter 2, the same questions could be applied to Plato's account of the death of Socrates.) In an extraordinary passage in the Gospel of John we are told that the "Jews" understood Jesus' repeated sayings about his "going away" as a death threat: "Again he said to them, 'I go away, and you will seek me and die in your sin; where I am going, you cannot come.' Then said the Jews, 'Will he kill himself, since he says, "Where I am going, you cannot come"?' " (John 8:21–22).[10]

In the Fourth Gospel the Jews often speak more wisely than they know. As we shall see in the next chapter, Tertullian described the death of Jesus as a form of voluntary martyrdom, and he was followed by Origen in affirming that Jesus gave up his spirit *voluntarily*, since it was impossible that the deity should be at the mercy of the flesh.[11] Even Augustine, as opposed to voluntary death as he was, could claim that "[Jesus'] spirit did not leave his body against his will, but because he willed it to happen and he willed when and how it happened."[12]

In strictly historical terms it is unlikely that Jesus of Nazareth ever expected to give his life as a "ransom for many" (Mark 10:45 par.). Rather, his intention was to bring about the restoration of Israel and to usher in the kingdom of God, a revolution that would be accomplished miraculously through Jesus himself acting as God's messianic agent.[13] So conceived, his death was a tragic failure.[14] By the time we reach the Gospel accounts, written a generation or more after Jesus' death, a transformation has occurred. Jesus' death was not a mistake; his was not the execution of a failed apocalyptic prophet. On the contrary, it was precisely for this reason that Jesus came: to redeem the world from sin through his sacrificial death. Hence the emphasis in all the Gospels on Jesus' prior knowledge of his fate and on his willing acceptance of it. The idea of vicarious atonement—that the self-sacrifice of a righteous individual had salvific consequences for others—was one of the most significant theological developments in Hellenistic Judaism. By interpreting the death of Jesus in this way, the early Christians were able to make sense of his otherwise tragic end.

The attempt to create a coherent and convincing explanation for Jesus' death was in part a response to the charge that Jesus' crucifixion *proved* that he could not have been the messiah, for the idea that the messiah was to suffer and die completely contradicted Jewish expectation. The historically undeniable fact of the crucifixion required a defense of Jesus' messianic status against the Jewish objection that "a hanged man is accursed by God" (Deut. 21:23). In his letter to the churches of Galatia, Paul turned this accusation into a badge of honor by arguing that Jesus took upon himself the "curse of the law" in order to redeem mankind:

> Christ redeemed us from the curse of the law, having become a curse for us—for it is written, "Cursed be every one who hangs on a tree"—that in Christ Jesus the blessing of Abraham might come upon the Gentiles, that we might receive the promise of the Spirit through faith (Gal. 3:13–14).

In the writings of Paul we find the earliest attempt to prove that Jesus' death occurred "according to the scriptures." Writing to the assembly at Corinth Paul reminds the Corinthians of the gospel he first preached to them:

> For I delivered to you as of first importance what I also received, that Christ died for our sins *in accordance with the scriptures*, that he was buried, that he was raised on the third day *in accordance with the scriptures*, and that he appeared to Cephas, then to the twelve (1 Cor. 15:3–5).

For Paul, Jesus' execution was not a tragic mistake but the fulfillment of what the ancient Hebrew oracles had predicted.[15]

This understanding of Jesus' death appears in the passion narratives of the four canonical Gospels. In all likelihood, the narrative of Jesus' arrest, trial, and execution represents one of the basic sources of the Gospel tradition, perhaps the first written unit in the tradition about Jesus. Since no first-century Jew expected the messiah to come *and* be executed as a criminal, the primary purpose of the passion narrative was to reconcile Jesus' divine or messianic status with his criminal's death. Thus, in all the Gospels there is a concern to demonstrate that Jesus' death took place "according to the scriptures."[16]

In the Gospel of Luke, for example, the resurrected Jesus upbraids two of his disciples for their failure to believe that the Jewish scriptures had predicted the suffering and death of the messiah. "O foolish men," Jesus admonishes them,

> "and slow of heart to believe all that the prophets have spoken! Was it not necessary that the Messiah should suffer these things and enter into his glory?" And beginning with Moses and all the prophets, he interpreted to them in all the scriptures the things concerning himself (Luke 24:25 –27).[17]

Nearly every detail in the events surrounding Jesus' death was explained as the fulfillment of one passage or another in the Jewish scriptures. The result was nothing less than astonishing. According to Luke, for example, Jesus deliberately provoked the Romano-Jewish authorities to arrest him as a revolutionary by instructing his disciples to buy swords! Why? So that the prophecy of Isaiah 53:12 might be fulfilled:

> And he said to them, "When I sent you out with no purse or bag or sandals, did you lack anything?" They said, "Nothing." He said to them, "But now, let him who has a purse take it, and likewise a bag. And let him who has no sword sell his mantle and buy one. For I tell you that this scripture must be fulfilled in me, 'And he was reckoned with transgressors'; for what is written about me has its fulfillment" (Luke 22:35– 37).

This passage is a good indication of the distance between the historical Jesus and the Jesus who emerges in the Gospels. We must take care not to confuse the two. Jesus of Nazareth proclaimed himself the messianic king and never expected to die, much less die on behalf of others. The Jesus of Luke's biography actually baited the Romans to kill him! It is not so much the historical Jesus as the Jesus imagined by the early Christians who is of interest to us here. Clearly, they understood his death not as the execution of a convicted criminal but as a divinely ordained event: predicted by the prophets and provoked by Jesus himself.

According to the Christians who preserved his memory, Jesus intended to die and embraced death willingly. In addition to claiming that Jesus' death took place "according to the scriptures," the author of the Gospel of Mark places the necessity for Jesus' suffering and death on the lips of Jesus himself. This occurs in the form of three prophecies Jesus utters about his impending death and resurrection:

> And they were on the road, going up to Jerusalem, and Jesus was walking ahead of them; and they were amazed, and those who followed were afraid. And taking the twelve again, he began to tell them what was to happen to him, saying, "Behold, we are going up to Jerusalem; and the Son of Man will be delivered to the chief priests and the scribes, and they will condemn him to death, and deliver him to the Gentiles; and they will mock him, and spit upon him, and scourge him, and kill him; and after three days he will rise" (Mark 10:32 –34).[18]

Jesus' death, according to Mark, was not only divinely ordained but also predicted by Jesus himself.

According to the Gospels, Jesus did not wait in Galilee to be arrested; he deliberately went to Jerusalem. Like Achilles, who chose to remain at Troy and die nobly, Jesus intentionally set out on a course that would inevitably lead to death. "When the days drew near for him to be received up," Luke tells us, "he set his face to go to Jerusalem" (Luke 9:51). It was Jesus who determined his course of action at the divinely appointed time. Previously in Luke there had been an attempt on his life: an angry mob at Nazareth tried to throw him over a cliff (Luke 4:29–30). But Jesus was in no real danger, for the time of his departure had not arrived: "Passing through the midst of them he went away" (Luke 4:30). In John, the Jews took up stones more than once to kill Jesus, but to no avail (John 8:59; 10:31). On another occasion, when the Jews tried to arrest Jesus, "no one laid a hand on him because his hour had not yet come" (John 7:30; cf. 8:20). Only Jesus knows the "hour" of his death.

All four Gospels relate that at the arrest of Jesus one of his disciples drew a sword and cut off the ear of the high priest's slave. But it is only Matthew who records the following reply of Jesus: "Put your sword back into its place. . . . Do you think that I cannot appeal to my Father, and he will at once send me more than twelve legions of angels? But how then should the scriptures be fulfilled, that it must be so?" (Matt. 26:52–54). Jesus rebuffs the efforts of one of his well-intending disciples to help him escape, in much the same way as Socrates rejected Crito's offer of assistance.[19] Even though the angels stand ready to save him, Jesus will not appeal for divine aid. The "scriptures must be fulfilled," and so, according to Matthew, Jesus goes to his death willingly, determined to die.

If it is not always easy to distinguish between "suicide" and "martyrdom," between killing oneself and provoking one's own death, then the Jews in the Fourth Gospel were not wrong when they described Jesus' "going away" as a death threat. Indeed, the author of the Fourth Gospel makes this explicit by having Jesus declare, "No one takes [my life] from me, but I lay it down of my own free will. I have power to lay it down, and I have power to take it again" (John 10:18).

The voluntary nature of Jesus' death is emphasized above all in the Fourth Gospel by that author's remarkable interpretation of the arrest, trial, and execution of Jesus. Throughout the Johannine account of the passion, Jesus' authority is repeatedly stressed. He is the one in control of the situation; he orchestrates the events that lead him to the cross. In the garden Jesus goes out to his arrest boldly identifying himself. In fact, it is Jesus who interrogates his captors! "Then Jesus, knowing all that was to befall him, came forward and said to them, 'Whom do you seek'?" (John 18:4). When Jesus finally reveals his identity, those who have come out to arrest him fall to the ground in terror. So Jesus must ask a second time, "Whom do you seek?" (John 18:6–7). Jesus' captors behave in much the same way as the young gladiator in the *Acts of Perpetua* (21.9–10), who could not bring himself to kill Perpetua until she compelled him.

During the trial, the Roman governor Pontius Pilate chided Jesus for his refusal to defend himself. "Do you not know," he asks, "that I have power to release you, and power to crucify you?" (John 19:10). Jesus' reply makes clear just who is in charge: "You would have no power over me unless it had been given you from above" (John 19:11). Pilate is no more than a pawn, an unwitting accomplice, for Jesus himself has determined the time and manner of his death. The sentence that is handed down is almost incidental.

The voluntary nature of Jesus' death is played out to the end in John. On the cross Jesus pronounces a solemn declaration: "It is finished"; then "he bowed his head and surrendered his spirit" (John 19:30). The cry, "It is finished," constitutes Jesus' last words in the Fourth Gospel. It is a victory cry replacing the cry of apparent defeat in Mark and Matthew: "My God, my God, why have you forsaken me?" The death of the Johannine Jesus is not a scene of suffering and ignominy; it is a great triumph. Jesus deliberately accepts death because it is the completion of God's plan, and death does not come until Jesus signifies his readiness (cf. 10:17–18).[20] This is illustrated by the fact that Jesus *first* reclines his head and then dies, whereas normally the reverse is said to occur. Even at the moment of death Jesus remains the subject of an active verb: *klinas ten kephalen* ("having reclined his head").[21]

The phrase "surrendered his spirit" (*paredoken to pneuma*) also deserves comment, for it is an unprecedented description of death. The other three

Gospels employ the usual expressions for dying. Mark (15:37, 39) and Luke (23:46) use the verb *ekpneo* ("expire") at the moment of Jesus' death; Matthew (27:50) has *aphiemi* ("give up"). So far as we can tell, John 19:30 is the first instance in Greek literature in which the expression *paradidomi to pneuma* is used to indicate an individual's death. What did the author of the Fourth Gospel intend by this unusual expression? Above all, he wished to stress the voluntary nature of Jesus' death. Death was not *forced* upon Jesus; he surrendered his spirit voluntarily.[22] As D. Moody Smith notes, "Jesus goes to the cross of his own volition and by his own decision. He decides when the hour for his departure in death has arrived, or rather he alone knows when the Father has decreed his hour has come. He lays down his own life; no one takes it from him (10:18). In John, Jesus' death is his glorification, not his humiliation."[23]

The Jesus created by his earliest followers became the paradigm for Christians to imitate, much as Plato's account of the death of Socrates served as a model for Greeks and Romans. Just as Socrates summoned those with a worthy interest in philosophy to come after him "as quickly as they could," so the Jesus of Christian imagination exhorted his followers to the cross. "If any man would come after me," Jesus declared, "let him deny himself and take up his cross and follow me. For whoever would save his life will lose it; and whoever loses his life for my sake and the gospel's will save it" (Mark 8:34–35 par.). Jesus' words did not fall on deaf ears; in the following centuries his followers were prepared to act on them. The representation of Jesus' death in the Gospels exercised a powerful influence on the imagination of the early Christian martyrs and those who preserved their memory. Behind every martyrdom lay the self-sacrifice of Jesus himself.

One such follower was the apostle Paul, whose fascination with death and his desire to escape from life were as intense as those of his contemporary Seneca, the Roman Stoic philosopher.[24] In his letter to the church at Philippi, written from prison in the middle of the first century, Paul offers us the earliest discussion of the problem of voluntary death by a Christian. In the first chapter of his letter the apostle agonizes over the decision to live or die. The passage is worth quoting in full.

> For me, to live is Christ and to die is gain. *Yet, which I shall choose I cannot tell.* I am hard pressed between the two. My strong desire is to depart and be with Christ, for that is far better. But to remain in the flesh is more necessary on your account. Convinced of this, I shall remain and continue with you all, for your progress and joy in the faith, so that in me you may have ample cause to glory in Christ Jesus, because of my coming to you again (Phil. 1:21–26).

The preceding passage concludes a section of the letter (1:12–26) in which Paul considers the relationship between his imprisonment and the proclamation of the gospel. In the final analysis, he declares that the gospel will be better served by his continued existence than by his departure in death. But first Paul carefully considers the advantages of each possibility. As commentators since Lightfoot have observed, "The grammar of the passage reflects the conflict of feeling in the apostle's mind. He is tossed to and fro between the desire to labour for Christ in life, and the desire to be united with Christ by death."[25] Although the former possibility is judged to be "more necessary" (*anangkaioteron*), the latter is, literally, "much more better" (*pollo mallon kreisson*).

At the outset it is important to note that Paul's reflections on death do not arise from the fact that he faces imminent execution. Admittedly, he is in prison (presumably in Ephesus), but by the time he writes his letter to the church at Philippi, Paul has every reason to expect that he will receive a favorable verdict from the Roman authorities (1:25–26). That is why he can say to the Philippians that he is looking forward to visiting them in the near future (2:24). Furthermore, full weight must be given to Paul's statement about life and death: "Which I *shall choose* I cannot tell" (1:22). This should be taken to mean what it says, that the question of life or death was a matter of Paul's *own* volition, not a fate to be imposed on him by others.

Philippians 1:21 is Paul's famous declaration about the meaning and significance he attached to life and death: "For me, to live is Christ," he declared, "and to die is gain." The meaning of the phrase "to live is Christ" is at first sight problematic, since it does not seem to be consistent with the tone of the rest of the passage. If, as Paul says in 1:23, death is preferable to life because it means union with Christ, then in what sense is living equivalent to Christ? Most commentators are inclined to read the phrase "to live is Christ" in light of Paul's pronouncement in Galatians 2:20: "I have been crucified with Christ; it is no longer I who live, but Christ who lives in me."[26] In other words, the life Paul lives is already a kind of postmortem existence. Paul's remarks in 2 Corinthians 4:8–11 are similar: "We are afflicted in every way . . . always carrying in the body the death of Jesus, so that the life of Jesus may also be manifested in our mortal flesh." As important as these parallels are, they still do not completely remove the difficulty of understanding the expression "to live is Christ" in its present context. For it is hard to see how Paul could say that his life is Christ and his death is gain when elsewhere he insists that all believers belong to Christ whether in life *or* death.[27]

A solution to this problem may be that Paul is deliberately playing on the similarity in sound between the title *Christos* and the word *chrestos* ("useful"). Alberto Giglioli, following the Arabic of Walton's Polyglot of 1657, has gone so far as to emend the text at this point from *Christos* to *chreston*, attributing the change from *e* to *i* to itacism.[28] Giglioli's emendation cannot be sustained, but that has no bearing on the possibility that Paul is engaging in a wordplay on the title *Christos*. Thus, Paul would be saying that "for me, to live is Christ," but also implying that "for me, to live is *useful* and to die is gain." The latter is entirely consistent with the tone of the passage. Even though Paul personally prefers death, it is nevertheless "useful" for him to remain alive for the continued progress of the Philippians (1:24–26).

Whatever the meaning of "to live is Christ" may be, there is no doubt about the interpretation of its counterpart, "to die is gain." Why is death a gain? The answer is given in 1:23, "My strong desire [*epithymia*] is to depart and be with Christ, for that is far better." For Paul, death is a gain because it means union with Christ and the attainment of immortality. And it is for this reason that Paul "lusts after death" (*epithymia eis to analysai*).[29]

Yet, as D. W. Palmer has shown, a complete answer to the question of why death is a gain is found not only in what Paul says but also in what is left unstated but may be assumed in the context.[30] Many others in addition to Paul affirmed the idea that death is a gain, and there was a conventional explanation that they offered: death brings release from life's troubles and afflictions. In chapter 2 we saw that many writers insisted that death should be entered into joyfully because it is a haven and refuge from the cares and torments of life. Paul Antin has drawn attention to a passage in Sophocles' *Antigone* (462–64) that closely parallels Paul's thinking in Philippians 1:21. Antigone declares, "I knew that I would die . . . even if you had not made a public proclamation. And if I am going to die before my time, I count it gain [*kerdos . . . ego lego*]. For death is a gain to one whose life, like mine, is full of misery."[31] Antigone did not wait for death; she took her own life.

In the *Apology* Socrates says that "the state of death is one of two things: either it is virtual nothingness . . . , or it is a change and a migration of the soul from this place to another. And if it is unconsciousness, like sleep in which a sleeper does not even dream, death would be a wonderful gain" (40cd).[32] The same attitude can be found especially when there is a strong hope of personal immortality, as in Revelation 14:13: "Blessed are the dead who die in the Lord henceforth. Blessed indeed, says the Spirit, that they may rest from their labors." These examples, which could easily be multiplied, express the sentiment that death is a gain because it brings an end to life's hardships.[33]

Although Paul declares that "to live is Christ," he also acknowledges the troubles that vex his earthly life. He repeatedly refers to his imprisonment (Phil. 1:7, 13, 14, 17), and he speaks of his own afflictions (1:17; 4:14) and his participation in the sufferings of Christ (3:10). For him, life is a struggle (1:30), full of grief (2:27), humiliation, deprivation, and hunger (4:11–12). In metaphorical language Paul speaks of being poured out as a libation (2:17) and of being conformed to the death of Christ (3:10).

References such as these can be found throughout Paul's letters. He boasts to the Corinthians that he "dies daily" (1 Cor. 15:31) and recounts his brush with death in Asia: "For we were so utterly, unbearably crushed that we despaired of life itself. We felt that we had received the sentence of death" (2 Cor. 1:8–9). In the *peristasis*-catalogues of 2 Corinthians 6:4–5 and 11:24–29 he gives detailed examples of his sufferings as an apostle, including imprisonments, beatings, and even shipwrecks. Death is a gain for Paul not only because it means union with Christ but also because it brings deliverance from life's miseries.

It is for these reasons that Paul "lusts after death." Although he finally rejects the "gain" of death, it is clearly death that he prefers. Of course, we should not underestimate the fact that Paul finds himself torn between two possibilities: the expressions "which I shall choose I cannot tell" and "I am hard pressed between the two" indicate as much. But in the final analysis the comparative *kreisson* ("better"), doubly strengthened by *pollo mallon* ("much more"), a combination unique in the New Testament, outweighs the simple comparative *anangkaioteron* ("more necessary"). For Paul, then, death is "much more better." This interpretation is confirmed by a similar statement in 2 Corinthians 5:1–8:

> For we know that if the earthly tent we live in is destroyed, we have a building from God, a house not made with hands, eternal in the heavens. Here indeed we groan, and long to put on our heavenly dwelling. . . . For while we are in this tent we sigh with anxiety; not that we would be unclothed, but that we would be further clothed, so that what is mortal may be swallowed up by life. . . . So we are always of good courage; we know that while we are at home in the body we are away from the Lord. . . . We are of good courage, *and we would rather be away from the body and at home with the Lord.*

The final sentence is important, for the phrase "we would rather" (*eudokoumen mallon*) does not express a preference but a decisive choice.[34]

If Paul prefers death, why does he finally choose life instead? Here attention must be given to the comparative *anangkaioteron* ("more necessary") in Philippians 1:24. In chapter 2 we saw that Socrates had left a single loophole for the justification of voluntary death: "An individual must not kill himself," Socrates says, "until God brings some necessity [*anangke*] upon him, such as has now come upon me" (*Phaedo* 62c). It appears that Paul, like many of his contemporaries, was aware of this Socratic principle and applied it to his own situation, for he says, "To remain in the flesh is *more necessary* on your account." While the option of voluntary death was considered and, indeed, personally desirable, it was ultimately rejected because it went against his understanding of the *present* will of God, namely, that Paul continue his earthly mission. In other words, the real sacrifice for Paul was remaining alive!

This is confirmed by what Paul says in 1 Corinthians 9:16: "For if I preach the gospel, that gives me no ground for boasting. For necessity [*anangke*] is laid upon me. Woe is me if I do not preach the gospel."[35] It is not that Paul rejected the option of voluntary death as such, only that it is was not (yet) the appropriate time for such an act. That Paul was not opposed to voluntary death is clear from his famous panegyric to *agape* in 1 Corinthians 13, where he classified self-destruction with other *worthy* but ineffectual approaches to salvation: "If I give away all I have, and if I deliver my body to be burned, but have not love, I gain nothing" (1 Cor. 13:3). Again, this is not a condemnation of voluntary death, only a condemnation of the act when committed for the wrong reason or without the appropriate motivation.

A similar position on voluntary death was endorsed by Paul's contemporary the Roman Stoic Musonius Rufus, in a statement that can be read as a virtual paraphrase of Paul's remarks in Philippians 1:21–26. "One who by living is of use to many," declares Musonius, "has not the right to die, unless by dying he may be of use to more."[36] Of course, Musonius did not share Paul's view of the afterlife, and so the rationale underlying their positions on voluntary death would no doubt have differed in this respect. But both were in agreement that, whatever the benefits death might hold, the decision to take one's life must be evaluated in light of an individual's responsibilities in this life.

Epictetus, Musonius's disciple, expressed the same view. He felt obliged to moderate against an excessive fascination with death on the part of certain young men who appealed to him in the following way:

> Are we not in a manner akin to God, and have we not come from him? Allow us to go back from whence we came; allow us to be freed from these fetters that are fastened to us and weigh us down. Here there are thieves and robbers, and courts of law, and those who are called tyrants. They think that they have some power over us because of this paltry body and its possessions. Allow us to show them that they have no power over us.[37]

The death wish of these young Greeks is based on a double desire: to return to the deity and to escape from earthly troubles, precisely the same reasons why Paul preferred death. In an attempt to restrain these men Epictetus exhorted them in the following manner: "And thereupon it were my part to respond: Men, wait upon God. When he shall give the signal to depart and set you free from this service, then you shall depart to him; but for the present endure to abide in the place where he has stationed you."[38]

Neither Musonius nor Epictetus opposed the right of an individual to take his own life; they only opposed the act when it was committed for the wrong reason or without sufficient justification. The same was true for Paul. He preferred death to life because it meant union with Christ and deliverance from the body and earthly troubles. But Paul also believed that a divine necessity (*anangke*) had been placed upon him and that he could not depart until that commission had been fulfilled.

In chapter 2 we saw that part of the debate about voluntary death revolved around the question of who owned an individual's body. Plato argued that one could not dispose of one's body (i.e., kill oneself) without first taking into consideration the question of ownership. Both the gods and the state, he claimed, exercised certain rights over an individual. The Cynics, by contrast, regarded themselves as completely independent and autonomous beings. The true Cynic, therefore, was at all times free to take his own life. Paul's position on voluntary death is analogous in this respect to that of Plato (at least in the *Phaedo*), for Paul also recognized that believers are not their own masters but belong to the Lord. In his first letter to the Corinthians Paul reminded them that they had been purchased by Christ—that is, that they were *his* property and did not belong to themselves: "Do you not know that your body is the temple of the Holy Spirit within you, which you have from God? You are not your own; you were bought for a price. So glorify God in your body" (1 Cor. 6:19–20). Likewise Paul repeatedly referred to himself as a "slave of Christ" (Rom. 1:1; Gal. 1:10; Phil. 1:1). The implication is that a Christian does not have the right to do with the body as he pleases, but only as his master (God) commands. The Christian, therefore, would not have the right to dispose of himself without his master's consent. Only when God gives his permission to depart is the individual free to act in this way. Conceivably, for Paul, an individual could kill himself and be "glorifying God with his body" by doing so.

That this was Paul's position on voluntary death is borne out by Ambrose in the fourth century. In his homiletical treatise *On Death as a Good*, Ambrose offered the following exposition of Philippians 1:21:

> For Christ is our king; therefore, we cannot abandon and disregard his royal command. How many men the emperor of this earth orders to live abroad in the splendor of office or to perform some function! Do they abandon their posts without the emperor's consent? Yet what a greater thing it is to please the divine than the human! Thus, for the saint, "to live is Christ and to die is gain." He does not flee the servitude of life like a slave, and yet like a wise man he does embrace the gain of death.[39]

Ambrose asserted with Paul that the Christian is to stay at the post to which God has assigned him *until* God gives the command to depart. When he does, the Christian embraces the gain of death.

In addition to Ambrose, we should mention a passage from John Donne's treatise *Biathanatos*, which likewise supports the interpretation we have set forth here. Commenting on Philippians 1:21–26, Donne wrote:

To this readiness of dying for his brethren Saint Paul had so accustomed him-self and made it his nature that, except for his general resolution of always doing what would promote their happiness, he could hardly have obtained for himself permission to live. At first he says he did not know which to wish for, life or death. Therefore, unless some circumstance inclines or averts us, life and death are generally equal to our nature. Then, after much perplexity, he made up his mind, and he desired to be released and to be with Christ. *Therefore, a holy man may wish it.* Still, he corrected that again, because he says, "For me to abide in the flesh is more needful for you" [Phil. 1:24]. Therefore, charity must be the rule of our wishes and actions in this matter.[40]

Our interpretation of Paul stands in sharp contrast to the view of most New Testament scholars, Ambrose and Donne notwithstanding. In his otherwise excellent monograph on Paul and Seneca, J. N. Sevenster gives careful consid-eration to Seneca's views on "suicide," but when he compares them to Paul's remarks in Philippians 1:23 and 2 Corinthians 5:8, his conclusions are entirely negative. "No immediate comparisons can of course be made," Sevenster asserts, "since Paul nowhere speaks of suicide or the possibility of it. . . . Paul's particular message concerning God and Christ prevents even the thought of suicide from arising."[41] Darrel W. Amundsen states it even more categorically. "The New Testament," he writes, "although it nowhere specifically condemns suicide, provides no implicit, much less explicit, encouragement of suicide. Rather it provides a structure of values and hopes antithetical, indeed inimi-cal, to suicide."[42] Why so sweeping and negative a judgment? Given the widespread acceptance of voluntary death among Paul's contemporaries, whether pagan or Jewish, is it so surprising that he would espouse a similar view? There can be little doubt that the barrier of Augustine has obscured our view of Paul on this point.

Despite the claim of Augustine and later theologians, the New Testament expresses no condemnation of voluntary death. This in itself is not surprising. In the *Umwelt* of early Christianity the act of taking one's life was judged to be acceptable and, in certain circumstances, noble. We have seen that this was Matthew's implicit judgment on Judas's death. Judas was condemned for betraying the messiah, not for killing himself. According to Matthew, Judas's act of self-destruction was the measure of his remorse and repentance. Yet, to say only that the writers of the New Testament did not condemn voluntary death is to miss the positive significance they attached to the act. The authors of the Gospels created a Jesus who died by his own choice, if not by his own hand. They claimed that Jesus died voluntarily and in accordance with God's plan, despite appearances to the contrary. This act, moreover, brought with it a singular benefit, both for Jesus and for those who put their confidence in him. God raised Jesus from the dead and exalted him to heaven, and he promised to do the same for those who "followed" Jesus. "If any man would come after me," Jesus exhorted his disciples, "let him deny himself and take up his cross and follow me. For whoever would save his life will lose it; and whoever loses his life for my sake or the gospel's will save it" (Mark 8:34–35 par.). For some Christians, "following" meant a *vicarious* reenactment of Jesus' death and resurrection through the ritual of baptism. But other Christians understood the idea of "following" more literally. They believed that salvation could only be *guaranteed* by actually reenacting the death of Jesus—that is, by voluntarily offering themselves up to death as he had done. The writers of the Gospels created a Jesus who became the prototype of the Christian martyr.

NOTES

1. Matt. 27:9–10 cites the prophet Jeremiah, though his quotation is actually a rather fanciful conflation of Zech. 11:12–13 and Jer. 18:1–3; 32:6–15. The book of Acts quotes Pss. 69:26 and 109:8. Both Matt. and Acts refer to the cemetery as the "Field of Blood." Despite some ingenious attempts, the two accounts cannot be reconciled, and it is unlikely that either account contains any historically reliable information. See J. Rendel Harris, "Did Judas Really Commit Suicide?" *American Journal of Theology* 4 (1900): 490–513.

2. If that is what *prenes genomenos* means (Acts 1:18). It is also possible to translate this phrase as "swelling up."

3. *Apelthon apengxato*; cf. Epictetus 1.2.3.

4. See Daube, "Death as a Release in the Bible," *Novum Testamentum* 5 (1962), pp. 88–89. The account in Acts treats Judas much more harshly: no mention of repentance or of giving up the blood money; but there is still no disapproval of the *means* of death. The church historian Eusebius relates a similar tradition about Pontius Pilate, who, he says, "fell into such great calamity that he was forced to become his own slayer and to punish himself with his own hand [*autocheir*], for the penalty of God, as it seems, followed hard after him" (*Church History* 2.7.1; cf. 9.6.1). Again, this is a condemnation not of voluntary death, but of Pilate.

5. Augustine, *City of God* 1.17; cf. Jerome, *Commentary on Matthew* 4.17.

6. In this respect, Judas's act is similar to a number of rabbinic accounts discussed in the previous chapter.

7. See Daube, "Death as Release," p. 88.

8. According to Acts 12:19, Herod had Peter's jailers executed after Peter's miraculous escape from prison.

9. This was already recognized by John Donne, *Biathanatos* 3.3.2.

10. The note on John 8:22 in *The New Oxford Annotated Bible* reads: "Suicide leads to hell, they [the Jews] suggest" (p. 1299). This comment tells us more about the prejudice of the modern editors than it does about the text. In fact, the passage in John implies no condemnation of voluntary death on the part of either the

Jews or the author of the Fourth Gospel (cf. 7:33–36; 13:33; and see Daube, "Death as Release," pp. 87–88). Compare Jesus' remark with Socrates' reply to Crito in the *Phaedo*. When Crito asked him how he wished to be buried, Socrates replied, "However you please, if you can catch me and I do not get away from you" (115c).

11. Tertullian, *Apology* 21.19; Origen, *Against Celsus* 2.11, 22.

12. Augustine, *On the Trinity* 4.16.

13. On this, see E. P. Sanders, *Jesus and Judaism* (Philadelphia: Fortress Press, 1985).

14. See the famous description of this in Albert Schweitzer, *The Quest of the Historical Jesus*, translated by W. Montgomery (London: Macmillan, 1968), pp. 370–71.

15. Note that this view of Jesus' death did not originate with Paul, for he says that he delivered to the Corinthians what he himself had received (1 Cor. 15:3). It must have been a very early attempt to explain the reasons for Jesus' death.

16. On this, see Sam K. Williams, *Jesus' Death as Saving Event: The Background and Origin of a Concept*, HDR 2 (Missoula, MT: Scholars Press, 1975) esp. pp. 203–54.

17. This theme is found again in Acts 3:18–25; 8:30–35; 26:22–23. The passages from the Hebrew Bible that figure prominently in this passion apologetic include Isa. 42–44; 49–53; 61; Pss. 22; 31; 34; 41–43; 69; 109; 118; and Zech. 9–14.

18. Almost identical predictions are found in Mark 8:31 and 9:30–31.

19. Plato, *Crito* 44bc *et passim*.

20. So A. Loisy, *Le quatrième évangile*, 2d ed. (Paris: Nourry, 1921), pp. 489–90.

21. On this, see C. K. Barrett, *The Gospel According to St. John*, 2d ed. (Philadelphia: Westminster Press, 1978), p. 554.

22. See BAGD s.v. *paradidomi* 1a. The last words of Jesus in Luke 23:46 are similar in tone: "Father, into your hands I commend [*paratithemai*] my spirit." As we shall see in the next chapter, the Johannine description of Jesus' death will be applied to the deaths of the Christian martyrs.

23. D. Moody Smith, *Johannine Christianity: Essays on Its Setting, Sources, and Theology* (Columbia: Univ. of South Carolina Press, 1984), p. 179. Smith further observes, "The tragic dimensions of Jesus' death, his own anguish and suffering in the face of it, are largely absent in John. He dies as man is scarcely known to die. If in Mark Jesus utters a cry of dereliction and in Luke a pious prayer, in John Jesus marks the end of his own earthly ministry and work with the imperious pronouncement, 'It is finished' " (pp. 179–80). Cf. C. H. Dodd, *The Interpretation of the Fourth Gospel* (Cambridge: Cambridge Univ. Press, 1953), p. 426.

24. Much of what follows is based on A. J. Droge, "MORI LUCRUM: Paul and Ancient Theories of Suicide," *Novum Testamentum* 30 (1988): 263–86.

25. J. B. Lightfoot, *St. Paul's Epistle to the Philippians* (London: Macmillan, 1891), p. 91.

26. See J.-F. Collange, *L'épître de saint Paul aux Philippiens*, Commentaire du Nouveau Testament Xa (Neuchâtel: Delachaux & Niestlé, 1973), p. 60, and the literature there cited.

27. See, for example, Rom. 8:38–39; 1 Thess. 5:9–10.

28. A. Giglioli, "Mihi enim vivere Christus est: Congeturra al texto di Phil. 1, 21," *Rivista Biblica* 16 (1968): 305–15. Giglioli was not the first to suggest this emendation; see C. Müller, *Commentatio de locis quibusdam Epistolae Pauli ad Philippenses* (Hamburg: Meissner, 1843), p. 17. Note that the Roman biographer Suetonius apparently confused the title "Christus" with the name "Chrestus" when he wrote, "Iudaeos impulsore Chresto assidue tumultuantis Roma expulit" (*Divus Claudius* 25.4).

29. See the comments of Albert Schweitzer, *The Mysticism of Paul the Apostle* (London: Adam & Charles Black, 1931), p. 136. Cf. Paul's "lust for death" with Seneca's reference to a *libido moriendi* among some of his contemporaries (*Epistle* 24.25).

30. D. W. Palmer, " 'To Die Is Gain' (Philippians i 21)," *Novum Testamentum* 17 (1975): 203–18.

31. P. Antin, "*Mori lucrum* et *Antigone* 462, 464," *Revue des sciences religieuses* 62 (1964): 259–60. The similarity goes beyond mere verbal parallel (*pace* Antin).

32. Cf. *Apology* 40e: "If such is the nature of death [i.e., unconsciousness], I count it gain."

33. See the passages assembled by Palmer, "To Die Is Gain," pp. 208–16.

34. Cf. Phil. 1:23: "But I am hard pressed between the two [life and death], having the strong desire to depart and be with Christ, for that is far better."

35. Note Paul's statement in the preceding verse: "I would rather die than have any one deprive me of my ground for boasting."

36. Fragment 29 in C. E. Lutz, "Musonius Rufus: 'The Roman Socrates'," *Yale Classical Studies* 10 (1947), pp. 132–33.

37. Epictetus 1.9.13–15.

38. Epictetus 1.9.16.

39. Ambrose, *On Death as a Good* 3.7.

40. John Donne, *Biathanatos* 3.4.8 (quoted from the edition by William A. Clebsch, *John Donne: Suicide*, Studies in the Humanities, Series 1 [Chico, CA: Scholars Press, 1983], p. 84).

41. J. N. Sevenster, *Paul and Seneca*, SNT 4 (Leiden: E. J. Brill, 1961), pp. 58 and 61.

42. Darrel W. Amundsen, "Suicide and Early Christian Values," in Baruch A. Brody, ed., *Suicide and Euthanasia: Historical and Contemporary Themes*, Philosophy and Medicine, no. 35 (Dordrecht, Boston, and London: Kluwer Academic Publishers, 1989), p. 80.

CHAPTER 6

❧

The Crown of Immortality

As Christianity expanded into and eventually took over the Greek and Roman worlds, it brought with it a preoccupation with death as intense as Paul's, or at least the surviving literary evidence would so suggest. "Nothing matters to us in this age," wrote Tertullian in 197, "but to escape from it with all speed."[1] The early Christian fascination with voluntary death was not simply a desire to escape from life's hardships; it was rather a statement about or judgment on life itself, both here and in the hereafter. For Christians like Tertullian, "life was at best unimportant; at worst, evil."[2] Death was therefore sought out with impatience as a means of *autoapotheosis*, as a shortcut to immortality. Addressing the governors of the empire, Tertullian asked, "Who does not join us, and joining us, does not wish to suffer, that he may purchase for himself the whole grace of God, that he may win full pardon from God by paying his own blood for it? For all sins are forgiven to a deed like this. That is why, on being sentenced by you, at that moment we render you thanks. . . . We are condemned by you, we are acquitted by God."[3] So much for the necessity of Christ's vicarious sacrifice! Now each Christian must become his own savior.

Martyrdom is one of the most fascinating and most studied aspects of early Christianity. In this chapter we have taken a somewhat different approach to the subject of martyrdom. The reader who is seeking an answer to the question of why the early Christians were persecuted or who wants to know how many of them died for their beliefs may be disappointed by our discussion. Legal, political, and historical questions remain in the background for the most part. Instead, our concern will be to explore how martyrdom was evaluated in early Christianity and then to place that evaluation within the larger debate about voluntary death among Greeks, Romans, and Jews. The primary evidence is abundant (letters, martyr acts, and treatises on the subject), and we do not pretend to offer a comprehensive survey. Rather, we will concentrate on those texts that reveal the variety of motives that inspired Christians to give themselves up, as well as on the relatively few passages that contain explicit statements about the manner in which this should, or should not, be done. It was

the Christians who were the first to draw the distinction between authentic
and inauthentic "witness" (*martyrion*)—between being a true martyr and merely killing oneself. When this distinction was made, by whom, and on what basis
are the fundamental questions we will seek to answer.[4]

IGNATIUS OF ANTIOCH

Early in the second century, Ignatius, bishop of Antioch, gave firsthand testimony to the motives that led some Christians to die voluntarily for Christ.
Condemned to death in 107, Ignatius was led as a prisoner from Antioch to
Rome, where he was to fight with the beasts. On his journey Ignatius wrote letters to various churches in Asia Minor, as well as one to the Roman community. In his letter to the Christians of Rome, Ignatius pleaded with them *not* to
make any effort to save him, and so rob him of his crown of immortality. The
letter is worth quoting at length.

> I am writing to all the churches, and I give injunctions to all men, that *I am
> dying willingly* for God's sake, if you do not hinder it. Allow me to be eaten by
> the beasts, through which I can attain to God. . . . Rather, entice the wild beasts
> that they may become my tomb, and leave no trace of my body, that when I fall
> asleep I be not burdensome to any. Then shall I be truly a disciple of Jesus
> Christ, when the world shall not even see my body. Beseech Christ on my
> behalf, that I may be found a sacrifice through these instruments.
>
> I long for the beasts that are prepared for me; and I pray that they may be
> found prompt for me. I will even entice them to devour me promptly; not as
> has happened to some whom they have not touched from fear; even if they be
> unwilling of themselves, I will force them to it. Grant me this favor. I know
> what is expedient for me; now I am beginning to be a disciple. . . . Let there
> come on me fire, and cross, and struggles with wild beasts, cutting, and tearing
> asunder, rackings of bones, mangling of limbs, crushing of my whole body, cruel
> tortures of the devil, may I but attain to Jesus Christ!
>
> . . . The pains of birth are upon me. Allow me, my brethren; hinder me not
> from living, do not wish me to die. . . . Allow me to receive the pure light; when
> I have arrived there I shall become a man. Allow me to follow the example of
> the passion of my God.
>
> . . . Even though when I come to you I beg you myself, do not be persuaded
> by me, but rather obey this which I write to you. For in the midst of life I write
> to you desiring death.[5]

Although Ignatius had been sentenced to death by the Roman authorities,
the point of his letter to the Roman Christians is to underscore the *voluntary*
nature of his impending death. "I am dying willingly for God's sake," Ignatius

tells them, and that is why they should do nothing to prevent his death. On the contrary, if possible, they should "entice" the wild beasts to devour Ignatius. And, if they will not, Ignatius himself will "force the beasts to it." He revels in the thought of fire and cross, of being cut, torn apart, and mangled: "May I but attain to Jesus Christ!"

Like Razis and the Jews of Maccabean tradition, Ignatius views his death in sacrificial terms:[6] "Beseech Christ on my behalf, that I may be found a sacrifice [*thusia*] through these instruments." Death, whether self-inflicted or deliberately sought out, will result in the attainment of salvation and the entry into eternal life. Thus, Ignatius can speak of death as life, and of life as death: "The pains of *birth* are upon me. . . . Do not hinder me from living, do not wish me to die." The transvaluation of life and death, already present in Plato, is now complete. That the dates of the deaths of the martyrs were celebrated annually in the church calendar as "birthdays" speaks volumes.[7]

The depiction of Jesus' death in the Gospels as a voluntary sacrifice exercised a powerful influence on the imagination of early Christians like Ignatius: "Behind every martyrdom, whether or not the texts chose to dwell on it, lay the self-sacrifice of Jesus himself."[8] Ignatius took quite literally Jesus' saying, "If any man would come after me, let him deny himself and take up his cross and follow me. For whoever would save his life will lose it; and whoever loses his life for my sake and the gospel's will save it" (Mark 8:34–35 par.). Ignatius urged the importance and necessity of an *imitatio mortis Christi*: "Allow me to follow the example of the passion of my God." Dying in this way, he will become a "true disciple" and, indeed, a "man." We find the same exhortation being given by Polycarp, the bishop of Smyrna and Ignatius' contemporary. "Let us then be imitators of [Christ's] endurance," Polycarp wrote to the Philippians, "and if we suffer for his name's sake let us glorify him. For this is the example which he gave us in himself."[9] Christians like Ignatius believed that they had to reenact the death of Jesus in order to become true disciples. His death was the paradigm. This is the reason why we have relatively few reports of Christians actually taking their *own* lives (though this did occur).[10]

Ignatius's language is also reminiscent of Paul, who expressed the desire to "share Christ's sufferings" in order to "attain the resurrection from the dead" (Phil. 3:10–11). "It is better to die in Christ," Ignatius tells the Roman Christians, "than to be king over the ends of the earth" (6.1). This is a clear echo of Paul's famous declaration, "For me, to live is Christ and to die is gain" (Phil. 1:21). Vicarious participation in Christ's suffering, death, and resurrection through baptism was not sufficient for Ignatius. Something more was required to ensure that an individual would be able "to attain to the resurrection."

Voluntary death was believed to bring with it special privileges, above all the assurance of immediate salvation. The narrator of the *Martyrdom of Polycarp* states explicitly that those who had died willingly for the faith "were no longer men but already angels."[11] As Robin Lane Fox observes, "The martyrs bypassed the long delays, the intervals of cooling and refreshment, the minor corrections and discipline, the years of waiting in Abraham's bosom. They sped straight to Christ and his Father."[12] The idea of death as transformation was present already in Paul, and we have seen a similar understanding among Greeks, Romans, and Jews. Ignatius cannot, therefore, be dismissed as an aberration, nor should his enthusiasm for martyrdom be attributed to "masochism" or "psychosis."[13] As W. H. C. Frend has noted, Ignatius's outlook was praised by the "orthodox" Irenaeus,[14] and his example was followed in the second century by Christians "who deliberately courted death at the hands of the authorities."[15]

One such Christian was Lucius of Rome, whose trial and execution are mentioned by Justin in his *Second Apology*.[16] Sometime between 152 and 156 a certain Ptolemaeus, who had converted an aristocratic Roman woman to Christianity, was denounced before the urban prefect Q. Lollius Urbicus on the sole ground that he was a Christian. The man who brought the charge was the woman's disaffected pagan husband. The story, probably accurate in general if not in detail, reveals the kind of circumstances in which Christians were coming to the attention of the Roman authorities. Ptolemaeus confessed to being a Christian and was summarily executed.[17] A bystander named Lucius objected to the sentence, telling the prefect that Ptolemaeus was not guilty of any crime. When the prefect asked whether Lucius was also a Christian, he replied, "I most certainly am." As Lucius was led away to execution, "he professed his thanks, knowing that he was delivered from such wicked rulers, and was going to the Father and King of the heavens."[18] Justin goes on to say that still another Christian was inspired to come forward in this way, and that he too was condemned and executed.

The actions of Lucius and his unnamed associate are examples of what has been described as "secondary martyrdom," a phenomenon we shall meet again. It appears that the courtroom in particular was the breeding ground of spontaneous acts of self-destruction. Not only individuals but also whole groups of Christians would give themselves up in the heat of the moment at "unfair sentences" handed down by the Romans. "Martyrdom," as Fox has noted, "proved infectious."[19]

THE MARTYRDOM OF POLYCARP

The earliest extant "history" of a Christian martyrdom is the *Martyrdom of Polycarp*.[20] The account is cast in the form of a letter, written by a certain

Evarestus, from the church in Smyrna to the church in Philomelium in Phrygia. The precise reasons for Polycarp's arrest are not stated, but it seems to have been related to a general prosecution of Christians in this region of Asia Minor.[21] The *Martyrdom* begins with an account of the death of "the most noble Germanicus . . . who fought gloriously with the wild beasts":

> For when the proconsul wished to persuade him and bade him have pity on his youth, he violently dragged the beast on top of him, intending to be freed all the more quickly from this unjust and lawless life. At this then all the mob was astonished at the courage of this pious and devoted race of Christians, and they shouted out: "Away with these atheists! Go and get Polycarp!"[22]

The charge of "atheism" was directed against the Christians' refusal to recognize the traditional gods. While this charge was fundamental in the Roman prosecution of Christians, no one really seems to have cared what the Christians did or did not believe. A gesture of respect to the traditional gods and a simple oath to the emperor were all that were required. The consistent leniency of the Roman authorities and their repeated efforts to strike a compromise only set the voluntary nature of Christian martyrdom in sharper relief.[23]

In the *Martyrdom of Polycarp* the Roman governor tried to persuade Germanicus to change his mind. "Have pity on your youth," he advised him. But Germanicus remained unmoved, so much so that he dragged a reluctant animal toward him in order that he could be eaten. The dynamics of the trial and execution of Germanicus are similar to those of Perpetua, discussed in the first chapter. Like Germanicus, Perpetua too refused the Roman governor's appeals and "forced" the gladiator to kill her. In both cases, the authorities are little more than reluctant accomplices. Germanicus's behavior is also reminiscent of what Ignatius promised to do in the arena if the wild beasts did not devour him promptly: he would force them to it![24] The implication is that Germanicus's death, like the deaths of Perpetua and Ignatius, was truly a voluntary act despite the legal setting and the presence of Roman authority. Finally, what motivated Ignatius and Perpetua to give themselves up also inspired Germanicus, namely, a desire to be released from this "unjust and lawless life" and to pass over into immortality.

As a result of his act Germanicus is praised by Evarestus as "most noble," "steadfast," and "courageous." Germanicus is a model for others to emulate. Why? The answer may seem obvious enough, but Evarestus gives an explicit justification of Germanicus's act in the second chapter. "Blessed indeed and noble," he tells us, "are all the witnesses [*ta martyria*] that took place *in accordance with God's will*. For we must be very careful to assign to God a providence over them all."[25] This statement indicates that only a death that has been carried out at the instigation and direction of God can be described as "blessed and noble." Despite five and a half centuries and a different religious tradition, the problem of voluntary death is still being evaluated in the terms set forth by Plato. We saw in the *Phaedo* that Socrates justified taking one's life only when a divine signal (the *anangke*) had been given. To kill oneself without having received such a sign would mean usurping a privilege that belonged only to God. The narrator of the *Martyrdom of Polycarp* expresses a similar view: only those who die *in accordance with God's will* are blessed and noble—that is, are true witnesses (*martyria*). "We must be very careful," he says, "to assign to God a providence over them all." The implication is that not every voluntary death is a true *martyrion*. The distinction made here between authentic and inauthentic martyrdom is unprecedented and represents a first step toward the Augustinian reversal.

The death of Germanicus provides the immediate occasion for the arrest of Polycarp, but first Evarestus relates the case of a certain Quintus:

> There was a Phrygian named Quintus who had only recently come from Phrygia, and when he saw the beasts he played the coward. Now he was the one who had given himself up and had forced some others to give themselves up *voluntarily*. With him the proconsul used many arguments and persuaded him to take the oath and offer sacrifice. This is the reason, brothers, that we do not approve of those who come forward of themselves, since this is not the teaching of the Gospel.[26]

Quintus is deliberately portrayed as the antitype to Germanicus and especially Polycarp, and his failed attempt to procure martyrdom is a negative example of what Evarestus had said in 2.1, that only those *martyria* that occur "in accordance with God's will" are "blessed and noble." Quintus, according to the narrator, acted outside the providence of God. What distinguished Quintus's act from Germanicus's? Evarestus would have us believe that Quintus acted voluntarily, whereas Germanicus did not.[27] But this distinction seems rather forced. Although we do not know how Germanicus came to the attention of the authorities, it is clear that he acted in a deliberately provocative manner, as did Quintus. Indeed, Germanicus literally took matters into his own hands by dragging the beast on top of him.

Both Germanicus and Quintus are examples of what G. E. M. de Ste. Croix has called "voluntary martyrdom." The surviving evidence shows that many Christians often went beyond what was expected of them by their communities and turned themselves over to the Roman authorities of their own free will or by acting in a deliberately provocative manner. De Ste. Croix has shown that in Palestine during the "Great Persecution" in the early fourth century, "very few [martyrs] were *sought out*: approximately twice as many (if not more) were volunteers or had otherwise attracted the attention of the authorities."[28] That Evarestus can condemn Quintus on scriptural grounds is astonishing, for, as we have seen, the Gospels placed a premium on voluntary death. Jesus did not wait to be arrested in Galilee; he "set his face to go to Jerusalem" (Luke 9:51). When the soldiers came for him in the garden, he boldly went out to his captors and identified himself (John 18:4–8). If there was a scriptural warrant, it was on the side of Quintus.[29]

What distinguished Quintus from Germanicus, then, was not simply that the former acted voluntarily whereas the latter did not. What distinguished them was the fact that Quintus "played the coward" at the moment of crisis. Here we should recall Justin's comment about the "confession" of Ptolemaeus: "He who denies anything, either denies it because he condemns the thing itself, or he shrinks from confession because he is conscious of his own unworthiness or alienation from it. Neither is the case of the *true* Christian."[30] Ptolemaeus did not deny the faith, but Quintus did by turning coward. His action revealed him as unworthy, indeed, as not even a Christian. That, it seems, was the real reason for the narrator's condemnation of him: it served as a warning of the danger of apostasy to those who would offer themselves to the authorities voluntarily. If Quintus had acted courageously, if he had embraced death in the manner of Germanicus, there can be little doubt that Evarestus would have praised his death as "blessed and noble," regardless of whether he gave himself up voluntarily or not.

While these events were taking place, Polycarp was persuaded to go into hiding outside the city. It was there that he had a vision in which he saw the pillow under his head in flames. Recognizing the meaning of the vision, Polycarp declared, "I must be burned alive" (5.2). Here again we note the appearance of the "divine signal" indicating death. Although Polycarp was eventually discovered by the authorities, in no sense did they compel him. On the contrary, the police displayed consideration toward him and were even reluctant to arrest him. Evidently, Polycarp was a man of high standing in Smyrna. He did not have to be brought back by force. Polycarp entered the city in triumph in the same way Jesus had entered Jerusalem: riding on an ass (8.1).[31] Along the way, he was met by Herod, the chief of police, and Herod's father, Nicetas, who took Polycarp into their carriage and tried to persuade him to save himself. When Polycarp refused, Herod and Nicetas threatened him and eventually tossed him out near the stadium (8.2–3). The Roman governor also tried to dissuade him: "Take the oath and I will let you go." Polycarp again refused. When the governor threatened Polycarp with the beasts, he deliberately baited the governor: "Call for them," he said. When the governor threatened to burn him alive, Polycarp replied, "Why are you waiting? Come, do what you will" (9–11). In the stadium, a voice came from heaven: "Be strong, Polycarp, and play the man" (9.1).[32] When the wood had been assembled for the bonfire, his executioners intended to fasten him to it in order to prevent him from fleeing. But Polycarp declined: "Leave me alone, for he who has given me strength to endure the flames will grant me to remain without flinching in the fire even without the firmness you will give me by using nails" (13.3). Polycarp deliberately and provocatively set out on a course that he knew would lead to certain death, but he also knew that his death was divinely ordained and that he would receive the "crown of immortality" (17.1). His vision was fulfilled, and he was burned alive.

The Romans seem not to have been prepared for the fact that Christians like Ignatius and Polycarp anxiously awaited, indeed, sought out, their deaths as a means of salvation. "We do not shrink from the struggle with your rage," Tertullian told Scapula, "even coming forward to the contest *of our own accord*; and condemnation gives us more pleasure than acquittal."[33] In times of persecution Christians would force themselves on the notice of Roman authorities by tearing down statues of the gods and by other provocative demonstrations. Tertullian relates that in 185 the proconsul of Asia, Arrius Antoninus, was approached by a group of Christians demanding to be executed. The proconsul obliged some of them and then sent the rest away, saying that if they wanted to kill themselves, there was plenty of rope available or cliffs they could jump off![34]

The Christians of Asia Minor who sought death at the hands of Arrius Antoninus have been plausibly identified as Montanists.[35] The implication is that it was only the Montanists and other "heretics" who *volunteered* for martyrdom, whereas "orthodox" Christians *waited* to be arrested. Hans von Campenhausen attempted to make this point with regard to the *Martyrdom of Polycarp*. According to von Campenhausen, the story of Quintus, who voluntarily gave himself up to the authorities, was added to the *Martyrdom* in the late second or early third century to condemn a Montanist fascination with voluntary death. In this way Quintus becomes a "proto-Montanist" and a foil for the "orthodox" Polycarp, who *waited* for the police to arrest him.[36]

The *Martyrdom of Polycarp* may well have been redacted, but not necessarily in the way von Campenhausen claims. To see in Quintus a "proto-Montanist" zeal for martyrdom and in Polycarp a "model death" in accordance with the Gospels cannot be derived from the *Martyrdom* itself. On the contrary, it depends on von Campenhausen's (and others') view of the debate about voluntary death in the late second and early third centuries. According to his view, it was the Montanists who *voluntarily* gave themselves up to death at the hands of the Romans and were condemned for this by the majority of orthodox Christians, who accepted martyrdom when it came to them but never sought it. The evidence does not bear out such a distinction. In most cases we simply do not know how individual Christians came to the attention of the Roman authorities, whether by volunteering or by being sought out. We do not know, for example, the circumstances of the arrests of Ignatius and Germanicus. What is clear is that Christians like Ignatius and Germanicus went to their deaths willingly despite the attempt of the Romans to find a compromise. The difference between Quintus and Ignatius or Germanicus or even Polycarp is one of degree. This is not to say that some Christians, including the narrator of the *Martyrdom of Polycarp*, did not distinguish between an authentic and inauthentic "witness" (*martyrion*)—between being martyred and merely killing oneself. A few Christians made this distinction, but the debate about voluntary death did not break down along the lines of "orthodoxy" and "heresy," at least as these categories are used by many historians of early Christianity.

More than half a century ago Walter Bauer's *Orthodoxy and Heresy in Earliest Christianity* did much to reconfigure our understanding of the theological complexity in Christianity of the first three centuries.[37] Within that period there were, strictly speaking, no such things as "orthodoxy" and "heresy." On the contrary, there was great diversity of belief among Christian communities and individual Christians, and the beliefs and practices of no single group or individual had achieved preeminence. All the great figures of this period—Paul, the author of the Fourth Gospel, Ignatius, Polycarp, Marcion, Tatian, Valentinus, Clement, and Origen—were orthodox or heretical *according to the point of view of the critic.* The terms *orthodox* and *heretical* were part of the lexicon of polemic, used by individuals and communities to condemn their *Christian* opponents and adversaries. The terms were employed as a means of self-definition vis-à-vis the *proximate other:* to claim for a particular community the privilege of being the "true church" over against the competing claims of other Christians. For the historian to brand, say, the Montanists as "heretics" and Polycarp as "orthodox," as is often done, is to retroject the views of a much later period into an earlier one. In the first three or four centuries there were no normative definitions of orthodoxy and heresy. It was Bauer who showed that so-called heretical movements were often the *earliest* expressions of Christianity in particular locales: Egypt, Asia Minor, Syria.

Not every Christian who "volunteered" for martyrdom was a "heretic" or, what amounts to the same thing, a Montanist. This point needs to be emphasized.[38] As de Ste. Croix has correctly noted, "Contrary to what is usually said, voluntary martyrdom was by no means confined mainly to heretical or schismatic sects such as the Montanists and Donatists, but was a good deal more common among the orthodox than is generally admitted."[39] This gives to voluntary martyrdom an importance in the history of the persecutions that has not been fully appreciated. As de Ste. Croix notes, "It seems to me impossible to doubt that the prevalence of voluntary martyrdom was a factor which, for obvious reasons, both contributed to the outbreak of persecution and tended to intensify it when already in being."[40]

VOLUNTARY MARTYRDOM I

The evidence that has survived indicates that Montanists were not the only Christians who gave themselves up voluntarily. At Pergamum, on the coast of Asia Minor, two Christians named Carpus and Papylus stood trial before the Roman governor for refusing to offer sacrifices to the gods.[41] Their behavior was deliberately provocative, despite the efforts of the governor to persuade them to save their lives. " 'Sacrifice to the gods,' the governor exhorted them, 'and do not play the fool.' Carpus, with a gentle smile, said, 'May the gods be destroyed who have not made heaven and earth' " (9–10). The governor, therefore, ordered Carpus and Papylus to be hung up and scraped with claws (23, 35). When the governor saw their extraordinary endurance, he ordered them to be burned alive. Although Carpus and Papylus had suffered much, they both "ran to the amphitheater that they might all the more quickly depart from the world" (36). A common motif in this and other *Acts* is that although their tortures were gruesome, the martyrs did not suffer, enjoying "anesthesia" and an "analgesic state."[42]

Papylus was nailed to the stake, and after the fire was brought near, "he prayed in peace and gave up his soul" (*paredoken ten psychen*, 37). Like Jesus in the Gospel of John, Papylus died voluntarily.[43] As Carpus was nailed down, he laughed at the bystanders. When they asked why, Carpus mocked them and replied, "I saw the glory of the Lord and I rejoiced." Then, uttering a prayer, he too "gave up his soul" (38–41). A woman named Agathonike, one of the onlookers, "saw the glory of the Lord, as Carpus said he had seen it. *Realizing that this was a call from heaven*, . . . she threw herself joyfully upon the stake. . . . And thus she gave up her spirit and died together with the saints" (42–47).

Here were three Christians who contrived the circumstances of their death by behaving in a deliberately provocative manner. The Roman governor attempted to dissuade them in vain. Indeed, both Carpus and Papylus ran to the amphitheater to meet death! Like Jesus, they are portrayed as dying voluntarily, yet there is no evidence to suggest that they were Montanists.

The death of Agathonike is especially worthy of note. On the basis of what the text says (or fails to say), it appears that Agathonike was not even a Christian but a pagan onlooker,[44] who was sparked off by the sight of Carpus's death. Her voluntary act of self-destruction was spontaneous, yet well judged and ennobling:

"She gave up her spirit and died together with the saints" (47). We have encountered a similar perspective on voluntary death among Greeks, Romans, and Jews. Among Greeks and Romans we saw that even the "fool" could be transformed into a sage by such a death. In Judaism voluntary death could be seen as an act of sincere contrition and simultaneous transformation, enabling the individual (whether Jew or pagan) to atone for his sins and to attain eternal life.[45] But the most striking feature of Agathonike's death was her recognition of the "divine signal." Having seen the glory of the Lord, she realized that "this was a call from heaven" (42) and so threw herself into the fire. The echo of the *Phaedo* is still being heard six centuries later. Agathonike is a Socrates gone mad![46]

The analogy with Socrates is one that the Christians themselves were quick to notice. Justin, for example, compared Christians with Socrates, who "was accused of the very same crimes as ourselves."[47] Even so, Justin points out, "no one believed in Socrates so as to die for [his] doctrine, but in Christ . . . not only philosophers and scholars believed, but also artisans and people entirely uneducated, despising glory and fear and death."[48] In the fourth century John Chrysostom argued that the Christian martyrs were far superior to Socrates, for, in the first place, Chrysostom claimed to be able to list "ten thousand" Christian martyrs for every Socrates the pagans could find, and, in the second place, Socrates had no choice but to accept death, whereas the martyrs went to their deaths *willingly*:

> For not against their will did the martyrs endure, but of their will, and being free not to suffer. . . . This you see is no great wonder: that he whom I was mentioning drank hemlock; it being no longer in his power not to drink, and also when he had arrived at a very great age. . . . But show me someone enduring torments for godliness' sake, as I show you ten thousand everywhere in the world. Who, while his nails were being torn out, nobly endured? Who, while his joints were being wrenched asunder? Who, while his body was being cut in pieces, member by member? Who, while his bones were being forced out by levers? Who, while being placed on frying-pans without relief? Who, when thrown into a caldron? Show me these instances. For to die by hemlock is like falling asleep, even more pleasant than sleep. . . . But if certain of them did endure torments, yet of these too the praise amounts to nothing. For on some disgraceful occasion they perished: some for revealing mysteries; some for wishing to rule; others detected in the foulest crimes; still others did away with themselves rashly, fruitlessly, and foolishly, there being no reason for it. But not so with us. Of their acts, therefore, nothing is said, but our deeds flourish and increase daily.[49]

Not only are Christian martyrs numerically superior to Socrates (indeed, ten thousand to one!); they are also nobler, more courageous, and above all *volunteers!*[50]

Were Christians really prepared to die in the manner and huge numbers Chrysostom claimed? Could it be that the importance placed on martyrdom by Chrysostom, the authors of the *Acta*, and those who avidly read these gory accounts was inversely proportional to their own chances of suffering martyrdom? In all probability, only a very small percentage of Christians actually died as martyrs. The counterpart to voluntary martyrdom was "voluntary apostasy," and the latter seems to have been far more common than the former. Cyprian tells us that during the Decian persecution (250) many of the Christians of Carthage "did not even wait to be arrested . . . or interrogated before they made their denial. . . . They ran to the market-place of their own accord, they hastened to death of their own will."[51] Note the reversal: to live as an apostate is to die; to die as a martyr is to live.

The actual number of martyrs was quite small. "It is by no means impossible," writes Timothy Ware, "that in the thirty years between 1918 and 1948 more Christians died for their faith than in the first 300 years after the Crucifixion."[52] Nevertheless, the *ideal* of martyrdom extends across too wide a range of evidence for anyone to doubt its significance. Despite the fact that more Christians probably committed apostasy than died for the faith, few Christians denied the importance and necessity of martyrdom. As Barnes notes, "It was left to later ages to elaborate a theological justification for its avoidance."[53]

In addition to immortality, martyrdom brought great publicity. The strident behavior of Christians like Carpus and Papylus made a noticeable impression on their pagan contemporaries. Agathonike was so moved by the "injustice" of their treatment and the miraculous spectacle of their execution that she was motivated to imitate them and in doing so was converted. Justin too owed his conversion to the martyrdoms of Christians who were "fearless of death."[54] This is no doubt what Tertullian meant when he wrote to the governors of the empire, "Nothing whatever is accomplished by your cruelties, each more exquisite than the last. It is the bait that wins men for our school. We multiply whenever we are mown down by you; the blood of Christians is seed."[55]

Others were not so impressed. Educated pagans in particular were shocked and horrified by the blind fanaticism of the Christians. Galen, who admired the high moral standards of the Christians, was nevertheless disgusted by their irrational zeal for martyrdom.[56] So, too, the Roman authorities were repulsed by the Christians' love of death and exasperated by the intransigence of the martyrs, so much so that even an emperor could remark about this in his private *Meditations*. Marcus Aurelius contrasted a dignified and rational choice of death with the Christians' spirit of opposition and theatrical behavior.[57]

CLEMENT OF ALEXANDRIA

Even certain Christians could be moved to embarrassment and irritation by such behavior. Clement of Alexandria, for example, criticized those Christians whose fascination with voluntary martyrdom led to theatrical displays. On this point he agreed with his Gnostic opponents: genuine martyrdom was a matter of *living* in accordance with the knowledge of God. Clement sets forth his views in an important passage in the fourth book of the *Stromateis:*

> Some of the heretics who have misunderstood the Lord, have at once an impious and cowardly love of life, saying that the true witness [*martyria*] is the knowledge [*gnosis*] of the real God (which we also admit), and that the man who makes confession by death is a self-murderer and self-killer. . . . Now we, too, blame those who have rushed on death, for there are some who are really not ours but share only the name, who are eager to hand themselves over in hatred against the creator, athletes of death. We say that these men take themselves out without witness [*exagein heautous amartyros*], even if they are officially executed. For they do not preserve the characteristic mark of faithful witness, because they do not know the real God, but give themselves up to a futile death, as the Gymnosophists of the Indians to useless fire.[58]

At first glance, Clement's condemnation of Christians "who have rushed on death" is reminiscent of the negative view expressed by educated pagans like Lucian.[59] But it would be incorrect to dismiss it as such. Clement's criticism of voluntary martyrdom reflects his theology and perhaps even his personal experience.

Clement presents us with two contrasting views of martyrdom. The first is that of the Gnostics, whom he calls "heretics" and who taught that martyrdom was unnecessary. Basilides of Alexandria appears to have been the first to advocate this view, claiming that "there was no harm in eating things offered to idols, or in light-heartedly denying the faith in times of persecution."[60] Heracleon, the pupil of Valentinus and Clement's older contemporary, did not go so far. He distinguished verbal confession (of the martyr) from the true confession of an individual's beliefs and manner of life. As Frend notes, Heracleon "did not deny the value of the martyr's death, but argued that it was only of relative importance."[61] Martyrdom was not a guarantee of salvation, according to Heracleon, because there were some who confessed Christ with their lips but denied him by their manner of life. "The confession that is made with the voice before the authorities," Heracleon maintains, "is what many reckon the only confession. Not soundly: for the hypocrites also can confess with this confession. . . . He will confess rightly with his voice who has first confessed with his disposition."[62] Put simply, not every "witness" (*martyrion*) is genuine.

The Gnostics are usually thought of as opposing martyrdom, but Heracleon's statements indicate that at least some Gnostics granted the legitimacy of martyrdom, so long as one's verbal confession was consistent with one's beliefs and disposition.[63] Despite Clement's disagreements with the Gnostics on other matters, it is clear that he agreed with Heracleon on the *relative* importance of martyrdom. "As many as fulfill the commands of the savior," says Clement, "bear witness [*martyrousi*] in each of their acts, by doing what he wills, consistently naming the Lord's name, and being witnesses [*martyrountes*] by deed to him whom they trust, crucifying the flesh with its desires and passions."[64]

But on one important point Clement parted company with Heracleon. Even if an individual had not confessed with his life, his willingness to suffer death rather than deny would result in salvation: "If some have not by conduct and in their life confessed Christ before men, they are shown to have believed with the heart by confessing him with the mouth at the tribunals, and not denying him when tortured to death. . . . For there is, so to speak, at the close of life a sudden repentance in action, and a true confession toward Christ, in the testimony of the voice."[65]

According to Clement, and in contrast to Heracleon, an individual could be transformed instantaneously through a martyr's death. We have encountered this understanding of voluntary death before among Greeks, Romans, and Jews. Martyrdom is not for everyone, Clement admits, "but it will be given to some" to become martyrs, so that Christians may be confirmed in their faith, pagans converted, and the rest astounded.[66] In contrast to Heracleon, Clement insists that martyrdom *is* necessary, but he insists that it "is not universally necessary, *for this [decision] is not within our power.*"[67] Like the author of the *Martyrdom of Polycarp*, Clement maintains that one can be a true martyr only if he acts in accordance with God's will. An individual Christian cannot choose to become a martyr without being called by God. Once again, the decision to allow one's life to be taken is evaluated in light of the Socratic tradition of the "divine signal." More precisely, the Socratic tradition is being employed as a means of moderating against an excessive fascination with voluntary death. The similarity between Clement and Socrates is by no means coincidental: Clement was a Platonist in addition to being a Christian, and he had read the *Phaedo*.[68]

Clement was in complete agreement with Heracleon on one point: death, though it was to be despised, was not to be courted. Nothing was to be said for the fanatic who demanded execution by the Roman authorities. The true Gnostic, according to Clement, "courageously awaits whatever comes. In this way he is distinguished from others who are called martyrs, inasmuch as some furnish occasions for themselves, and rush into the heart of dangers." True Gnostics, "in accordance with right reason, protect themselves; then, when God really calls them, promptly surrender themselves and confirm the call. . . . From love of God they voluntarily obey the call, with no other aim in view than pleasing God, and not for the sake of reward."[69] To be noted again is Clement's appeal to a "divine call" as the only justification for voluntary death. When such a call is received, the true Gnostic willingly obeys by accepting death. But the person who seeks martyrdom without a divine call is guilty of his own death:

> He who presents himself before the judgment-seat becomes guilty of his own death. And such is also the case with him who does not avoid persecution, but out of daring presents himself for capture. Such a person . . . becomes an accomplice in the crime of the persecutor. And if he also uses provocation, he is wholly guilty, challenging the wild beast.[70]

In the *Martyrdom of Polycarp*, Evarestus had condemned Quintus for voluntarily giving himself up and then playing the coward. Clement goes further: he denounces as "self-murderers" Christians who had been *officially executed*. This takes us one step closer to Augustine.

Clement attempted to steer a course between a rejection of martyrdom, on the one hand, and an excessive fascination with it on the other. He did so by arguing that martyrdom was necessary only in cases when God provided a sign. Clement's evaluation of the relative importance of martyrdom and the manner in which it should be performed represents the first sustained discussion of the problem of voluntary death by an early Christian. Clement attempted to construct a theory of martyrdom that would be consistent with his general theological position, but we should not overlook an important personal factor that may have influenced his view of martyrdom. When a persecution of Christians broke out in Alexandria in 202/3, Clement refused to offer himself up and prudently left the city. Others, however, chose to remain and face the consequences. Among them was the young Origen, Clement's pupil.[71] Eusebius tells us that "countless numbers were wreathed with the crowns of martyrdom." Origen's father, Leonides, was one of the victims. While Leonides was awaiting execution, Origen wrote to him in prison, urging him not to change his mind or be swayed by family considerations. "Origen's soul," Eusebius reports, "was possessed with such a passion for martyrdom . . . that he was all eagerness to come to close quarters with danger, and to leap forward and rush into the conflict." Only by hiding his clothes was Origen's mother able to hold him back.[72]

Clement's reflections on martyrdom in the fourth book of the *Stromateis* may well have been written after the persecution of 202/3. If so, his antimartyr perspective may have been in part an attempt to justify his flight. Presumably,

Clement would have excused himself on the ground that he had not received a divine call, that it had not been "given to him" to make a public witness (*martyrion*). This would also explain why Clement was so critical of other Christians who had volunteered for martyrdom. Many, according to Clement, had acted on their own initiative, without a divine call. They lacked "the characteristic mark of faithful witness." These Christians he condemned as "self-killers" and "self-murderers," because they took themselves out "without witness" (*amartyros*). Their deaths were no more efficacious than the "vain deaths" of the Indian philosophers.[73]

We should not overlook the polemical and apologetic context of Clement's discussion of martyrdom. Despite Clement's theological sophistication, in the final analysis his distinction between the martyr and the self-murderer is rather arbitrary and a result, perhaps, of his personal situation. After all, Clement was condemning the actions of men he considered heretics: "those who are really not ours but share only the name." Heretics, by definition, cannot believe or act in an acceptable manner or, in Clement's terms, as the "true Gnostic" believes and acts. It did not matter that they both read the same Bible, celebrated the same liturgy, and dispensed the same sacraments, for what is good in the hands of the true Gnostic becomes a bad thing in the hands of a heretic. This applies to martyrdom as well. Depending, therefore, on the perspective or prejudice of the critic, the act of taking one's life or allowing it to be taken could be evaluated positively, as an authentic witness, or negatively, as the equivalent of self-murder.[74] The claim that not all forms of voluntary death are true *martyria* is uniquely Christian, and it is a distinction that arises out of an internal polemic. Like Augustine two centuries later, Clement would not allow the "heretics" to appeal to their martyrs as a justification for their beliefs and actions. Indeed, he claimed they were not true martyrs.

There was a fundamental problem in Clement's evaluation of voluntary death, a problem that was faced by Greeks and Romans but was never resolved satisfactorily. Like Socrates and many of his epigones, Clement justified voluntary death only when God provided a divine sign. But how was the divine sign to be recognized? How did Clement know whether those Christians he praised and condemned had received it or not? This problem still had not been resolved.

TERTULLIAN

Tertullian stands in sharp contrast to his Alexandrian contemporary. Clement's "true Gnostic" might have to face martyrdom, *if God called him*, but such a death would be only one of several means of salvation. According to Tertullian, martyrdom was the only *sure* way of escape—the key that unlocked the prison door. To Christians awaiting execution in prison, he wrote,

> If we reflect that the world is more really the prison, we shall see that you have gone out of a prison rather than into one. The world has the greater darkness blinding men's hearts. The world imposes the more grievous fetters, binding men's very souls. The world breathes out the worst impurities: human lusts. The world contains the larger number of criminals, even the whole human race. . . . Then, last of all, it awaits the judgment, not of the proconsul but of God. Wherefore, O blessed, you may regard yourselves as having been translated from prison to, we may say, a place of safety. It is full of darkness, but you yourselves are light. It has bonds, but God has made you free.[75]

Tertullian claims that human beings have been placed in a prison, but God has provided a way of escape. Deliverance from the prison does not come through the vicarious identification in baptism with Christ's atoning sacrifice. Salvation can be guaranteed only by a "second baptism," not in water but in blood. According to Tertullian, God foresaw the weakness of human beings; he predicted that some Christians would be in danger from sin even after baptism: "God therefore appointed as a second supply of comfort, and the last means of relief, the fight of martyrdom and the baptism—thereafter free from danger—of blood. . . . For, strictly speaking, nothing can any longer be reckoned against the martyrs, by whom life itself is laid down in the baptism of blood."[76]

The passage just quoted comes from Tertullian's treatise *Antidote for the Scorpion's Sting*, a work usually thought to have been written after Tertullian's conversion to Montanism. But T. D. Barnes has shown that "the *Scorpiace* must be redated to 203/4, and therefore understood as representative of orthodox opinion in Carthage."[77] The tract was composed during a time of persecution. Some Christians had been arrested and executed, but others—Valentinian Gnostics—had come forward to denigrate martyrdom. "Innocent persons are suffering," the Gnostics said. "Men are perishing without reason."[78] Tertullian wrote to strengthen the resolve of the Christians of Carthage, to provide an "antidote for the sting of scorpions" like the Gnostics.

Tertullian's thesis is twofold: first, martyrdom is a duty and a necessity; second, it is good and useful because God commands it.[79] The thesis is supported by a dizzying array of scriptural citations, punctuated by occasional refutations of Gnostic objections. The duty and necessity of martyrdom are connected with God's proscription of idolatry. It is the first commandment, "You shall have no Gods but me" (Exod. 20:3), that creates the necessary precondition for martyrdom. "Otherwise," Tertullian says, "martyrdoms would not take place."[80] God forbade idolatry because he desired martyrdom!

The Gnostics objected to this line of reasoning because it called into question the goodness of God's will. Tertullian responds that whatever God wills is

good because he himself is good. And martyrdom is good because it frees people from the evil of idolatry: "I strongly maintain that martyrdom is good, as
required by the God by whom idolatry is also forbidden and punished. For
martyrdom strives against and opposes idolatry. To strive against and oppose
evil cannot be anything but good."[81]

Using a medical analogy, Tertullian argues that martyrdom is the divine
medicine that heals with eternal life: "He [God] has chosen to contend with a
disease and to do good by imitating the malady: to destroy death by death, to
dissipate killing by killing, to dispel tortures by tortures, to disperse in a vapor
punishments by punishments, to bestow life by withdrawing it, to aid the flesh
by injuring it, to preserve the soul by snatching it away."[82]

The Gnostics objected that Tertullian's theology of martyrdom turned God
into a murderer. This is blasphemous, according to Tertullian. He admits that
God kills, but for a purpose: to keep the victim from dying![83] The Gnostics
would probably not have been persuaded by this kind of peculiar logic, but
Tertullian was not writing for them. He wanted to provide the simple and weak-
minded Christians of Carthage with enough scriptural proofs, and just enough
argumentation, so that they would be able to defend themselves against the
sophistry of the Gnostics. The thesis is simple. Martyrdom is ordained by God
and therefore reasonable, for God would not do anything contrary to reason.[84]
Scripture is unanimous in its support of this thesis. From the violent death of
Abel to the persecution and deaths of Peter and Paul, the Bible offers clear and
uniform testimony to the necessity and importance of martyrdom.[85]

In the *Scorpiace* Tertullian dealt with only two possible responses to persecution: martyrdom and apostasy. Some Christians, however, had found a third
alternative: flight. Tertullian did not discuss the option of flight in the *Scorpiace*,
but from what he says in two other early (i.e., pre-Montanist) works it is clear
that he condoned flight in the face of persecution.

In his treatise *On Endurance* Tertullian argued that the virtue of *patientia*
("endurance") was essential to salvation. Above all, it is through *patientia* that
the Christian is able to face persecution and accept martyrdom.[86] In this
way the Christian repays the *patientia* Christ displayed on behalf of mankind.[87]
The word *patientia* denotes both endurance and suffering, and Tertullian
would seem to be saying that martyrdom should be sought. Yet, as T. D.
Barnes observes, "Tertullian permits patience to have a double application. Not
only will patience prevent apostasy and enable a Christian to endure torture
and barbarous modes of execution, but it also overcomes the inconveniences of
flight."[88] In other words, martyrdom and flight are both acceptable responses
to persecution.

Tertullian shifts his position slightly in the treatise *To His Wife*. Flight is
still permitted, but it is not necessarily good. Tertullian derives this principle

from Paul's discussion of sex and marriage in 1 Corinthians 7. Paul condoned marriage as a means to keep sexual immorality in check: "It is better to marry than to be consumed by lust" (1 Cor. 7:9). Nevertheless, Paul maintained that celibacy was to be preferred. Tertullian applies this principle to martyrdom and flight. The latter is condoned for weaker Christians as a preventive measure: flight is certainly preferable to apostasy. But because a thing is permitted does not mean it is necessarily good.[89] Martyrdom, like celibacy, is the best way.

In a later work, On Flight in Persecution, Tertullian rejected this view. He argued that, since persecution ultimately comes from God, to avoid persecution by fleeing would be to shun God's will. On Flight was written after Tertullian's conversion to Montanism, but his argument against fleeing cannot be attributed solely to this. Although his position in On Flight differs from what he says in To His Wife, it coheres with the view expressed in the Scorpiace, a pre-Montanist work, even though in that treatise the subject of flight was not directly addressed. In the Scorpiace Tertullian argued that God ordained martyrdom as a means of salvation. It is a duty and cannot be avoided. On Flight in Persecution elaborates this view with respect to flight: "For if persecution proceeds from God, in no way will it be our duty to flee from what God has ordained. There are two reasons for this: on the one hand, what proceeds from God ought not to be avoided, and, on the other, it cannot be avoided. . . . Therefore those who think that they should flee either reproach God with doing what is evil . . . , or consider themselves stronger than God . . . by imagining it possible to escape when it is God's pleasure that such events should occur."[90]

Against this view, a fictive (or real) opponent raises the following objection: "I flee . . . that I may not perish [eternally!] if I deny."[91] This sounds like the Tertullian of To His Wife. Here, however, he responds differently. "Are you sure," he asks his opponent, "that you will deny if you do not flee, or are you not sure? For if you are sure, you have denied already. . . . But if you are doubtful on this point, why do you not in the uncertainty of your fear . . . presume that you are able to act the confessor's part and so add to your safety . . . ?"[92]

Tertullian's opponent now raises another objection: Christ commanded his disciples to flee from city to city when they were persecuted (Matt. 10:23). Flight, not martyrdom, is the fulfillment of what the Lord commands.[93] Matthew 10:23 is one of the key passages in the debate about martyrdom, and we will find Augustine using it as a weapon against the Donatists in the early fifth century. But Tertullian, usually the master of the "proof text," will not allow his opponents to use this isolated saying of Jesus to justify the possibility of flight. Here is a rare occasion when Tertullian insists on reading a passage in context. He stresses the particularity of Jesus' saying. It was spoken as part of Jesus' instructions to his disciples to preach only to "the lost sheep of the house of Israel." That command is now obsolete: "We maintain that this belongs especially to the persons of the apostles, and to their times and circumstances."[94] Furthermore, the saying about flight cannot be reconciled with the numerous sayings of Jesus that speak of "confession before men" (Matt. 10:32), of being "persecuted for my name's sake" (Matt. 5:10, 11), and of "endurance to the end" (Matt. 10:22).

Tertullian emphasizes that martyrdom is a duty for every Christian, regardless of rank. "Thus ought every servant of God to feel and act, even one in an inferior place, that he may come to have a more important one, if he has made some upward step by his endurance of persecution. But when persons in authority—deacons, presbyters, and bishops—take flight, how will the layman be able to see with what view it was said, 'Flee from city to city?' Most assuredly a good shepherd lays down his life for the sheep" (John 10:11).[95] Tertullian's condemnation of clerical runaways (and his quote from the Gospel of John) will be used by Donatists against Catholics in the fourth and fifth centuries.

Tertullian's condemnation of flight has been attributed to his Montanist bias. But that is a misplaced criticism. The argument of *On Flight* is constructed independently of his Montanist convictions, as T. D. Barnes has shown.[96] It is true that in an earlier work Tertullian condoned flight as a means of preventing apostasy, but what requires an explanation is how he could have come to such a conclusion, given his defense of martyrdom in the *Scorpiace*. The view expressed in *On Flight*, though written during his Montanist period, is entirely consistent with his position in the *Scorpiace* or, for that matter, in the short tract *To the Martyrs*, one of Tertullian's earliest works. In all probability Tertullian's treatise *On Flight* was occasioned by the majority of Christians fleeing Carthage whenever persecution threatened.[97] His condemnation of flight was not so much an expression of Montanist bias as a belief that Christians should have the courage of their convictions.

Tertullian placed such a premium on martyrdom that he made no distinction between an authentic and inauthentic "witness," as did Clement and others. He may have criticized the excesses (notably drunkenness and sexual immorality) to which some Christians were prone while they awaited martyrdom in prison,[98] but he never condemns anyone for "volunteering" or "rushing headlong into death." Every individual who suffered as a result of persecution was a martyr. There was no need to wait for a special divine command. The reason is that God desired martyrdom; he ordained it as the only sure means of salvation. Martyrdom was not only good; it was also necessary.

There is a tendency among historians of early Christianity to push Tertullian to the periphery. The importance he attached to martyrdom is often attributed to his Montanist bias and compared negatively to the more moderate views of his Alexandrian contemporary Clement. We have seen, however, that the essentials of Tertullian's view of martyrdom were already in place in his pre-Montanist phase, and there is good reason to suppose that they were in line with what many Christians of Carthage thought about martyrdom, at least in theory, if not in practice. A comparison between Tertullian and Origen reveals that martyrdom was an ideal to which many Christians aspired, in both the West and the East.

ORIGEN

On the subject of martyrdom Origen has more in common with Tertullian than with Clement, his Alexandrian predecessor. Indeed, Origen might well be described as an Alexandrian Tertullian.[99] We have already met the young Origen, who encouraged his father to go to martyrdom and whose mother was barely able to restrain him from rushing to a voluntary death. What Origen thought about martyrdom is revealed in a heated outburst to a council of bishops at Caesarea in about the year 245:

> Bring wild beasts, bring crosses, bring fire, bring tortures. I know that as soon as I die, I come forth from the body, I rest with Christ. Therefore let us struggle, therefore let us wrestle, let us groan being in the body, not as if we shall again be in the tombs in the body, because we shall be set free from it, and shall change our body to one which is more spiritual. Destined as we are to be with Christ, how we groan while we are in the body.[100]

In Origen's outburst we hear the echoes of Ignatius and Paul. For Origen, martyrdom is not one among many means of salvation, as it was for Clement. Like Tertullian, Origen stresses the *duty* and *necessity* of martyrdom: sins committed after the baptism of water can only be forgiven by the baptism of blood.[101]

Origen composed an *Exhortation to Martyrdom* during a persecution of Christians at Caesarea in 235. The treatise is addressed to Ambrose and Protoctetus, a deacon and a priest, respectively, of the Christian community in that city. The faith of both men had been tested, and Origen writes to encourage them to remain steadfast. What occasioned the treatise, however, was the appearance of certain "opponents" who thought it did not matter if Christians agreed to sacrifice according to the demands of the Roman authorities or invoked the Christian God under the name of Zeus or Apollo.[102] These opponents sound like the Gnostics mentioned by Clement and attacked by

Tertullian in his *Scorpiace*. Origen's *Exhortation* is intended to refute their "false arguments."

Origen begins by stating that a true Christian (like a good Platonist) tries as much as possible to keep his soul separate from the body. Death therefore should not be feared, because it simply means the final removal of the soul from the body. Martyrdom is the means to attain this goal: "When he [the martyr] sees that he has been delivered from the body of death by his confession, he will make a holy proclamation, 'Thanks be to God.' "[103] It is not enough, Origen maintains, "to believe in your heart"; only those who confess will be saved. Their words must correspond to their disposition.[104] This leads Origen into a discussion about the dangers of apostasy and idolatry.[105]

Chapters 11 to 21 constitute the heart of his exhortation. Origen encourages the Christians of Caesarea in the same way he encouraged his father: they should take no thought of family or possessions. Their reward will be greater in proportion to what they leave behind.[106] Only those who take up their cross and follow the example of Jesus will be saved: "If we wish to save our life in order to get it back better than a life, let us lose it by our martyrdom. For if we lose it for Christ's sake . . . , we shall gain possession of true salvation for it."[107] Paul ascended to the third heaven, Origen says, but he eventually had to return. Not so with the martyrs: "You will not come down if you take up your cross and follow Jesus."[108]

Next Origen appeals to biblical examples of suffering and endurance, placing special emphasis on the *voluntary* nature of the deaths: "Who would be so rightly praised as the person who died *of his own accord*, welcoming death for his religion. This is what Eleazar was like, who, welcoming death with honor rather than life with pollution, went up to the rack *of his own accord*."[109] Origen is especially impressed by Eleazar's last words and quotes them verbatim: "By manfully giving up my life now, I will show myself worthy of my old age and leave to the young a noble example of how to die a good death *willingly* and *nobly* for the revered and holy laws."[110] He then deals at length with the deaths of the seven brothers in 2 Maccabees 7. In the process, Antiochus is turned into a Roman proconsul and the Maccabean heroes into Christians.[111]

One of the lessons to be learned from these Maccabean heroes, Origen claims, is that martyrdom is the way of repaying the debt Christians owe to God: "Nothing else can be given to God from a person of high purpose that will so balance his benefits as perfection in martyrdom."[112] Here Origen begins a complex exegetical argument that carries over into the next chapter. Psalm 116, he says, poses a question: "What shall I give back to the Lord for all his bounty to me?" (Ps. 116:12). The answer is given in the next verse: "I will take *the cup of salvation* and call on the name of the Lord" (116:13). Origen connects "the cup of salvation" with martyrdom on the basis of Jesus' question to his disciples, "Are you able to drink the *cup* that I am to drink?" (Matt. 20:22). The conclusion Origen draws from this is: "He who drinks that cup which Jesus drank will sit with him and rule and judge with the King of kings."[113]

But now a problem arises. In the garden Jesus said, "Father, if it be possible, let this *cup* pass from me" (Matt. 26:39). Origen recognizes that this would seem to imply that "the Savior proved a coward at the time of the passion."[114] Origen, of course, will not admit such a conclusion, so he constructs an ingenious (if unconvincing) exegetical escape. He begins by noting that all three Gospels have Jesus refer to *this* cup (Matt. 26:39; Mark 14:36; Luke 22:42). From this Origen concludes: "[Jesus] does not refuse martyrdom in general, but only one kind. Otherwise he would have said, 'Let *the* cup pass from me.' Consider carefully whether it is not possible that the savior saw, so to speak, what the different kinds of cups [i.e., martyrdoms] were and what would happen because of each of them. . . . He refused one kind of martyr's death, while in secret he asked for another kind that was probably harder."[115] We have already noted the powerful influence the death of Jesus exerted on the imagination of some early Christians. But Origen's "exegesis of the cup" indicates that the influence could also flow in the opposite direction. The importance Origen attached to martyrdom has transformed the poignant and almost too human prayer of Jesus in Gethsemane into a death wish that strained even the ability of the Father to grant. According to Origen, Jesus did not ask to be spared execution; he demanded a fate worse than crucifixion!

Like Tertullian, Origen describes martyrdom as a *second* baptism. "It is impossible," he says, "according to the laws of the Gospel to be baptized again with water and the spirit for the forgiveness of sins. And that is why the *baptism of martyrdom* has been given to us."[116] Moreover, those who have died a martyr's death "grant forgiveness of sins to those who pray," a clear reference to the cult of the martyrs.[117]

In his letter to the Colossians Paul had described his sufferings as completing "what was lacking in Christ's afflictions" (Col. 1:24), thereby implying that Paul thought of himself as a *second* Christ whose suffering and death would bring to completion what the *first* Christ left unfinished. Origen cites this passage and applies it to Protoctetus and his fellow Christians. The implication is that the vicarious participation in Christ's death is not sufficient to guarantee salvation. Each Christian must reenact the death of Jesus for himself.[118]

On the basis of a saying of Jesus recorded in Luke 14:26 Origen enjoins Ambrose and Protoctetus to "hate your souls because of eternal life, persuaded that the hatred Jesus teaches is noble and useful. And just as we must hate our souls so that they may be kept for eternal life, so you . . . must hate your wife and children, your brothers and sisters, so that you may help the ones you hate by becoming a friend of God through that very hatred and so receiving the freedom to benefit them."[119] Rather than attempting to place controls on the act of voluntary death (as Clement had and Augustine would), Origen does the opposite by inverting the categories of judgment. He has turned the world upside down: hatred is love; prison is freedom; torture is exaltation; death is life. "Why then do we hang back," he asks, "and hesitate to put off the perishable body, the earthly tent that hinders us and weighs down the soul?"[120] Martyrdom is the path to immortality.

Nowhere does Origen suggest that Christians should be circumspect in their attitude toward martyrdom. Nowhere does he condemn voluntary death. For Origen, martyrdom is a duty and a necessity, and he holds up the Maccabean heroes and above all Jesus as exemplary for their *willingness* to die a noble death. In spite of this Origen is often represented as having opposed voluntary martyrdom. It is a constant refrain of historians of early Christianity that voluntary martyrdom was condemned by the "orthodox." Even G. E. M. de Ste. Croix has fallen prey to such a view. In his brilliant essays on the persecutions, de Ste. Croix correctly stresses the importance and prevalence of voluntary martyrdom. He argues persuasively that voluntary martyrdom was a factor that contributed to the outbreak of persecution and tended to intensify it when already in being. Nevertheless, de Ste. Croix maintains that "the heads of the churches, *sensibly enough*, forbade voluntary martyrdom again and again, and were inclined to refuse to these zealots the very name of martyr."[121] He states categorically that "voluntary martyrdom was officially condemned by the orthodox."[122] De Ste. Croix claims that there are references to the condemnation of voluntary martyrdom in "a dozen different sources," but he cites only six.[123] Whichever figure is correct, the overwhelming evidence supports the opposite conclusion: voluntary martyrdom was a widespread phenomenon. From the second century on, voluntary martyrdom was practiced and idealized by both "orthodox" and "heretic" alike, in the East as well as in the West. It is true that we find occasional references—Evarestus, Clement, Cyprian—condemning voluntary martyrdom, but there was no official, universally recognized judgment on the matter. Nor were the criteria on which these occasional objections were based clearly articulated.

VOLUNTARY MARTYRDOM II

Voluntary martyrdom was believed to be a necessary reenactment or *mimesis* of the death of Christ. Like Christ, the Christian martyrs were victims—albeit in appearance—of a sinister alliance between pagans and Jews, orchestrated by Satan. But appearances could be deceiving, at least so the early Christians argued. The Gospels revealed that Christ had not been executed as a criminal; rather, he went to his death of his own accord. The pagans and Jews, even Satan, were little more than unwitting accomplices in Christ's death. The same interpretation was applied to the deaths of Christ's followers, as can be seen in the *Martyrdom of Pionius*, bishop of Smyrna, in about the year 250. "What these people [the Jews] forget," Pionius told his comrades in prison, "is that this 'criminal' [Christ] departed from life at his own choice" (*ho idia proairesei exagon heauton tou biou*).[124] "Thus," Pionius declared, "in obedience to my Teacher I choose to die" (*apothneskein hairoumai*).[125] Death was not forced on Pionius. Like Christ, he *chose* it. Refusing the appeals of the Roman authorities, Pionius said, "Light the fire and we shall climb upon it of our own accord."[126] "Many others have offered sacrifice," the proconsul objected, "and they are now alive and of sound mind. Why do you rush toward death?" "I am not rushing toward death," Pionius answered, "but towards life."[127] For Pionius, the categories of life and death had been turned inside out.

Sometimes Christians would go to their deaths to provoke others to do the same. On their way to execution in c. 257, Agapius and Secundius, two North African bishops, stopped to exhort their fellow Christians to follow their example. "It was not enough," the narrator says, "that they were to devote their own precious blood to glorious martyrdom; they wished to make others martyrs by the inspiration of their own faith."[128] Before the sword struck their comrade Marian, he prophesied revenge on the pagans. His words, the narrator says, "sounded a trumpet call, as it were, to arouse his brethren to emulate his courage, so that in the midst of these temporal plagues the saints of God might grasp at the opportunity for a death that was precious and holy."[129] Marian and his fellow martyr James believed, like Socrates, that they had received the divine signal to depart. In the words of the narrator, they *"possessed the signs they had always desired, that the divine choice had fallen on them. . . . They recognized that their footsteps had been guided by the providence of Christ to the very spot where they would receive their crowns."*[130] Marian and James are examples of those who responded to the call and in doing so became signals to many others who were provoked by the sight of Christians being tried, tortured, or executed.[131]

On other occasions Christians would go to their deaths to prevent others from committing apostasy. At Antioch in 303 a Christian from Palestine named Romanus became enraged at men, women, and children "going up in crowds to the idols and sacrificing." When he tried to intervene, he was immediately arrested and executed.[132] That same year at Caesarea a similar episode took place. A certain Alpheus was arrested as a result of his attempt to intervene and prevent mass apostasy. He refused the order to sacrifice and was beheaded.[133]

From the period of the Great Persecution (303–12/3) Eusebius preserves numerous accounts of individuals in Palestine either "volunteering" for martyrdom or killing themselves outright. The information Eusebius offers is geographically specific, and his statistics do not provide a reliable index of the numbers of Christians who died for their religion. But the evidence, such as it is, suggests that very few Christians were *sought out* by the Roman authorities. As de Ste. Croix has shown, "nearly twice as many (if not more) were volunteers."[134]

One famous "volunteer" was Euplus. On 29 April 304 he stood outside the governor's chamber in the city of Catania, Sicily, and shouted, "I want to die; I am a Christian." Calvisianus, the governor, replied, "Come in, whoever it was who shouted out." Euplus entered the council chamber, carrying copies of the forbidden Gospels. Following an interrogation, Euplus was tortured and executed. "So it was," the narrator of his martyrdom says, "that the blessed Euplus received the unfading crown."[135]

In the following year Eusebius describes how a rumor spread that Christians would be thrown to the beasts as part of a festival at Caesarea. While the Roman governor was en route to the amphitheater, he was met by six Christians, young men, who demanded to be thrown to the beasts with their comrades. The governor and his entourage were overcome by astonishment at the request. The six men were arrested, but instead of having them thrown to the beasts as they had requested, the governor had them beheaded.[136]

Eusebius says he was an eyewitness in the Thebaid in upper Egypt to the execution of "many" Christians "in a single day." His description goes into great and gory detail, but it reveals that most of the martyrs were volunteers: "It was then that we observed a most marvelous eagerness and a truly divine power and zeal in those who had placed their faith in the Christ of God. For as soon as sentence was pronounced against the first one, some from one quarter and others from another would leap up to the tribunal before the judge and confess themselves Christians, . . . receiving with joy and laughter and gladness the final sentence of death."[137] Far from condemning such behavior, Eusebius praises these "volunteers" for their courage and endurance.

Admittedly, some Christian leaders disapproved of such conduct. At the opening of the Great Persecution, Mensurius, bishop of Carthage, forbade Christians to honor those who "gave themselves up of their own accord and volunteered the information that they possessed Scriptures which they would not hand over, when no one had asked them to do so." Mensurius accused these so-called Christians of being "criminals and debtors . . . , who took advantage of the persecution to rid themselves of a life burdened with many debts, or hoped to purge themselves and, so to speak, wash away their crimes, or at any rate to live like fighting-cocks in prison on the charity of the Christians."[138]

Mensurius's denunciation of voluntary martyrdom was by no means universally recognized, and his call for restraint seems to have gone unheeded. In fact, it was this kind of negative judgment that contributed to the rise of the Donatists. That Mensurius condemned voluntary martyrs as "criminals and debtors" should come as no surprise, for Mensurius himself was accused of being a *traditor*—of handing over the sacred books to the persecutors.

In addition to individuals who volunteered for martyrdom, Eusebius reports a number of instances of Christians who deliberately killed themselves. At Alexandria a year before the Decian persecution, an angry mob assaulted an elderly woman named Apollonia, threatening to burn her alive if she did not recite with them their "blasphemous sayings" (*ta tes asebeias kerygmata*). According to Eusebius, Apollonia asked for some time to think it over, and "as soon as she was left alone she eagerly threw herself into the fire and was consumed."[139] Describing the persecution of Diocletian in Nicomedia, Eusebius reports that "men and women leaped upon the pyre with a divine and unspeakable fervor." Far from condemning these Christians, Eusebius calls them "martyrs" and says that "they were perfected by fire."[140]

At Antioch, also during the Great Persecution, Eusebius tells of a woman and her two daughters who opted for "flight to the Lord" rather than be raped by their captors: "She exhorted both herself and her daughters that they ought not to submit to listen to even the least whisper of such a thing, and said that to surrender their souls to the slavery of demons was worse than all kinds of death and every form of destruction. So she submitted that to flee to the Lord was the only way of escape from it all. And when they had both agreed to her opinion, and had arranged their garments suitably around them, on coming to the middle of their journey they quietly requested the guards for a little time for retirement, and threw themselves into the river that flowed by. Thus they became their own executioners."[141]

SUMMARY

We cannot be certain that the stories Eusebius and other Christian writers relate are historical. The accounts of the deaths of Polycarp, Perpetua, Carpus, Agathonike, and the other Christian martyrs are probably no more or less historical than Plato's description of the death of Socrates, or Cicero's account of the death of Cato, or even the Johannine version of the death of Jesus. That some early Christians died for their religion cannot be disputed. Nor can it be denied that some gave themselves up voluntarily. Even the testimony of Evarestus, Clement, and Mensurius indicates that they did so. But in the first three centuries only a very small percentage of Christians died for their religion.

The evidence indicates that far more chose flight or committed apostasy. Nonetheless, the ideal of martyrdom enjoyed an importance that belied the relatively insignificant number of actual martyrs. Of interest to us, therefore, is not so much what the early Christians did but how their actions were described and evaluated by their fellow Christians and contemporaries.

The martyrs are portrayed as going to their death in one of three ways: either as a result of being sought out, by deliberately volunteering, or by actually taking their own lives. On the basis of the evidence that has survived, it would appear that the majority of Christian martyrs chose death by the second and third means. But even in those cases where individuals "waited" for the persecutors to arrest them, the emphasis is placed on their willingness to embrace death. Like Jesus, they went to execution "of their own accord."

Behind every description of martyrdom lay the example of Jesus. Martyrdom was believed by many to be a necessary reenactment of his death and to hold out the prospects of a similar reward: "the crown of immortality." The authors of the Gospels described the death of Jesus as divinely ordained. He went to death in willing obedience to God. Those who preserved and revered the memory of the martyrs explained their deaths in the same way. Both the martyrs themselves and even some of their critics emphasized the importance and necessity of a divine signal or command. Only when such a sign had been given could martyrdom be justified. Plato had said much the same thing about the death of Socrates, and it is tempting to think that the early Christians were familiar enough with the Socratic tradition on voluntary death to apply it to their martyrs. With a few authors—Clement, for example—we can establish a direct link with the *Phaedo*, but not in most cases. It may be, as Rudolf Hirzel has suggested, that the early Christians arrived at the same conclusion independently.[142] In any case, the problem of voluntary death was discussed by Christians in terms similar to those of Plato.

As important as the requirement of a divine sign was thought to be, it did not solve the problems of definition and evaluation. To state it in Foucaultian terms: the early Christians failed to "problematize" voluntary death, despite considerable debate and polemical squabbling. They recognized an ambiguity in the act of voluntary death and attempted to force a distinction between "martyrdom" and "self-killing," but they never developed a language of problematics or criteria of evaluation. There was no agreed-upon definition of what constituted *martyria* ("witness"), nor was there a pejorative term (like *suicide*) to denote its negative counterpart. A further complication was the appeal to the divine sign. How was the "sign" to be recognized, and what was the criterion to determine that it was "divine"? Insofar as these questions were left unanswered, the debate about voluntary death never went beyond polemics to problematization.

The condemnation of voluntary martyrdom was a factor of self-definition and self-justification. Clement denounced the voluntary deaths of heretics as acts of "self-killing." They took themselves out, he says, "without witness" (*amartyros*). Clement's judgment was not an evaluation of the act, only an expression of self-definition vis-à-vis the proximate other: those who falsely claimed the name "Christian." Heretics qua heretics could not be true martyrs. That was a title reserved only for Clement's "Gnostic." Mensurius likewise condemned voluntary martyrs as "criminals and debtors." However, once the categories of "orthodoxy" and "heresy" are removed, it becomes impossible to distinguish between authentic and inauthentic "witness"—between "martyrdom" and "self-killing." There are only a handful of references in early Christian literature in which voluntary martyrdom is condemned, and, significantly, they come from Christians who either fled in the face of persecution or in some way collaborated with the authorities. Clement prudently left Alexandria when persecution broke out in 202/3. During the Great Persecution Mensurius handed over copies of the sacred books to the Romans. It is hardly surprising, therefore, that they were opposed to voluntary martyrdom.

In his otherwise excellent discussion of persecution and martyrdom, Robin Lane Fox offers the following judgment:

> [Martyrdom] had no use for sophistication or for a complex awareness of the complexities in human choices. It required a simple, persistent response, which was admirable even if it irritated others and had only to be repeated to attain its end. This compound of qualities has an appeal for various sorts of person, but it appeals especially to the young or the inexperienced and to those who do not reflect habitually that all may not be quite as it seems. Such a habit of reflection does not come easily, and among the early Christians there were particular forces working against it, the certainty of faith, the misguided ideals of single-mindedness and simplicity of heart. To the overachiever, the rewards and esteem of martyrdom had a clear and final attraction. Why live, if death brought a martyr to Christ?[143]

Fox's evaluation of Christian martyrdom could hardly be more misleading. Although he expresses a certain empathy for the men and women about whom he writes, in the final analysis they are dismissed as simpleminded and misguided. Admittedly, this is preferable to attributing the early Christian fascination with voluntary death to "morbid desire," "psychopathological impulse," or even "sexual abnormality," all of which still characterize much of the secondary literature on martyrdom.[144] But the historian should not be too quick to hold the ideals and practices of an ancient culture accountable to those of his own day.

We have seen that, far from being simpleminded or misguided, the early Christians displayed considerable sophistication in their thinking about voluntary death. The evidence belies Fox's assertions that martyrdom appealed mostly to the "young and inexperienced" and that the early Christians failed "to reflect habitually that all may not be quite as it seems." In fact, that was precisely their point. All was *not* as it seemed. The early Christians shifted the center of gravity from this world to the next. The radical transvaluation of reality that had begun with Plato reached its apex in early Christianity. That meant that, for the early Christians, life was at best unimportant and at worst evil. Death was a release, anxiously awaited and sometimes eagerly sought out. To be sure, the world they constructed and inhabited is no longer one that many of us in the modern West share, and therefore the answers they found to their questions about the meaning of life and death are not likely to have much appeal. More often than not, the answers at which they arrived, as well as their application of them, repel the modern reader, especially if he or she does not happen to live under the threat of "persecution." Professor Fox (it appears) is one who does not like their conclusions. It would seem that the problem of voluntary death terrifies him in a way that would not have been possible for the early Christians—at least those early Christians who had the courage of their convictions.

NOTES

1. Tertullian, *Apology* 41.5.
2. Alfredo Alvarez, *The Savage God: A Study of Suicide* (New York: Random House, 1970), p. 68.
3. Tertullian, *Apology* 50.15–16. Cf. his remarks in *On the Soul* 55.4–5: "Observe, then, the difference between a pagan and a Christian in their death: if you have to lay down your life for God, *as the Paraclete counsels*, it is not in mild fevers and on soft beds, but in the sharp pains of martyrdom. You must take up the cross and bear it after your Master, as he himself instructed you. *The sole key to unlock paradise is your own life's blood.*"
4. The literature on Christian martyrdom is enormous. In addition to W. H. C. Frend's *Martyrdom and Persecution in the Early Church: A Study of a Conflict from the Maccabees to Donatus* (Oxford: Basil Blackwell, 1965), which contains rich bibliographies, mention should be made of the following studies that inform our discussion in this chapter: D. W. Riddle, *The Martyrs: A Study in Social Control* (Chicago: Univ. of Chicago Press, 1931); G. E. M. de Ste. Croix, "Aspects of the 'Great' Persecution," *Harvard Theological Review* 47 (1954): 75–113; G. E. M. de Ste. Croix, "Why Were the Early Christians Persecuted?" *Past and Present* 26 (1963): 6–38 (reprinted in M. I. Finley, ed., *Studies in Ancient Society*, Past and Present Series [London: Routledge & Kegan Paul, 1974], pp. 210–49); H. Musurillo, *The Acts of the Christian Martyrs*, Oxford Early Christian Texts (Oxford: Clarendon Press, 1972); T. D. Barnes, *Tertullian: A Historical and Literary Study*, rev. ed. (Oxford: Clarendon Press, 1985); and Robin Lane Fox, *Pagans and Christians* (New York: Knopf, 1987), pp. 419–92.

5. Ignatius, *To the Romans* 4–7. Ignatius was executed during the reign of Trajan, c. 107/8 A.D.

6. Cf. 2 Macc. 6:18–20; 12:39–45; 14:37–46 ; 4 Macc. 5:29–32; 9:1–11; and our discussion in chap. 3.

7. The earliest reference to "birthdays" occurs in the *Martyrdom of Polycarp* 18.2; cf. Tertullian, *On the Crown* 3; Cyprian, *Letters* 33.3; 36.2.

8. Fox, *Pagans and Christians*, p. 441.

9. Polycarp, *To the Philippians* 8.2. The martyrdom of Polycarp will be discussed below.

10. Eusebius and other writers mention numerous instances of Christians taking their own lives to procure martyrdom, to avoid apostasy, or to retain the crown of virginity. See our discussion below.

11. *Martyrdom of Polycarp* 2.3; cf. Hermas, *Similitudes* 2.2, 7 and *Visions* 9.25.2; 9.28.6.

12. Fox, *Pagans and Christians*, p. 435 (with important references, p. 751, n. 8).

13. See the perceptive comments of R. G. Tanner, "Martyrdom in Saint Ignatius of Antioch and the Stoic View of Suicide," in E. A. Livingstone, ed., *Studia Patristica*, vol. 16.2, Texte und Untersuchungen 129 (Berlin: Akademie-Verlag, 1985), pp. 201–5.

14. See Irenaeus, *Against Heresies* 5.28.4.

15. Frend, *Martyrdom and Persecution in the Early Church*, p. 198. Ignatius himself mentions "those who have preceded me from Syria to Rome to the glory of God" (*To the Romans* 10.2), which indicates that his was not an isolated case. He also mentions two Christians, Philo and Rheus Agathopous, from Cilicia and Syria respectively, who had "renounced this life" and were being sent to Rome after him (*To the Philadelphians* 11.1; *To the Smyrneans* 10.1).

16. Justin, *Second Apology* 2.1–20; discussed by Frend, *Martyrdom and Persecution in the Early Church*, pp. 252–53.

17. Note Justin's description of Ptolemaeus's confession: "Being convinced of his duty, and the nobility of it through the teaching of Christ, he confessed his discipleship in the divine virtue. For he who denies anything, either denies it because he condemns the thing itself, or he shrinks from confession because he is conscious of his own unworthiness or alienation from it. Neither case is that of the true Christian" (*Second Apology* 2.13–14).

18. Justin, *Second Apology* 2.19.

19. Fox, *Pagans and Christians*, pp. 442–43.

20. Eusebius places the martyrdom in the reign of Marcus Aurelius, but an earlier date (c. 156/57) seems more plausible. See the discussion in T. D. Barnes, "Pre-Decian *Acta Martyrum*," *Journal of Theological Studies* 19 (1968): 510–14. The *Martyrdom* survives in six Greek manuscripts as well as in a Latin version. Substantial portions of it are preserved by Eusebius in his *Church History* 4.15.2–45. On the reliability of the *Acta Martyrum*, their form, and transmission, see Musurillo, *Acts of the Christian Martyrs*, pp. l–lvii; and Fox, *Pagans and Christians*, pp. 434–35.

21. On this, see Frend, *Martyrdom and Persecution in the Early Church*, p. 270.

22. *Martyrdom of Polycarp* 3.1–2.
23. See Fox, *Pagans and Christians*, pp. 421 and 425.
24. The refusal of the beasts to touch Christian martyrs was a commonplace. See, for example, the *Acts of Paul and Thecla* 28; Eusebius, *Church History* 5.1.42; 8.7.2ff.
25. *Martyrdom of Polycarp* 2.1. It is not altogether clear whether *martyrion* (*–ia*) should be translated as "martyrdom" or "witness" (or perhaps "testimony"). There is an untranslatable play on words.
26. *Martyrdom of Polycarp* 4.1. In his famous study of the *Martyrdom of Polycarp*, Hans von Campenhausen ("Bearbeitungen und Interpretationen des Polykarp-martyriums," in *Sitzungsberichte der Heidelberger Akademie der Wissenschaft*, Phil.-hist. Klasse [1957], 3. Abh., pp. 1–48), argued that the Quintus story was "an anti-Montanist insertion" of the late second or early third century (p. 20). While leaving open the possibility that the *Martyrdom* was redacted, we see no evidence that demands that the Quintus story was a later addition or, if it was, that it was inserted as a piece of anti-Montanist polemic. The fact that Quintus is said to be from Phrygia, the place where Montanism originated, is not sufficient to warrant von Campenhausen's conclusion. See below, pp. 136–137.
27. A similar injunction occurs about a century later in the *Acts of Cyprian*. During his interrogation Cyprian informed the proconsul that "our discipline forbids anyone to surrender voluntarily" (1.5). In light of all the evidence to the contrary, it is difficult to believe that such a view was very widespread. We shall return to this below.
28. De Ste. Croix, "Aspects of the 'Great' Persecution," p. 103. His statistics are based on Eusebius's list in the *Martyrs of Palestine*, which de Ste. Croix takes to be relatively complete (p. 101). De Ste. Croix recognizes that these statistics are not absolutely reliable and that his conclusions for Palestine do not necessarily apply to other provinces in the empire (pp. 102–3). Even so, de Ste. Croix has seen what no one else has been able (or willing) to see, namely, the importance and prevalence of "voluntary martyrdom." We shall have more to say about this below.
29. It is significant that the narrator appeals to "the teaching of the Gospel," but does not (or cannot!) provide a specific passage.
30. Justin, *Second Apology* 2.13–14.
31. Note the emphasis on Polycarp's willing compliance with the authorities, and this despite the narrator's condemnation of Quintus's voluntary act.
32. Note the contrast with Quintus, who "played the coward" (4.1).
33. Tertullian, *To Scapula* 1.1.
34. Tertullian, *To Scapula* 5.1. Tertullian's claim that *all* the Christians of Asia presented themselves before the governor is probably an exaggeration, but there is no reason to doubt the reliability of the account.
35. See, for example, Frend, *Martyrdom and Persecution in the Early Church*, p. 293: "Here was the Montanist equivalent of the Donatist Circumcellions two centuries later."

36. See n. 26, above.

37. Walter Bauer, *Orthodoxy and Heresy in Earliest Christianity*, 2d ed., translated by the Philadelphia Seminar on Christian Origins (Philadelphia: Fortress Press, 1971). Bauer's work was first published in 1934.

38. Note Eusebius's astonishing claim that *no* Montanists were martyred either "by the Jews or the wicked" (*Church History* 5.16.12, quoting from an anonymous treatise *Against Miltiades*, a Montanist bishop). Further on, the same source states, "They [the Montanists] take refuge in martyrs, saying that they have many martyrs and that this is trustworthy proof of the power of the alleged prophetic spirit among them. But this appears to be actually further from the truth than anything. For some of the heresies have innumerable martyrs, but I do not suppose that we shall accept them for that reason, nor admit that they have the truth" (5.16.20–21). In another place, and again quoting from the same source, Eusebius alleges that Montanus and Maximilla actually killed themselves, "inspired by a mind-destroying demon . . . like the traitor Judas" (5.16.13–14). Eusebius admits, however, that his source is not certain of this. The connection made between Montanus's death and Judas's act anticipates Augustine's polemic against the Donatists (see Augustine, *Against Gaudentius* 1.37.49; cf. *City of God* 1.17).

39. De Ste. Croix, "Why Were the Early Christians Persecuted?", p. 234.

40. De Ste. Croix, "Why Were the Early Christians Persecuted?", p. 234.

41. *The Martyrdom of Carpus, Papylus, and Agathonike* survives in Greek and Latin recensions. We cite the Greek text and English translation of Musurillo, *Acts of the Christian Martyrs*, pp. 22–29. Eusebius (*Church History* 4.15.48) refers to these three martyrs immediately after Polycarp and Pionius, who are both dated to the reign of Marcus Aurelius. Some scholars, however, prefer to date Carpus *et al.* in the reign of Decius. See the discussion in Musurillo, *Acts of the Christian Martyrs*, p. xv.

42. See, for example, Blandina in *The Martyrs of Lyons* 18, 56; and Sanctus in Eusebius, *Church History* 5.1.22.

43. Cf. John 19:30: Jesus "gave up his spirit" (*paredoken to pneuma*); and see our discussion in chap. 5, pp. 118–19.

44. At least she is not referred to as a Christian according to the Greek recension of the *Martyrdom*. Note the meaning of her name: "Good Victory." Agathonike conquers death by dying.

45. See our discussion in chap. 4, pp. 101–02 and 105.

46. This is but one of a large number of similar examples of voluntary martyrdom. See further de Ste. Croix, "Aspects of the 'Great' Persecution," pp. 83, 93, 101–3; de Ste. Croix, "Why Were the Early Christians Persecuted?", pp. 235–36; and Fox, *Pagans and Christians*, pp. 441–45.

47. Justin, *Second Apology* 10.5. The crime, according to Justin, was the introduction of new deities and refusal to worship the gods recognized by the state (i.e., "atheism").

48. Justin, *Second Apology* 10.8.

49. John Chrysostom, *Homilies on 1 Corinthians* 4.7.

50. Note that Chrysostom interprets Socrates' *anangke* to mean that he had no choice but to accept death. This is a sharp break with the view that Socrates drank the poison willingly.

51. Cyprian, *On the Lapsed* 8. For a similar response in Alexandria during the persecution of Decius, see Dionysius's letter to Fabius, preserved by Eusebius, *Church History* 6.41.12. Eusebius also reports that during the persecution of Diocletian Christian leaders "hid" and "thousands" of bishops offered sacrifice (8.2.1; 8.3.1).

52. Timothy Ware, *The Orthodox Church* (Harmondsworth: Penguin Books, 1985), p. 20.

53. Barnes, *Tertullian*, p. 167; cf. pp. 161–63.

54. Justin, *Second Apology* 12.1.

55. Tertullian, *Apology* 50.13; cf. *Acts of Perpetua and Felicitas* 17.2–3; *Martyrdom of Pionius* 7.1. On the importance of martyrdom for conversion, see the famous discussion by A. D. Nock, *Conversion: The Old and the New in Religion from Alexander the Great to Augustine of Hippo* (Oxford: Clarendon Press, 1933), pp. 187–98.

56. On Galen, see R. Walzer, *Galen on Jews and Christians* (London: Oxford Univ. Press, 1949), pp. 14ff. and 48ff.

57. Marcus Aurelius, *Meditations* 11.3. Marcus was not thinking only of "voluntary martyrdom," as noted by Barnes, *Tertullian*, p. 165, n. 7. For the often-repeated charge that Christians were "in love with death," see S. Benko, *Pagan Rome and the Early Christians* (Bloomington: Indiana Univ. Press, 1984), pp. 39–43, with important references.

58. Clement, *Stromateis* 4.16.3–17.3.

59. Lucian, *The Death of Peregrinus* 13. Like Clement, Lucian also noted the parallel with the Gymnosophists (20–25, 38–39).

60. This saying is preserved by Eusebius, *Church History* 4.7.7.

61. Frend, *Martyrdom and Persecution in the Early Church*, p. 354. Heracleon's position is summarized by Clement in *Stromateis* 4.71.1–72.4.

62. Quoted by Clement, *Stromateis* 4.71.2, 4.

63. The Gnostic texts from Nag Hammadi support Heracleon's position. For example, an openness to martyrdom can be found in the first and second *Apocalypses of James*. The *Apocryphon of James*, in addition to containing an exhortation to martyrdom, holds t..at many Christians died as martyrs for the wrong reasons. These texts are available in J. M. Robinson, ed., *The Nag Hammadi Library*, 3d rev. ed. (San Francisco: Harper & Row, 1988). See the recent study by Clemens Scholten, *Martyrium und Sophiamythos im Gnostizismus nach den Texten von Nag Hammadi*, Jahrbuch für Antike und Christentum Ergänzungsband 14 (Münster: Aschendorffsche Verlagsbuchhandlung, 1987).

64. Clement, *Stromateis* 4.43.4.

65. Clement, *Stromateis* 4.73.1–3.

66. Clement, *Stromateis* 4.73.5.

67. Clement, *Stromateis* 4.74.1.
68. There are over fifty quotations and allusions to the *Phaedo* in Clement's extant writings. See Otto Stählin, *Clemens Alexandrinus, 4.1: Register*, 2. Auflage, GCS (Berlin: Akademie-Verlag, 1980), pp. 52–53 (s.v. "*Phaidon*").
69. Clement, *Stromateis* 7.66.
70. Clement, *Stromateis* 4.77.1.
71. On this, see Eusebius, *Church History* 6.1.1–6; 6.6.
72. Eusebius, *Church History* 6.1.1, 3–5.
73. Clement, *Stromateis* 4.17.1–3, quoted above, p. 141.
74. Note that Clement did not have a pejorative term like *suicide* to wield against the "heretics." He was forced to take otherwise neutral terms and invest them with a negative meaning. His phrase *to take oneself out* (*exagein heauton*), for example, is a good Stoic expression.
75. Tertullian, *To the Martyrs* 2. The reference to the "prison" recalls the *Phaedo* (62b).
76. Tertullian, *Antidote for the Scorpion's Sting* 6.
77. Barnes, *Tertullian*, p. 172; cf. pp. 34–35. Our discussion of Tertullian is indebted to Barnes at several points.
78. Tertullian, *Antidote for the Scorpion's Sting* 1.
79. Tertullian, *Antidote for the Scorpion's Sting* 2.
80. Tertullian, *Antidote for the Scorpion's Sting* 4.
81. Tertullian, *Antidote for the Scorpion's Sting* 5.
82. Tertullian, *Antidote for the Scorpion's Sting* 5. Socrates also used "medical" terminology when he asked Crito to offer a cock to Asclepius, the god of healing. See chap. 2, p. 21.
83. Tertullian, *Antidote for the Scorpion's Sting* 7.
84. Tertullian, *Antidote for the Scorpion's Sting* 8.
85. Tertullian, *Antidote for the Scorpion's Sting* 8–15.
86. *On Endurance* 15.2.
87. *On Endurance* 16.5.
88. Barnes, *Tertullian*, p. 177, referring to *On Endurance* 13.6–8.
89. *To His Wife* 1.3.4.
90. *On Flight in Persecution* 4.
91. *On Flight in Persecution* 5.
92. *On Flight in Persecution* 5.
93. *On Flight in Persecution* 6.
94. *On Flight in Persecution* 6.
95. *On Flight in Persecution* 11.
96. Barnes, *Tertullian*, p. 183.
97. As Barnes notes, "No African bishop was martyred before Cyprian" in the mid-third century (*Tertullian*, p. 183, n. 1).
98. See, for example, the bizarre case of Pristinus in *On Fasting* 12. He had gotten so drunk in prison that he could not even make a proper confession before the

Roman governor. "Hiccoughs and belchings" were all he could manage to get out. Although he was executed, he did not suffer. Therefore, Tertullian says, he was "no *Christian* martyr."

99.   *Pace* Frend, *Martyrdom and Persecution in the Early Church*, p. 394.

100. Origen's remarks are preserved in a document known as the *Dialogue with Heraclides*. The text survives in a sixth-century codex found among a number of papyri at Toura near Cairo in 1941. It is not a literary work, but the record of an actual discussion between Origen and the bishop Heraclides regarding the latter's view on the trinitarian question. See A. D. Nock, *American Journal of Archaeology* 55 (1951): 283–84; and B. Capelle, "L'Entretien d'Origène avec Héraclide," *Journal of Ecclesiastical History* 2 (1951): 143–57.

101. Origen, *Exhortation to Martyrdom* 30. In his *Homilies on Leviticus* 2.4, Origen placed martyrdom second only to baptism as the means of achieving forgiveness of sins.

102. *Exhortation to Martyrdom* 45–46.

103. *Exhortation to Martyrdom* 3.

104. *Exhortation to Martyrdom* 5.

105. *Exhortation to Martyrdom* 6–10.

106. *Exhortation to Martyrdom* 11, 14–16.

107. *Exhortation to Martyrdom* 12.

108. *Exhortation to Martyrdom* 13.

109. *Exhortation to Martyrdom* 22; cf. 2 Macc. 6:18–28.

110. *Exhortation to Martyrdom* 22, quoting 2 Macc. 6:27–28.

111. *Exhortation to Martyrdom* 23–27.

112. *Exhortation to Martyrdom* 28.

113. *Exhortation to Martyrdom* 28.

114. *Exhortation to Martyrdom* 29.

115. *Exhortation to Martyrdom* 29.

116. *Exhortation to Martyrdom* 30.

117. *Exhortation to Martyrdom* 30.

118. *Exhortation to Martyrdom* 36.

119. *Exhortation to Martyrdom* 37.

120. *Exhortation to Martyrdom* 47. Note the allusions to Paul here and throughout the treatise.

121. De Ste. Croix, "Why Were the Early Christians Persecuted?", p. 234 (our emphasis).

122. De Ste. Croix, "Aspects of the 'Great' Persecution," p. 83.

123. De Ste. Croix, "Why Were the Early Christians Persecuted?", p. 234, referring to "Aspects of the 'Great' Persecution," p. 83, n. 40.

124. *Martyrdom of Pionius* 13.7 See Fox, *Pagans and Christians*, pp. 462–92, who presents a convincing case for dating the *Martyrdom* to the reign of Decius. His entire discussion is excellent, except on one point. He asserts that "Pionius shared the Church's execration of suicide, a death, naturally, which was quite distinct from martyrdom" (p. 480). This claim is anachronistic and without textual

support. On the contrary, Pionius insists that Jesus was not executed by the Jews, but "departed from life at his own choice." In other words, Jesus' death, like Pionius's, was *voluntary!*

125. *Martyrdom of Pionius* 4.7.

126. *Martyrdom of Pionius* 18.2. Pionius will not allow himself to be compelled.

127. *Martyrdom of Pionius* 20.3, 5. The Roman governor implies that Pionius is mad. This is what Augustine will say of the Donatist martyrs.

128. *Martyrdom of Marian and James* 3.5.

129. *Martyrdom of Marian and James* 12.8.

130. *Martyrdom of Marian and James* 2.3.

131. On secondary martyrdom, see, for example, Lucius, in Justin, *Second Apology* 2.19; Agathonike, in *Martyrdom of Carpus, Papylas, and Agathonike* 42–47 (Greek); Vettius Epagathus, in *Martyrs of Lyons* 9; a crowd, in *Acts of Cyprian* 5.1; a bystander, in *Acts of Marian and James* 9.2–4; Philoromus, in *Martyrdom of Phileas* 7.1–3.

132. Eusebius, *The Martyrs of Palestine* 2.1.

133. Eusebius, *The Martyrs of Palestine* 1.5. Eusebius mentions a similar episode involving a certain Zacchaeus, an exorcist from Gadara.

134. De Ste. Croix, "Aspects of the 'Great' Persecution," p. 102. According to Lactantius, some Roman governors boasted of not having executed any Christians (*Divine Institutes* 5.11). Many governors simply looked the other way.

135. *The Martyrdom of Euplus* 1–2 (Greek).

136. Eusebius, *The Martyrs of Palestine* 3.2–4.

137. Eusebius, *Church History* 8.9.5; cf. his similar description of the martyrs of Lyons and Vienne (5.1.9–11).

138. Quoted by Augustine, *Summary of the Conference with the Donatists* 3.13.25. We owe this reference to de Ste. Croix, "Aspects of the 'Great' Persecution," p. 83.

139. Eusebius, *Church History* 6.41.7.

140. Eusebius, *Church History* 8.6.6.

141. Eusebius, *Church History* 8.12.3–5; cf. 8.14.16–17: a Roman aristocratic woman killed herself rather than be outraged.

142. Rudolf Hirzel, "Der Selbstmord," *Archiv für Religionswissenschaft* 11 (1908): 473–74. Earlier we suggested that Josephus and perhaps even Paul were aware of the Socratic tradition on voluntary death. It is not until Augustine, however, that an *explicit* connection can be drawn.

143. Fox, *Pagans and Christians*, pp. 441–42.

144. Of the many examples of this, see Riddle, *The Martyrs*, pp. 60–76.

☙

CHAPTER 7

The Augustinian Reversal

In his detective novel *The Three Taps*, Ronald Knox has one of his characters say of suicide, "I think it is a fine thing, quite often, and the Christian condemnation of it merely echoes a private quarrel between St. Augustine and some heretics of his day."[1] We have seen that Augustine was not the first Christian to oppose voluntary death. Two centuries earlier, Clement of Alexandria had distinguished between genuine martyrdom and a mere killing of oneself. He condemned some of the heretics of his day as "self-murderers," even though they had been officially executed.[2] There were other Christians who denied that an individual had the right to take his own life, but it is to Augustine more than anyone else that Christianity and the West owe their condemnation of suicide.[3]

Augustine discussed the problem of voluntary death in a minor polemical tract *Against Gaudentius* and in the first book of his magnum opus, *Concerning the City of God Against the Pagans*.[4] His position was the same in both works, although the occasion for each was different. In the former treatise, a bitter attack on the Donatist bishop Gaudentius, Augustine refused to recognize as martyrs Donatist Christians who had killed themselves under the threat of persecution. They were no more martyrs, Augustine argued, than the traitor Judas.

The treatise *Against Gaudentius*, and the views about voluntary death expressed in it, can only be appreciated in light of the bitter division within North African Christianity following the last, "great" persecution of Diocletian in 303–5. As Peter Brown aptly describes the situation, "The African communities found themselves in a position similar to that of a Resistance movement whose country had begun to settle down to the complexities and compromises of peacetime."[5] During the persecution many bishops had collaborated by handing over copies of the Bible to the Roman authorities. In the eastern half of the empire the Romans had required Christians to sacrifice and swear an oath of allegiance to the emperor; in the West, Christian clergy were ordered to hand over copies of their sacred books for burning. Those who complied

were branded *traditores* ("traitors"). When the persecution ended, many
Christians refused to recognize the authority of those clerics who had collaborated with the Romans.

The conflict was exacerbated in 311 by the death of Mensurius, bishop of
Carthage. When Caecilian was elected in his place, a sizable and strong faction
of Christians refused to recognize him, claiming that he had been ordained by
a *traditor*. The dissidents appointed Majorinus as a rival bishop. In 315 Majorinus
was succeeded by another Numidian cleric, Donatus, and it was he who gave his
name to the *pars Donati*, "the party of Donatus."

Although the Donatists were a majority in North Africa, the Catholic bishop Caecilian enjoyed the support of the Roman emperor. In 347 Donatus was
exiled, and an imperial commissioner, Macarius, attempted to force the
Donatists to rejoin the Catholic church by threatening them with violence. A
series of imperial rescripts in 405 banned the movement, and at Carthage in
411 a conference of over five hundred bishops condemned the "heretics." No
longer were the persecutors pagans; now Christians were killing Christians. The
years of violence that followed were ended only by the arrival of the Vandals in
429. The Donatist church, however, managed to survive down to the Arab con-
quest.

The Donatists were rigorists in the tradition of Tertullian and Cyprian,
maintaining that the true church must remain holy, composed only of the righteous and separated from a world ruled by demonic powers. There was no salvation outside the body of the elect. Other Christians believed that the church
was a mixed body, containing both righteous *and* sinners. The "wheat and the
tares" must grow together, they claimed, until the Lord returns and separates
them. The differences between Donatists and Catholics, however, should not
be exaggerated. Both read the same Bible, professed the same creed, and celebrated an identical liturgy. The Donatists only refused to recognize the domi-
nation of the Catholic church. Against the Catholic claim to universality the
Donatists claimed integrity.

We gain an understanding of what it was like to be a Donatist by reading
their *Acts of the Martyrs* and their descriptions of the persecution they suffered
at the hands of both pagans and Catholics.[6] The Donatists conceived of their
religion as a law, and, like the Jews of Maccabean tradition, they were prepared
to die for it. "I care for nothing," one Donatist declared, "but the Law of God
which I have learned. This I guard, for this I die; in this I shall be burned up.
There is nothing in life other than this Law."[7] The Donatists thrived on martyrdom, often deliberately courting death and at times even killing themselves
outright. It was above all the spectacular death of the Maccabean hero Razis (2
Macc. 14:37–46) from which the Donatists drew their inspiration, but they also
appealed to other biblical figures as precedents for their acts of martyrdom.

Augustine gives the following description of the Donatists' fascination with voluntary martyrdom:

> While the worship of the idols still continued, vast numbers of them used to come in procession to the most well attended ceremonies of the pagans, not with the intention of breaking the idols, but that they might be put to death by those who worshipped them. For if they had sought to break the idols under the sanction of legitimate authority, they might, in the case of anything happening to them, have had some shadow of a claim to be considered martyrs. But their only object in coming was, that while the idols remained uninjured, they themselves might meet with death. . . . Some went so far as to offer themselves for slaughter to any travellers whom they met with arms, using violent threats that they would murder them if they failed to meet with death at their hands. Sometimes, too, they extorted with violence from any passing judge that they should be put to death by the executioners, or by the officer of his court. . . . It was their daily sport to kill themselves, by throwing themselves off cliffs, or into the water, or into the fire. For the demon taught them these three modes of self destruction, so that, when they wished to die, and could not find any one whom they could terrify into slaying them with his sword, they threw themselves over the rocks, or committed themselves to the fire or the swirling pool. . . . Since they have given place within themselves to the demon, they either perish like the herd of swine, whom the legion of demons drove down the hillside into the sea, or, being rescued from that destruction and gathered together into the loving bosom of our Catholic Mother, they are delivered just as the boy was delivered by our Lord, whom his father brought to be healed of the demon, saying that he frequently fell into the fire and into the water.[8]

Despite Augustine's obvious disgust with the Donatists, there was nothing new in their behavior. The Donatists sustained the tradition and importance of voluntary martyrdom in the fourth and fifth centuries.

The occasion for Augustine's tract *Against Gaudentius* was this: at the approach of the imperial official Dulcitius in 420, Gaudentius, the Donatist successor of Optatus, barricaded himself in his magnificent basilica at Timgad and threatened to burn it down with himself and his congregation in it. From his church Gaudentius wrote two letters to Dulcitius, explaining his refusal to follow imperial policy and justifying his intention to die rather than compromise. Dulcitius turned these letters over to Augustine, who replied to them in the two books entitled *Against Gaudentius*. This treatise, as Peter Brown observes, "is noticeably the most heartless of Augustine's writings in defence of the suppression of the Donatists."[9]

It did not matter to Gaudentius that it was a *Christian* emperor, Honorius, who was demanding his allegiance. In Gaudentius's eyes, what Honorius was doing to the Donatists was no different than what the pagan emperors had done to Christians during the "great persecution" about a century earlier. Gaudentius saw himself as a martyr ("witness") for his faith. Since the Council of Carthage in 411, many Donatists had preferred to kill themselves rather than "convert" to Catholicism, and they drew their inspiration from the martyrs of an earlier period.

Augustine denied Gaudentius's claim. He refused to recognize as martyrs those Donatists who had chosen death rather than submit to the Catholic church. Death and martyrdom were not the same, according to Augustine, for what is good in the hands of Christians becomes a bad thing in the hands of heretics. The death of a heretic is never a true martyrdom.

In a celebrated formulation, Augustine declared: *Martyres veros non facit poena sed causa* ("Punishment does not make true martyrs but the reason [for the punishment]").[10] Not content with refusing to recognize the Donatists as martyrs, Augustine likened them to criminals who had broken the law. Seen in this light, the violence directed against the Donatists by the state-supported Catholics was not "persecution" but "prosecution"—the necessary and legal repression of criminals.[11] Imperial policy was only an expression of divine anger: God was "inviting" the Donatists to renounce their heresy and rejoin the ranks of the church.[12] Augustine claimed, in effect, that the Catholics were trying to save the Donatists from themselves. The blood being shed was the result not of Catholics killing Donatists but of Donatists killing themselves. It was this that provoked God's anger in this world, and it would provoke it yet again in the next. In other words, Augustine made an explicit connection between the act of killing oneself and eternal punishment.[13]

Barricaded in his cathedral, Gaudentius presented the following ultimatum:

> In this church, in which the name of God and his Christ, as you yourself have recognized, have always been worshipped in the truth by a large congregation, we will either remain in life, as long as that pleases God, or else, as it becomes the family of God, within the walls of this camp of the Lord, we will put an end to our life, yet on this condition [*sub ea scilicet conditione*]: if one should do us violence, in that case the act will be realized. No one is so insane that he would run to death without being driven to it.[14]

This passage reveals that Gaudentius's position was more subtle and complex than Augustine cared to admit. Gaudentius was not advocating an unwarranted or unjustified killing of himself, as Augustine claimed. Gaudentius denies that he and his congregation are rushing headlong toward death. Only a madman (*demens*) would do such a thing, he says. On the contrary, Gaudentius claims that he and his followers are being compelled in the same way the martyrs had been compelled during times of persecution. He justifies his intended act of self-destruction for a specific reason (*sub ea conditione*): "If someone does us violence . . . (etc.)." It appears that Gaudentius agreed with the Augustinian definition of martyrdom, even if his application of it differed. According to Gaudentius, he and his congregation were prepared to act on the basis of a *causa iusta.*

Gaudentius appealed to the "noble death" of Razis in the Old Testament as a scriptural warrant for his view of voluntary death.[15] Gaudentius justified the death of Razis and, by implication, the deaths of the Donatist faithful by interpreting 2 Maccabees 14:37–46 in light of a saying of Jesus: "The spirit is willing but the flesh is weak" (Matt. 26:41). The "weakness of the flesh" indicates, according to Gaudentius, that there is a certain limit of suffering beyond which the body cannot endure. When faced with persecution, the Christian should die voluntarily for God, either by killing himself or by hurling himself into a ravine, in order to escape suffering and the risk of apostasy. By acting in this way the Christian displays his recognition of the weakness of the flesh and avoids the possibility of denying his faith. When suffering, or the possibility of suffering, presents itself, the Christian will not hesitate: he will kill himself for fear of renouncing the faith. Far from separating himself from God, he affirms by this act his commitment to God.

By appealing to Razis, Gaudentius introduced a new argument into the debate: the use of biblical figures *other than Jesus* as a justification for voluntary martyrdom. Gaudentius's claim to scriptural precedent could not be dismissed lightly. In addition to Razis, the Old Testament records the self-inflicted deaths of Abimelech, Samson, Saul and his armor-bearer, Ahithophel, and Zimri. In the New Testament there is the example of Judas, who hanged himself out of remorse for having betrayed Jesus. Augustine deals with three of these examples: Samson, Razis, and Judas. Gaudentius was a clever exegete and more than a match for Augustine. In attempting to refute Gaudentius's claim to biblical precedent, Augustine had to call upon all his interpretive skills. On occasion he reads into the text ideas that are not present; at other times he denies what the text explicitly says. His exegesis reveals something of the frustration and desperation provoked in him by the Donatists.

For Augustine it is significant that Razis had *no escape* from his enemies.[16] He would have been killed even if he had not taken his own life. According to Augustine, the situation of Razis stands in sharp contrast to that of the Donatists. Their lives are not in danger, and they should find "a way out." Citing Matthew 10:23, Augustine stresses that it is preferable to *flee* from persecution when possible. "When they persecute you in one town," Jesus told his disciples, "flee to the next one." Augustine, therefore, advises Gaudentius to "ask Christ; he orders you to flee. Ask the tribune; he permits you to flee. If you could ask Razis, he would respond: 'I was not able to flee.' Therefore, you neither have Christ for a savior, nor the tribune for a persecutor, nor Razis for a respondent."[17] Augustine's reasoning is nothing less than astonishing, for if the same logic was applied to his own (Catholic) martyrs, he would be forced to conclude that they too were self-murderers.

Ignoring the explicit statement of the text, that Razis "preferred to die nobly rather than fall into the hands of sinners" (2 Macc. 14:42), Augustine claims that the author of 2 Maccabees did not praise Razis' death. According to Augustine, the "nobility" the Donatists see in Razis is a pagan, not a Christian, virtue. And, in any case, the books of the Maccabees do not command the authority of the other books of scripture, "the Law and the Prophets and the Psalms" (quoting Luke 24:44).

Samson, too, had no way out. When he pulled down the temple on himself and the Philistines, Augustine argues, Samson "wanted to share with them the death which they were soon going to inflict on him, *since he was not able to escape it. Indeed, he did not act of his own accord. His act must be attributed to the spirit of God that was using him by its presence to do what he could not do when the same spirit was lacking.*"[18] Augustine has clearly bent the text to his own purposes, for the account of Samson's death in Judges 16:23–31 does not mention that Samson was faced with imminent execution or that his returning strength was the result of the spirit of God working through him.

Augustine will not allow the Donatists to compare themselves to the biblical heroes Samson and Razis. Instead they should emulate Job, who refused to kill himself and chose to endure despite his extreme suffering.[19] In addition, Augustine suggests another, and this time very sinister, comparison: the Donatists who kill themselves resemble the traitor Judas: "Although many of you have rushed into voluntary death [*in mortem voluntariam*] by different means, it is under the instigation of the same demon that you imitate the traitor [Judas] by slaying yourselves."[20] The Donatists are the real *traditores*, according to Augustine. They betrayed the Church just as Judas, the faithful disciple of Satan, betrayed Jesus.

Although Augustine drew a sharp distinction between martyrdom and a simple killing of oneself, he did not have an explicitly pejorative term, like our word *suicide*, to denote the latter. In his treatise *Against Gaudentius* we see Augustine taking great care to keep separate the vocabulary he uses for Catholic, as opposed to Donatist, martyrs.[21] The former gave their lives for the glory of God, as members of the *ecclesia catholica* and on the basis of a *causa iusta.*[22] By contrast, Augustine uses numerous expressions to denote the deaths of the Donatists: "a rushing toward death" (*ad mortem festinatio*),[23] "to kill oneself" (*se ipsum occidere*),[24] "extorters of their souls" (*extortores animarum*),[25] "spontaneous death" (*mors spontanea*),[26] "voluntary destruction" (*interitus voluntarius*),[27] "voluntary death" (*mors voluntaria*),[28] and "to slay themselves" (*ipsos necare*).[29] All these expressions emphasize the voluntary nature of the act Augustine condemned: that is, the intentional and willing decision of an individual to die, either by killing himself or by provoking his own death.

Augustine offers a more extensive and theoretical treatment of the morality of voluntary death in the first book of his magnum opus, *Concerning the City of God against the Pagans*. On 24 August 410 the unimaginable had happened: an army of "barbarians" (Goths), led by Alaric, invaded the city of Rome. The invasion heightened the bitterness and hostility many pagans felt toward Christianity. They blamed the catastrophe on the Christians, who had caused the worship of the traditional gods to be neglected.[30]

Augustine's discussion of voluntary death was occasioned by the abuse suffered by Roman women during the barbarian invasion of 410. Some of these women had killed themselves either to avoid being raped or out of shame in having been violated. Were they justified in taking their lives, as many claimed, or had they sinned in trying to avoid sin? It is commonly held that Augustine's discussion concerned only *Christian* women. But the text does not support such an assumption. It was *pagan* women who had killed themselves in the invasion of 410, and Augustine's pagan opponents held the Christians ultimately responsible for this. "Our adversaries," Augustine writes, "certainly think they have a weighty attack to make on Christians, when they make the most of their captivity [by the Goths in 410] by adding stories of the violation of wives, of maidens ready for marriage, and even in some cases of women in the religious life. . . . Some women killed themselves to avoid suffering anything of the kind."[31]

Augustine will not allow his pagan opponents to hold Christianity responsible for the deaths of these women, nor will he permit his opponents to transform them into "pagan martyrs." On the contrary, these women are guilty of a crime: they killed themselves! They alone bear responsibility for their acts of self-destruction. "It is clear," Augustine argues, "that if no one has a private right to kill even a guilty man . . . , then anyone who kills himself is a murderer [*homicida*], and is the more guilty in killing himself the more innocent he is of the charge on which he has condemned himself to death."[32] Augustine invokes the example of Judas. Ignoring Matthew's view, that Judas's death was the measure of his remorse and repentance, Augustine claims that Judas *increased* rather than atoned for the guilt of his betrayal: "How much less right has anyone to indulge in self-slaughter when he can find in himself no fault to justify such a punishment!"[33]

There is an obvious problem with Augustine's first argument. Aside from his distortion of the Matthean account of Judas's death, Augustine appears not to recognize that there are cases of *justifiable* homicide (though he concedes this point in a later chapter).[34] The term *homicide* is morally neutral, since it could apply to criminal acts as well as to justifiable and even commendable ones. If killing oneself is a form of "self-homicide," then presumably there would be instances when an individual could justifiably take his own life.[35]

In the next chapter Augustine deals with a possible objection from his pagan opponents: if a woman allows herself to be raped, will she not be polluted by another's lust? Augustine's answer is no, for purity (*pudicitia*) "is a virtue of the soul and is not lost when the body is violated. . . . Therefore when a woman has been ravished without her consent, forced by another's sin, she has no reason to punish herself with a voluntary death [*mors spontanea*]. Still less should she do so before the event lest she should commit certain murder [*homicidium certum*] while the offence . . . remains uncertain."[36] Put simply, it is better to be raped than to kill oneself.

In defending the deaths of their women, Augustine's pagan adversaries appealed to the example of the legendary Roman heroine Lucretia, in much the same way as the Donatists invoked the biblical hero Razis. Lucretia killed herself after being raped by the son of King Tarquin.[37] "There were two persons involved," Augustine says of Lucretia's rape, "but only one committed adultery." Augustine holds Lucretia guilty of having killed an innocent woman: herself![38] But he also offers another argument, one that is as clever as it is sinister. Perhaps, he suggests, Lucretia was not innocent but guilty: "For suppose (a thing that only she herself could know) that, although the young man attacked her violently, she was so enticed by her own desire that she consented to the act and that when she came to punish herself she was so grieved that she thought death the only expiation."[39] Even if such was the case, Lucretia should not have killed herself. Instead she should have offered "a profitable penitence to the false gods." Augustine has tried to put his pagan opponents on the horns of a dilemma: "If [Lucretia's] self-homicide is extenuated, her adultery is established; if she is cleared of adultery, the murder is abundantly proved. There is no possible way out."[40]

Augustine contrasts the behavior of Roman women with that of Christian women who refused to follow the example of Lucretia: "When they [i.e., Christian women] were treated like this they did not take vengeance on themselves for another's crime. They would not add crime to crime by committing murder on themselves in shame because the enemy had raped them in lust."[41] To do so, Augustine argues, would have been to violate the authority of God's law.

This brings Augustine to his second argument against voluntary death, an argument based on the Bible. "It is significant," he contends, "that in the sacred canonical books there can nowhere be found any command or permission to inflict death on ourselves either to ensure immortality or to avoid or escape any evil."[42] Augustine is correct that the Bible contains no explicit opinion about the morality of voluntary death. But his statement conveniently ignores the eight accounts in the Bible of individuals who took their own lives. Despite Augustine's claim to the contrary, these individuals killed themselves *in order to avoid shame and dishonor*. Since none of them is condemned by the biblical authors, one might conclude that their acts of self-destruction were considered acceptable and some, perhaps, even heroic. In the case of Razis it is explicitly stated that he died nobly, with the full assurance of attaining immortality. If, as Augustine argues, there is a biblical precedent, it would appear to sanction voluntary death in certain circumstances.

Augustine makes the bold claim that, far from condoning voluntary death, the Bible actually forbids it. His appeal is to the sixth commandment, *Non occides* ("You shall not kill," Exod. 20:13).[43] Since the sixth commandment does not have the qualification "your neighbor," as do the ninth and tenth commandments, Augustine takes this to mean that the commandment applies both to other people *and* to oneself: "For to kill oneself is to kill a human being."[44] Lactantius had earlier expressed a similar view, though he did not appeal to the sixth commandment. "If a homicide is guilty because he is a destroyer of a man," Lactantius says, "he who puts himself to death is under the same guilt, because he puts to death a man."[45]

Augustine's interpretation of the sixth commandment would appear to rule out any situation in which killing could be justified. But if that were the case, what right would the state have to execute criminals convicted of capital offenses, or how could the examples of killing *in the Bible* be explained? Augustine is quick to make a qualification. He recognizes that "there are exceptions to the commandment against killing, made by the authority of God himself. There are some[46] whose killing God orders, either by a law, or by the express command to a particular person at a particular time."[47] Samson is a case in point. He destroyed himself and the Philistines by pulling down the temple of Dagon. "This can only be excused," Augustine contends, "on the ground that the Spirit . . . secretly ordered him to do so."[48] There is, of course, no mention of this in Judges 16:23–31, but Augustine could probably count on his opponents' ignorance of the Bible. What is more important is that Augustine justifies Samson's death in the same way Plato excused Socrates'. Like Plato, Augustine grants that an individual may take his own life when— and only when—God has commanded him to do so. Apart from such a command, "anyone who kills a human being, whether himself or anyone else, is involved in a charge of murder" (*homicidii crimine innectitur*).[49]

In the next three chapters (22–24) Augustine deals with the problem of voluntary death as understood by the pagans, above all by Plato and the Stoics. Augustine is well aware that the Stoics defend the right of an individual to take his own life when faced with the indignities of hardship, suffering, or shame.

Such an act, according to the Stoics, is an expression of "greatness of soul" (*magnitudo animi*). Augustine counters the Stoic view by arguing that the individual who kills himself displays "weakness of soul" in not being able to endure such indignities. The willingness to suffer pain and humiliation is the mark of the Christian, as opposed to the Stoic, wise person. And it is precisely this willingness to endure that is true *magnitudo animi*.[50]

Here Augustine appeals to Plato, not the Bible. If voluntary death was a sign of greatness of soul, then "Plato would have been the first and foremost to take this action, and he would have recommended it to others, had not the same intelligence which gave him his vision of the soul's immortality enabled him to decide that this step was not to be taken—was, indeed, to be forbidden."[51] Augustine is referring to the *Phaedo*, but his exegesis of Plato is as suspect as his exegesis of the Bible. Although Plato wanted to restrict the circumstances in which an individual might justifiably kill himself, he did not *forbid* voluntary death. In the *Phaedo* Socrates' death was justified on the ground that God provided a divine sign—the *anangke*. In the *Laws* voluntary death was permitted if an individual was ordered to do so by the state, or if he suffered devastating misfortune or intolerable shame. By concentrating on the Pythagorean element in the *Phaedo*, Augustine makes Plato's argument about voluntary death appear less complex and more straightforward than it was.[52]

Augustine readily admits the claim of his opponents that "many people did away with themselves to avoid falling into the hands of the enemy," but he contends that they should not have done so. "Sound reason," says Augustine, "is certainly to be preferred to examples."[53] Then, in an astonishing tour de force, Augustine asserts that "neither the patriarchs nor the prophets acted thus; nor did the apostles, since the Lord Christ himself, when he advised them to escape from one town to another in case of persecution [Matt. 10:23], could have advised them to take their own lives to avoid falling into the hands of their persecutors."[54] What has happened to Saul, Zimri, and Razis? All three killed themselves in order to avoid falling into the hands of their enemies. For obvious reasons Augustine consigns them to silence.

The argument from example leads Augustine into a discussion of the famous death of Cato of Utica, the paradigm of the Stoic martyr.[55] Instead of praising Cato as the embodiment of Roman virtue, Augustine condemns him: Cato's self-inflicted death came not from "greatness of soul" but from weakness in the face of adversity. It is a measure of Augustine's opposition to voluntary death that he goes out of his way to condemn Roman heroes like Lucretia and Cato. He could just as easily have exonerated Cato as he did Samson, especially in light of the fact that Augustine had read Cicero's account of Cato's death:

Cato departed from life with a feeling of joy in having found a reason for death; for the God who is master within us forbids our departure without permission. When, however, God himself has given a valid reason [*causam iustam*], as he did in the past to Socrates and in our day to Cato and to many others, then with certainty your true wise man will joyfully go forth from the darkness here into the light beyond.[56]

Cicero justified Cato's death on the basis of a divine sign in much the same way that Augustine defended Samson's act. Furthermore, Cicero's reference to Cato's having received a *causa iusta* for killing himself would have qualified Cato as a martyr according to Augustine's own definition of martyrdom: *martyres veros non facit poena sed causa.*[57] Why then did Augustine condemn Cato?

In the first place, Augustine no doubt would have disputed Cicero's claim that Cato had received a divine call. Cato may have been ordered by a god to kill himself, but certainly not by the God of the Christians. Second, and more to the point, it seems that Augustine wanted to keep the list of "exceptions that prove the rule" as short as possible. The names on that list could only be those of biblical heroes or "martyrs venerated in the Catholic Church."[58]

For Augustine the paradigmatic figure is Job: "Our adversaries object to our giving preference over Cato to the holy Job or to other saints recorded in our literature—writings of supreme authority and worthy of all credence. Job would rather suffer horrible bodily distresses than free himself from all those torments by self-inflicted death. And other saints chose to endure captivity and oppression at the enemies' hands, rather than take their own lives."[59] Augustine realizes that his pagan opponents are unlikely to be swayed by the example of Job. He therefore offers them a "Roman Job," Marcus Regulus, who chose to endure slavery and torture at the hands of the Carthaginians rather than kill himself: "In our adversaries' literature I should put Marcus Regulus above Marcus Cato. . . . He chose to let his life be ended by any kind of torture, rather than die by his own hand."[60] Among the Romans, Augustine declares, no one is more deserving of praise than Regulus. Augustine's adversaries should learn a lesson from his example: voluntary death is "a great crime" (*magnum scelus*).[61]

The argument against voluntary death culminates in the twenty-sixth chapter of the first book. Here Augustine is forced to deal with the most difficult of his opponents' objections, namely, that *Christian* women had killed themselves during persecution to avoid being raped! "'But,' they say, 'in time of persecution there were holy women [*sanctae feminae*] who escaped those who threatened their chastity by throwing themselves into rivers for the stream to whirl them away to death; and after such a death they were venerated as martyrs in the Catholic Church, and crowds thronged to their tombs.'"[62] Although earlier Augustine had boasted that Christian women did not follow the example of pagan women during the barbarian invasion in 410, he is now forced to admit that *in the past* Christian women *did* kill themselves in order to preserve their chastity. Since these women are venerated as martyrs in the church, Augustine cannot dismiss them, as he did the pagan women, as self-murderers, but he is hard pressed to justify their behavior. "I would not presume to make a hasty judgment in their case," he says. "I do not know whether divine authority convinced the church by cogent evidence that their memory should be honored in this way; it may well be so. It may be that they acted on divine instruction and not through a human mistake—not in error but in obedience."[63]

Both Ambrose and Jerome, Augustine's older contemporaries, agreed with him that an individual did not have the right to kill himself. But they made an exception in the case of young women when their virginity was at stake. In such a situation a woman could take herself out.[64] The parade example was Pelagia, a girl of fifteen, who drowned herself at Antioch during the Great Persecution (c. 306) in order to avoid being raped. In contrast to Ambrose, who praised Pelagia's heroism, Augustine denies that the threat of being violated is a legitimate pretext for voluntary death. How then does he justify the deaths of these Christian women? Augustine appeals to the argument of Plato in the *Phaedo* and to a Platonizing interpretation of the death of Samson: "When God orders, and shows without ambiguity that he orders, no one will bring an accusation against obedience. Who will lay a charge against a loyal compliance? This is what we are bound to believe in Samson's case. So let anyone who is told that he has no right to kill himself, do the deed if he is so commanded by him whose orders must not be slighted. There is just one proviso: let him take care that there is no uncertainty about the divine command."[65]

This is the only "loophole" in Augustine's otherwise absolute condemnation of voluntary death. The appeal to Plato is clear: Augustine justifies voluntary death only when a divine order has been received. Despite all his criticism of Cato, Augustine defends the death of Samson in the same way that Cicero justified Cato's act: on the basis of the divine sign. This is also how it *might* be possible for Augustine to defend those Christian women who killed themselves in times of persecution. But he withholds a final judgment in their case. Augustine fears the "slippery slope." He is concerned that if voluntary death is permitted as a means of avoiding sin, then "we shall not be able to stop it until we reach the point when people are encouraged to kill themselves as soon as they have received baptism. For that would be the time to forestall all future sins—the moment when all past sins have been erased. If self-inflicted death is permitted, surely this would be the best moment for it!"[66]

It is instructive to compare Augustine's position on voluntary death with that of his pagan contemporary Macrobius.[67] Both men agree that the only exception to the prohibition of voluntary death is the explicit command of

God to do so, and both quote the *Phaedo* with approval. Augustine and Macrobius also agree that voluntary death defiles the soul, but their reasons for this differ in a decisive way. For Macrobius, the act of taking one's life springs from passions, and as a result the soul of the person who takes his own life retains something corporeal and cannot find its way to heaven. For Augustine, voluntary death is "a damnable sin and a detestable crime."[68] It is a form of murder and explicitly forbidden by the sixth commandment.

Augustine went beyond Macrobius by attempting to draw a distinction between two kinds of voluntary death: "self-homicide" and "martyrdom." The former was condemned as reprehensible; the latter was praised as noble and ennobling. Augustine was not the first to draw this distinction, as we have seen, but it was he who reinforced it and established it in a way that has endured to the present day. It is a measure of the strength of Augustine's legacy that nearly all post-Augustinian thought on the subject of voluntary death bears this distinction between "suicide" and "martyrdom."

It should be remembered, however, that the Augustinian distinction was only one factor among many in a bitter struggle between Donatists and Catholics, on the one hand, and pagans and Christians, on the other. Despite the importance of the Platonic underpinning of Augustine's condemnation of voluntary death, we should not forget the polemical contexts in which Augustine's view was set forth.

In confrontation with the Donatists, Augustine sought to define the terms *martyrdom* and *voluntary death* in such a way as to turn the Donatists' "martyrs" into "self-murderers." What is good in the hands of the orthodox—baptism, the Eucharist, ordination—becomes evil in the hands of heretics. So conceived, no heretic could be a true witness, a true martyr. Similarly, Augustine would not condone, much less take responsibility for, the deaths of pagan women during the sack of Rome. To have done so would have lent credence to the pagan claim that Christianity was ultimately to blame for the disaster of 410. Augustine argued that these Roman women were wrong to have imitated Lucretia or Cato. Their acts of self-destruction sprang from "weakness of soul" and an inability to persevere in the face of adversity. Since God had not ordered their deaths, they too were condemned as "self-murderers." No pagan could be a true martyr.

What is so curious about all of this is that both Gaudentius and Cato—the Donatists and the women of Rome—would likely have found little to object to in Augustine's definition of martyrdom or in his use of the *Phaedo*. Augustine's opponents believed that they were taking, or had taken, their lives for a *causa iusta* and that they had received the *divina auctoritas* to do so. Put simply, their acts of self-destruction could be justified on precisely the same grounds as those on which Augustine condemned them. This only serves to set the polemical character of the debate about voluntary death in antiquity into sharper relief. And, lest the reader feel superior, it should be noted that this kind of polemic finds its modern equivalent in the conflicting evaluations of the self-immolation of Buddhist monks in Vietnam, the persistent cases of *sati* in northern India, the Jonestown episode, and the activities of Islamic fundamentalist groups.

We saw that Augustine's evaluation of voluntary death was based on Plato and only secondarily on the Bible. Aside from his appeal to the sixth commandment, Augustine took over the argument of the *Phaedo* that to sever the bonds of body and soul prematurely was to usurp a privilege that belonged only to God. Only God could determine the time for an individual to quit this life, and he would do so by providing a divine sign. This view Augustine shared with many of his predecessors and contemporaries, pagan and Christian. But despite the eight centuries of debate between Socrates and Augustine, the problem of how to recognize the sign and determine that it is from God was never resolved.

NOTES

1. Ronald A. Knox, *The Three Taps* (London: Penguin Books, 1960), p. 43 (first published in 1927). I owe this reference to Christopher Kirwan, *Augustine* (London and New York: Routledge, 1989), p. 204.

2. See our discussion in chap. 6, pp. 141–44.

3. Despite its obvious importance, Augustine's discussion of voluntary death has not received the attention it deserves. Aside from the general and at times superficial treatments of it in introductions to his thought and in books on the history of suicide, we know of no monograph on the subject. The best study is an article, to which we are much indebted, by Jacques Bels, "La mort volontaire dans l'oeuvre de saint Augustin," *Revue de l'histoire des religions* 187/2 (1975): 147–80. Darrel W. Amundsen offers a very thorough treatment of Augustine's views on the problem of voluntary death, though he underestimates the importance of Plato in this regard ("Suicide and Early Christian Values," in Baruch A. Brody, ed., *Suicide and Euthanasia: Historical and Contemporary Themes*, Philosophy and Medicine, no. 35 [Dordrecht, Boston, and London: Kluwer Academic Publishers, 1989], pp. 123–41). The burden of Amundsen's argument is to show that "it is simply wrong to suggest that Augustine formulated what then became the 'Christian position' on suicide. Rather, by removing certain ambiguities, he clarified and provided a theologically cogent explanation of and justification for the position *typically* held by earlier and contemporary Christian sources" ("Suicide and Early Christian Values," pp. 123–24, our emphasis). While it is clear that Augustine's position on voluntary death was anticipated by a *few* earlier Christian writers (notably Clement) and shared by some of his contemporaries (Ambrose and Jerome), Amundsen's claim that this position was "typically held" oversimplifies an extraordinarily complex debate, as our analysis in the previous chapter attempts to make clear.

4. *Against Gaudentius* (a Donatist bishop) was written c. 421/2. Unfortunately, there is no English translation of this treatise. We have followed the Latin text of M. Petschenig in *Corpus Scriptorum Ecclesiasticorum Latinorum* (Vienna: F. Tempsky, 1910), vol. 53, pp. 201–74. There is a superb French translation by G. Finaert, *Oeuvres de Saint Augustin*, vol. 32, Quatrième Série: *Traités Anti-Donatistes* (Paris: Desclée de Brouwer, 1965), vol. 5, pp. 511–685 (with Petschenig's text, and introduction and notes by E. Lamirande). The first book of the *City of God*, in which Augustine's other discussion of voluntary death is found, was composed in c. 413 and published in 414 along with books 2 and 3. We have followed the Latin text of G. E. McCracken in the *Loeb Classical Library* (Cambridge, MA: Harvard Univ. Press, 1972). There is a very readable English translation by Henry Bettenson, *St Augustine: Concerning the City of God Against the Pagans* (Harmondsworth: Penguin Books, 1984). These two treatises are the most important, but by no means the only, evidence for Augustine's views on voluntary death. For a summary and discussion of other relevant passages, see Amundsen, "Suicide and Early Christian Values," pp. 123–41.

5. Peter Brown, *Augustine of Hippo: A Biography* (Berkeley and Los Angeles: Univ. of California Press, 1967), p. 215. The classic study of this conflict is W. H. C. Frend, *The Donatist Church: A Movement of Protest in Roman North Africa* (Oxford: Clarendon Press, 1952).

6. See the "Monumenta ad Donistarum historiam pertinentia," in J. P. Migne, *Patrologiae Cursus Completus, Series Latina*, 8.673–784.

7. Migne, "Monumenta" 8.693 (*Acta Saturnini* 4). We owe this reference to Brown, *Augustine*, p. 218.

8. Augustine, *The Correction of the Donatists* 3.12. This passage was the basis for the famous description of the Donatists by Edward Gibbon, *The History of the Decline and Fall of the Roman Empire*, edited by J. B. Bury (London: Methuen, 1896–1900), vol. 2, pp. 389–90. On the Donatists' fascination with voluntary martyrdom, see Lamirande's note in Finaert, *Oeuvres de Saint Augustin*, pp. 747–48.

9. Brown, *Augustine*, p. 335, n. 10.

10. Augustine, *Letter* 89.2; cf. *Against Gaudentius* 1.20.22. On this general principle, see Lamirande's note in Finaert, *Oeuvres de Saint Augustin*, p. 747.

11. See Augustine, *After the Meeting Against the Donatists* 17.22.

12. See Augustine, *On the Unity of the Church* 20.53.

13. Augustine, *Against Gaudentius* 1.27.31; 1.29.33. On this, see Bels, "La mort volontaire," pp. 160–61. The connection between killing oneself and eternal punishment is extremely rare in Christian literature before Augustine. The only instances we have found are in the *Clementine Homilies* 12.14 (probably fourth century); and John Chrysostom, *Commentary on Galatians* 1.4.

14. Augustine, *Against Gaudentius* 1.6.7. Augustine is here quoting directly from Gaudentius's letter to Dulcitius. There is a striking similarity between the rationale of Gaudentius and that of Jim Jones. Both destroyed themselves and their communities when hostile outsiders threatened to intervene. On the Jonestown episode, see Jonathan Z. Smith, "The Devil in Mr. Jones," in *Imagining Religion*

(Chicago: Univ. of Chicago Press, 1982), pp. 102–20; and David Chidester, *Salvation and Suicide: An Interpretation of Jim Jones, the Peoples Temple, and Jonestown* (Bloomington and Indianapolis: Indiana Univ. Press, 1988), esp. pp. 129–59.

15. Augustine, *Against Gaudentius* 1.28.32.

16. Augustine, *Against Gaudentius* 1.31.36–38.

17. Augustine, *Against Gaudentius* 1.31.40.

18. Augustine, *Against Gaudentius* 1.31.39; cf. *City of God* 1.21.

19. Augustine, *Against Gaudentius* 1.30.35; cf. *City of God* 1.24.

20. Augustine, *Against Gaudentius* 1.37.49; cf. *City of God* 1.17. Note a similar connection made by Eusebius between the Montanists and Judas (*Church History* 5.16.13–14).

21. On this, see Bels, "La mort volontaire," p. 165.

22. See, for example, Augustine, *Against Gaudentius* 1.30.34; 1.37.31; 1.38.32.

23. Augustine, *Against Gaudentius* 1.6.7.

24. Augustine, *Against Gaudentius* 1.11.12; 1.30.35; 1.31.39; 1.32.41; 1.37.49.

25. Augustine, *Against Gaudentius* 1.27.31.

26. Augustine, *Against Gaudentius* 1.30.34.

27. Augustine, *Against Gaudentius* 1.30.34.

28. Augustine, *Against Gaudentius* 1.37.49.

29. Augustine, *Against Gaudentius* 1.37.49.

30. Alaric and the Goths may have been "barbarians," but they were also Christians (more precisely, Arians).

31. Augustine, *City of God* 1.16–17.

32. Augustine, *City of God* 1.17.

33. Augustine, *City of God* 1.17.

34. Cf. Augustine, *City of God* 1.21: "There are, however, certain exceptions to the commandment against killing [Ex. 20:13], made by the authority of God himself. There are some whose killing God orders, either by a law, or by an express command to a particular person at a particular time." We shall return to this Augustinian "loophole" shortly.

35. It is worth noting that only a year before Augustine wrote this, a considerable number of Donatists had killed themselves because Augustine had taken such extreme measures against them. See P. W. van der Horst, "A Pagan Platonist and a Christian Platonist on Suicide," *Vigiliae Christianae* 25 (1971): 284–85, n. 11.

36. *City of God* 1.18.

37. The story is found in Livy, *Roman Antiquities* 1.57–58.

38. *City of God* 1.19.

39. *City of God* 1.19.

40. *City of God* 1.19.

41. *City of God* 1.20. This passage further indicates that it was the deaths of *pagan* women that occasioned Augustine's discussion of voluntary death.

42. *City of God* 1.20.

43. *City of God* 1.20.

44. *City of God* 1.20; cf. Augustine's similar remarks in *On Patience* 10.
45. Lactantius, *Divine Institutes* 3.18; cf. *Epitome* 39; both passages condemning pagan "(self-) homicides." Like Augustine, Lactantius condemned the Stoics, and above all Cato, for their excessive fascination with voluntary death. But he held Christian martyrs in high esteem (*Divine Institutes* 5.13; 6.17).
46. Notably the Donatists!
47. *City of God* 1.21.
48. *City of God* 1.21.
49. *City of God* 1.21.
50. *City of God* 1.22.
51. *City of God* 1.22.
52. See our discussion in chap. 2, pp. 20–22.
53. *City of God* 1.22.
54. *City of God* 1.22.
55. *City of God* 1.23.
56. Cicero, *Tusculan Disputations* 1.74. See our discussion in chap. 2, pp. 32–34.
57. See n. 10, above.
58. See *City of God* 1.26.
59. *City of God* 1.24; cf. Augustine's treatment of Job in *On Patience* 10.
60. *City of God* 1.24. Regulus was the commander of the Roman troops in Africa during the First Punic War (c. 256 B.C.). When the Carthaginians sought peace, Regulus proposed terms that were unacceptable to them. The war continued, and Regulus was defeated and captured. In 250 Regulus was sent to Rome on a peace mission, but he recommended to the senate that the war be continued. He then returned to Carthage, where he died as a result of torture.
61. *City of God* 1.24. Note Augustine's extreme language throughout this section of the first book: voluntary death is a *detestabile facinus et damnabile scelus*, a *peccatum gravissimum*, a *crimen homicidii*. The deed is *non licet*; it is *nefas*, a deviation *ab auctoritate legis divinae*, for which *nulla causa iusta* is possible. Augustine's strident tone is that of a man railing against general acceptance of the act of voluntary death (*pace* Amundsen, "Suicide and Early Christian Values," p. 138).
62. *City of God* 1.26.
63. *City of God* 1.26.
64. See Ambrose, *On Virgins* 3.7.32–39; *Letter* 37; Jerome, *Commentary on Jonah* 1.6; cf. Eusebius, *Church History* 8.12.3–4; 8.14.14, 17.
65. *City of God* 1.26.
66. *City of God* 1.27. The implication, of course, is that only *Catholic* Christians would be able to receive and recognize the divine command.
67. For what follows, we are much indebted to P. W. van der Horst, "A Pagan Platonist," pp. 287–88. For the views of Macrobius, see our discussion in chap. 2, pp. 41–42.
68. *City of God* 1.25.

Conclusion

Why did the Augustinian condemnation of voluntary death succeed in reversing the perspective of an entire period of history, a period that Augustine himself is often thought to have brought to a close? We confess not to have a satisfying answer to that question, save for the obvious one of the enormous influence of Augustine's legacy in the West. But this does not explain why a similar attitude toward voluntary death came to be held in Eastern Christianity, where Augustine was little read. Have we then misinterpreted the evidence by making too much of the Augustinian "reversal"?

Augustine was not alone in condemning voluntary death. We have seen that the Platonists of late antiquity also opposed the act, and that Augustine's argument against voluntary death had several points in common with the view of a contemporary Platonist, Macrobius. Furthermore, both Augustine and the Neoplatonists constructed their arguments in a polemical context: the Neoplatonists criticized the Stoics as Augustine did the Donatists. Given the prominence of Neoplatonism from the third century on, and its influence on Christian theology in particular, is it possible that the opposition to voluntary death in this period was a *general tendency* and not the *reversal* we have described? Perhaps, but the former possibility fails at three crucial points.

First, despite the similar arguments employed by Augustine and the Neoplatonists, the evidence that survives indicates that it was only Augustine who, for all practical purposes, closed the Platonic "loophole" by virtually eliminating any justification for voluntary death. Admittedly, Augustine considered the act justifiable when an individual (like Samson) had been commanded to do so by God, but he clearly thought that an exceedingly remote possibility.

Second, despite the polemical contexts in which Augustine and the Neoplatonists set forth their views, the difference in tone between them could hardly have been sharper. The dispassionate discussion of voluntary death by a Plotinus or a Macrobius stands in stark contrast to Augustine's strident—indeed, at times, vicious—rhetoric. Opposed to voluntary death as, for the most part, the Neoplatonists were, they never condemned anyone for having killed himself. They may have opposed the Stoic position on voluntary death, but they never condemned, say, Cato as a "self-murderer." By contrast, Augustine dismissed Cato as having acted out of weakness, and he thought Judas more damned for his self-inflicted death than for his betrayal of Christ. Augustine even went so far as to suggest that some (Catholic!) Christians, who were revered as martyrs by the Church, were in fact nothing more than self-murderers.

Third, if Augustine's condemnation of voluntary death reflected a "general tendency" in late antiquity, then one would have to explain why it was that earlier Christian Platonists (save for Clement) did not similarly oppose the act.

How, then, did Augustine succeed in overturning the perspective of an entire period? One of the few scholars bold enough to attempt an explanation was Henry Fedden, who attributed the Augustinian reversal to

> the general decline in world civilization that set in about the third century and grew steadily more marked until the complete collapse of the Empire in the West and the coming of the Dark Ages. The *elite* and the educated, who in the previous centuries had opposed reason to the suicide-horror of the common people, grew fewer and less influential. All through the Empire, and particularly among the common Christians who were drawn from the most instinctive and credulous elements of the people, the old pagan-religious fear of suicide, with its roots in a tribal and pre-historic past, found no opposition. As the intellectual impetus and order of society failed, suicide again became a social crime.[1]

The reader may find it difficult to keep from smiling over Fedden's quaint and utterly erroneous analysis, but it seems that his answer to the question is wrong in a remarkably instructive way. Fedden is at least correct to call attention to the *terror* (whether primitive or not) attached to the act of voluntary death, for even in the modern, "rational" West, voluntary death continues to terrify. And we have attempted to mollify, or repress, that terror in ways that differ only by degree from the efforts of Augustine and his successors. In the article on suicide in the *Encyclopaedia of Religion and Ethics*, H. J. Rose wrote, with an almost audible sigh of relief, that "perhaps the greatest contribution of modern times to the *rational* treatment of [suicide] is the consideration . . . that many suicides are non-moral and entirely the affair of specialists in mental diseases."[2] Despite fifteen hundred years there is very little that separates Augustine's denunciation of Gaudentius as a "mad man" (*demens*) and Rose's judgment about suicide. We do not think that either Socrates or Jesus, Seneca or Paul, the Gymnosophists or the Donatists, would find much in Rose's "rational" approach for which to be grateful.

The title of our book reflects a fundamental aspect of the discussion of voluntary death in Western antiquity. In the texts and traditions over which we have ranged—from the Bible, through Greek and Roman philosophy, to Judaism and Christianity—the decision to take one's life, or allow it to be taken, was considered a *noble* choice, provided there was *sufficient justification*. The entire debate turned on this issue, even if no consensus was reached about when or under what circumstances such a choice was justified. What emerges instead is a fairly broad spectrum of opinion, from Socrates' insistence on the requirement of a divine sign to Seneca's emphasis on the unqualified freedom of the individual. But the very attempt to find a consensus indicates that the decision to die could be a *conscientious* one.

The debate about voluntary death was conducted in terms established by Plato's account of the death of Socrates. Indeed, the discussion of voluntary death in antiquity could well be described as the history of the interpretation of *Phaedo* 62c, for it was this text that remained central to the discussion down to the close of antiquity. The inherent ambiguity in the Platonic "loophole"— Socrates' insistence on the necessity of a divine sign—allowed this text to be used both as a justification for and as a means of moderating against the act of voluntary death. Yet, even in authors for whom no knowledge of the *Phaedo* can be presumed, the deity was thought to play an important role in an individual's decision to embrace death. The dramatic deaths of many Jewish and Christian martyrs, for example, were justified on the basis of a divine calling. Despite eight centuries of discussion, however, no agreement was reached on what constituted the divine sign or how it might be recognized.

Another important element in the debate was the dualistic cosmology presumed by many of the texts and traditions we have surveyed. When this world is contrasted with the one beyond, body with soul, mortality with immortality, reality itself is transformed. Life becomes death, and death the entry into life. Seen in this light, the question of voluntary death assumes a different aspect. In a world-negating system like the apostle Paul's, the question became how to justify continued existence in this world rather than voluntary death. At the same time, however, the cosmic dualism characteristic of the ancient world does not *in itself* explain why voluntary death was considered noble and ennobling. For we have seen that, on the pagan side at least, the two philosophies with the strongest belief in an afterlife—Pythagoreanism and Neoplatonism—both exercised the greatest restraint in the matter of voluntary death.

In this book we have attempted to deconstruct the "linguistics of suicide" by examining the precise terms and formulations employed in antiquity to denote the act of voluntary death. We have seen that when the conventional distinction between "suicide" and "martyrdom" is read back into antiquity, it conceals rather than reveals the issues at stake in the debate. We have also attempted to show historically how that distinction came about as the result of internecine Christian polemics. One person's martyr was another person's suicide, and vice versa. It is our contention, moreover, that no distinction can be made philosophically (that is, by means of definition) between "suicide" and "martyrdom." In the final analysis, the distinction devolves upon personal commitment.

The contours of the debate about voluntary death in antiquity stand in sharp contrast to those of the last hundred years. To the extent that the discourse on voluntary death has been controlled by medical doctors and social scientists, to that extent has it ceased to be discussed as an enduring moral and religious problem. Since the 1970s, however, voluntary death has reemerged as a topic of moral concern, both in the academy and in society at large. The last two decades have witnessed the growth of the "right-to-die" movement and the creation of a new academic discipline, medical ethics. The renewal of the debate about voluntary death suggests that it is being reevaluated. Having fought a long battle with theology for control of voluntary death, the medical and social scientific hegemony is now in decline. The nature and precise terms of this new debate about voluntary death are far from clear. But in order for it to be an informed debate, what is needed is an awareness of our classical heritage on this enduring problem. That, in part, is what we have attempted to provide in this book. Whether that heritage can be brought to bear on the contemporary discussion of voluntary death we leave to others more competent than ourselves to determine. We are not so naive as to suppose that ancient answers can easily be found to the questions now being raised about voluntary death. Yet, as Alasdair MacIntyre has argued, our contemporary moral disagreements often prove so intractable because we have inherited a variety of moral concepts, terms, and principles, each originally at home in different historical contexts. Only by being grounded in the history of our own tradition, he contends, will we be able to restore rationality and intelligibility to our moral attitudes and commitments.[3]

What, finally, is to be learned from the discussion of voluntary death in antiquity? Are there occasions when the taking of one's life is justifiable in the light of other ends? Are there occasions when one ought not to intervene even when it is possible to keep another from self-destruction? Is the right to dispose of oneself either by an act of commission or by refusing the means to sustain or heal life an absolute right, so that freedom to take one's own life ought never to be interfered with? These are questions that James Gustafson explores in the second volume of his *Ethics from a Theocentric Perspective*. His response is summarized nicely in the following passage:

> I believe that the fact that few if any persons morally condemn any given suicide . . . both reflects compassion for the conditions which led to the act and an

ambivalence that mirrors a moral ambiguity inherent in the act itself. Suicide is always a tragic moral choice; it is sometimes a misguided choice. But it can be, I believe, a conscientious choice.[4]

Although Gustafson does not deal with the texts and traditions we have treated in this book, his conclusions are remarkably in line with the discussion of voluntary death in Western antiquity before Augustine. The "ambiguity" of the act, the "morality" and "tragedy" of it, and above all the idea of "conscientious choice"—all were recognized and discussed in antiquity in ways that may still prove instructive. Both Jews and Christians, Greeks and Romans, gave meaning to their lives through their deaths. Their way of exiting from this life affirmed the values for which they lived and gave a legacy to those who valued them and their commitments.

In a review of Gustafson's book, James Childress and William Boley offer praise for his "sensitivity and insight" on this problem, but in the final analysis they urge that "defenders of traditional Western religious morality, especially within the Christian tradition, might raise questions about Gustafson's claim that suicide is often not only understandable, excusable, and forgivable, but also *justifiable*," especially since "the Christian tradition of moral reflection has maintained a strong prohibition against suicide in almost all circumstances."[5] They admit to certain "complexities and problems within the tradition itself" but insist nevertheless that "this tradition [should be] understood as the deposit of communal wisdom across space and time."[6] Reactionary and erroneous assertions such as this will not serve to advance the new debate about the problem of voluntary death. Childress and Boley, like so many, seem to have forgotten that voluntary death was one of the ideals on which the church was founded.

NOTES

1. H. R. Fedden, *Suicide: A Social and Historical Study* (London: Davies, 1938), p. 111.
2. H. J. Rose, "Suicide (Introductory)," in J. Hastings, ed., *Encyclopaedia of Religion and Ethics*, vol. 12 (1922), p. 24.
3. Alasdair MacIntyre, *After Virtue: A Study in Moral Theory*, 2d ed. (Notre Dame, IN: Univ. of Notre Dame Press, 1984).
4. James A. Gustafson, *Ethics from a Theocentric Perspective*, Vol. 2, *Ethics and Theology* (Chicago: Univ. of Chicago Press, 1984), p. 215.
5. James F. Childress and William H. Boley, *Journal of Religion* 67 (1987): 392–95, quotation from p. 394.
6. Childress and Boley, p. 394.

Bibliography

Adkins, Arthur W. H. "Values in Euripides' *Hecuba* and *Hercules Furens*." *Classical Quarterly* 16 (1966): 193–219.

Alvarez, Alfredo. *The Savage God: A Study of Suicide*. New York: Random House, 1970.

Amundsen, Darrel W. "Suicide and Early Christian Values." In *Suicide and Euthanasia: Historical and Contemporary Themes*, edited by Baruch A. Brody, pp. 77–153. Philosophy and Medicine, no. 35. Dordrecht, Boston, and London: Kluwer Academic Publishers, 1989.

Anderson, Olive. *Suicide in Victorian and Edwardian England*. Oxford: Clarendon Press, 1987.

Antin, Paul. "*Mori lucrum* et *Antigone* 462, 464." *Revue des sciences religieuses* 62 (1964): 259–60.

Barnes, T. D. "Pre-Decian *Acta Martyrum*." *Journal of Theological Studies* 19 (1968): 509–31.

———. *Tertullian: A Historical and Literary Study*. Rev. ed. Oxford: Clarendon Press, 1985.

Barrett, C. K. *The Gospel According to St. John*. 2d ed. Philadelphia: Westminster Press, 1978.

Battin, Margaret. "Age Rationing and the Just Distribution of Health Care: Is There a Duty to Die?" *Ethics* 97 (1987): 317–40.

Bauer, Walter. *Orthodoxy and Heresy in Earliest Christianity*. 2d ed. Translated by the Philadelphia Seminar on Christian Origins. Philadelphia: Fortress Press, 1971.

Beauchamp, Tom L. "Suicide in the Age of Reason." In *Suicide and Euthanasia: Historical and Contemporary Themes*, edited by Baruch A. Brody, pp. 183–219. Philosophy and Medicine, no. 35. Dordrecht, Boston, and London: Kluwer Academic Publishers, 1989.

Bels, Jacques. "La mort volontaire dans l'oeuvre de saint Augustin." *Revue de l'histoire des religions* 187/2 (1975): 147–80.

Benko, Stephen. *Pagan Rome and the Early Christians*. Bloomington: Indiana Univ. Press, 1984.

Bickerman, Elias. *Der Gott der Makkabäer*. Berlin: Schocken Verlag, 1937.

Blidstein, Gerald J. "Rabbis, Romans, and Martyrdom—Three Views." *Tradition* 21 (1984): 54–62.

Bonhoeffer, Adolf. *Die Ethik des Stoikers Epictet*. Stuttgart: Enke, 1894.

Borowitz, Michael. "Some Ruminations on Suicide: A History of its Problematization." Unpublished paper, March 1988.

Brandon, S. G. F. *The Judgment of the Dead*. New York: Scribner's, 1967.

Brewer, Julius A. *A Critical and Exegetical Commentary on Haggai, Zechariah, Malachi and Jonah*. The International Critical Commentary. New York: Scribner's, 1912.

Brody, Baruch A. "Jewish Casuistry on Suicide and Euthanasia." In *Suicide and Euthanasia: Historical and Contemporary Themes,* edited by Baruch A. Brody, 39–75. Philosophy and Medicine, no. 35. Dordrecht, Boston, and London: Kluwer Academic Publishers, 1989.

Brown, Peter. *Augustine of Hippo: A Biography.* Berkeley and Los Angeles: Univ. of California Press, 1967.

Browne, Sir Thomas. *Religio Medici and Other Writings.* Everyman's Library. New York: Dutton, 1965.

Burkert, Walter. *Greek Religion.* Translated by John Raffan. Cambridge, MA: Harvard Univ. Press, 1985.

Callahan, Daniel. *Setting Limits: Medical Goals in an Aging Society.* New York: Simon & Schuster, 1987.

Cameron, Alan. "The Date and Identity of Macrobius." *Journal of Roman Studies* 56 (1966): 25–38.

Camus, Albert. *The Myth of Sisyphus and Other Essays.* Translated by Justin O'Brien. New York: Random House, 1955.

Capelle, Bernard. "L'Entretien d'Origène avec Héraclide." *Journal of Ecclesiastical History* 2 (1951): 143–57.

Cavallin, H. C. C. *Life After Death: Paul's Argument for the Resurrection of the Dead in I Cor. 15: Part I: An Enquiry into the Jewish Background.* Lund: Gleerup, 1974.

Charles, R. H. *Eschatology: The Doctrine of a Future Life in Israel, Judaism, and Christianity, A Critical History.* 1913. Reprint. New York: Schocken Books, 1963.

Charlesworth, James H. *The Pseudepigrapha in Modern Research with a Supplement.* Septuagint and Cognate Studies, no. 7S. Missoula, MT: Scholars Press, 1981.

Chidester, David. *Salvation and Suicide: An Interpretation of Jim Jones, the Peoples Temple, and Jonestown.* Bloomington and Indianapolis: Indiana Univ. Press, 1988.

Childress, James F., and William H. Boley. Review of *Ethics from a Theocentric Perspective.* Vol. 2, *Ethics and Theology,* by James A. Gustafson. *Journal of Religion* 67 (1987): 392–95.

Clebsch, William A., ed. *John Donne: Suicide.* Studies in the Humanities Series, no. 1. Chico, CA: Scholars Press, 1983.

Clemons, James T. *What Does the Bible Say About Suicide?* Minneapolis, MN: Fortress Press, 1990.

Collange, J.-F. *L'épître de saint Paul aux Philippiens.* Commentaire du Nouveau Testament Xa. Neuchâtel: Delachaux & Niestlé, 1973.

Collingwood, R. G. *The Idea of History.* Oxford: Clarendon, 1946.

Collins, John J. "Apocalyptic Eschatology as the Transcendence of Death." *Catholic Biblical Quarterly* 36 (1974): 21–43.

———. "The Root of Immortality: Death in the Context of Jewish Wisdom." *Harvard Theological Review* 71 (1978): 177–92.

Cooper, John M. "Greek Philosophers on Euthanasia and Suicide." In *Suicide and Euthanasia: Historical and Contemporary Themes,* edited by Baruch A. Brody, pp. 9–38. Philosophy and Medicine, no. 35. Dordrecht, Boston, and London: Kluwer Academic Publishers, 1989.

Crocker, Lester G. "Discussion of Suicide in the Eighteenth Century." *Journal of the History of Ideas* 13 (1952): 47–72.

Cumont, Franz. "Comment Plotin détourna Porphyre du suicide." *Revue des études grecques* 32 (1919): 113–20.

Daube, David. "Death as a Release in the Bible." *Novum Testamentum* 5 (1962): 82–104.

———. "Suicide." In *Studi in onore di Giuseppe Grosso*, pp. 117–27. Torino: G. Glappichelli, 1971.

———. "The Linguistics of Suicide." *Philosophy and Public Affairs* 1 (1972): 387–437.

Deshaies, Gabriel. *Psychologie du suicide*. Paris: Presses Universitaires de France, 1947.

de Ste. Croix, G. E. M. "Aspects of the 'Great' Persecution." *Harvard Theological Review* 47 (1954): 75–113.

———. "Why Were the Early Christians Persecuted?" *Past and Present* 26 (1963): 6–38. Reprinted in *Studies in Ancient Society*, edited by M. I. Finley, pp. 210–49. Past and Present Series. London: Routledge & Kegan Paul, 1974.

Dodd, C. H. *The Interpretation of the Fourth Gospel*. Cambridge: Cambridge Univ. Press, 1953.

Dodds, E. R. *Pagan and Christian in an Age of Anxiety: Some Aspects of Religious Experience from Marcus Aurelius to Constantine*. Cambridge: Cambridge Univ. Press, 1965.

Dörrie, Klaus. *Exemplum Socratis: Studien zur Sokratesnachwirkung in der kynisch-stoischen Philosophie der frühen Kaiserzeit und ihm frühen Christentum*. Hermes Einzelschriften, no. 42. Wiesbaden: Steiner, 1979.

Douglas, Jack. *The Social Meanings of Suicide*. Princeton, NJ: Princeton Univ. Press, 1967.

Droge, Arthur J. "MORI LUCRUM: Paul and Ancient Theories of Suicide." *Novum Testamentum* 30 (1988): 263–86.

Dudley, Donald R. *A History of Cynicism from Diogenes to the Sixth Century* A.D. London: Methuen, 1937.

Durkheim, Emile. *Le suicide: Etude de sociologie*. 1897. English translation, *Suicide: A Study in Sociology*. Glencoe, IL: Free Press, 1951.

Edelstein, Ludwig. *Ancient Medicine: Selected Papers of Ludwig Edelstein*. Edited by O. Temkin and C. L. Temkin. Baltimore, MD: Johns Hopkins Univ. Press, 1967.

Fedden, Henry R. *Suicide: A Social and Historical Study*. London: Davies, 1938.

Feldman, Louis. "Flavius Josephus Revisited: The Man, His Writings, and His Significance." In *Aufstieg und Neidergang der römischen Welt*, II.21.2, pp. 763–862. Berlin: Walter de Gruyter, 1984.

———. *Josephus and Modern Scholarship (1937–1980)*. Berlin: Walter de Gruyter, 1984.

Fox, Robin Lane. *Pagans and Christians*. New York: Knopf, 1967.

Frankfort, Henri, H. Frankfort, John A. Wilson, and Thorkild Jacobsen. *Before Philosophy: The Intellectual Adventure of Ancient Man*. Baltimore, MD: Penguin Books, 1949.

Frend, W. H. C. *The Donatist Church: A Movement of Protest in Roman North Africa*. Oxford: Clarendon Press, 1952.

———. *Martyrdom and Persecution in the Early Church: A Study of a Conflict from the Maccabees to Donatus*. Oxford: Blackwell, 1965.

Frey, Raymond G. "Did Socrates Commit Suicide?" *Philosophy* 53 (1978): 106–8.

Gibbon, Edward. *The History of the Decline and Fall of the Roman Empire*. 3 vols. Edited by J. B. Bury. London: Methuen, 1896–1900.

Giglioli, Alberto. "Mihi enim vivere Christus est: Congeturra al texto di Phil. 1, 21." *Revista Biblica* 16 (1968): 305–15.

Goldstein, Sidney. *Suicide in Rabbinic Literature*. Hoboken, NJ: KTAV, 1989.

Goodenough, E. R. *By Light, Light: The Mystic Gospel of Hellenistic Judaism*. New Haven, CT: Yale Univ. Press, 1935. Reprint. Amsterdam: Philo Press, 1969.

Gordis, Robert. *The Book of God and Man: A Study of Job*. Chicago: Univ. of Chicago Press, 1965.

————. *Koheleth, the Man and His World*. 3d ed. New York: Schocken Books, 1968.

Griffin, Miriam T. *Seneca: A Philosopher in Politics*. Oxford: Clarendon Press, 1976.

Grisé, Yolande. *Le suicide dans la Rome antique*. Montreal: Bellarmin, 1982.

Gustafson, James A. *Ethics from a Theocentric Perspective*. Vol. 2, *Ethics and Theology*. Chicago: Univ. of Chicago Press, 1984.

Hackforth, Reginald. *Plato's Phaedo*. Cambridge: Cambridge Univ. Press, 1952.

Hankoff, L. D. "The Theme of Suicide in the Works of Flavius Josephus." *Clio Medica* 2 (1976): 15–24.

Harran, Marilyn J. "Suicide." In *The Encyclopedia of Religion*, edited by Mircea Eliade, vol. 14, pp. 125–31. New York: Macmillan, 1987.

Harris, J. Rendel "Did Judas Really Commit Suicide?" *American Journal of Theology* 4 (1900): 490–513.

Hengel, Martin. *Judaism and Hellenism*. 2 vols. Philadelphia: Fortress Press, 1974.

Henten, J. W. van, ed. *Die Entstehung der jüdischen Martyrologie*. Studia Post-Biblica, no. 38. Leiden: Brill, 1989.

Hirzel, Rudolf. "Der Selbstmord." *Archiv für Religionswissenschaft* 11 (1908): 75–104, 243–84, 417–76. Reprinted separately as *Der Selbstmord*. Darmstadt: Wissenschaftliche Buchgesellschaft, 1967.

Hoenig, Sidney. "The Sicarii in Masada—Glory or Infamy?" *Tradition* 11 (1970): 5–30.

Inge, W. R. *The Philosophy of Plotinus*. 3d ed. London: Longmans, Green, 1929.

Jaeger, Werner. "The Greek Ideas of Immortality." In *Immortality and Resurrection: Death in the Western World*, edited by Krister Stendahl, pp. 97–114. New York: Macmillan, 1965.

Kirwan, Christopher. *Augustine*. London and New York: Routledge, 1989.

Klausner, Samuel Z. "Martyrdom." In *The Encyclopedia of Religion*, edited by Mircea Eliade, vol. 9, pp. 230–38. New York: Macmillan, 1987.

Ladouceur, David J. "Josephus and Masada." In *Josephus, Judaism, and Christianity*, edited by L. Feldman and G. Hata, pp. 95–113. Detroit, MI: Wayne State Univ. Press, 1987.

Lightfoot, J. B. *St. Paul's Epistle to the Philippians*. London: Macmillan, 1891.

Loisy, Alfred. *Le quatrième évangile*. 2d ed. Paris: Nourry, 1921.

Lutz, Cora E. "Musonius Rufus: 'The Roman Socrates.' " *Yale Classical Studies* 10 (1947): 3–147.

McCarter, P. Kyle, Jr. *I Samuel*. The Anchor Bible. Garden City, NY: Doubleday, 1980.

————. *II Samuel*. The Anchor Bible. Garden City, NY: Doubleday, 1984.

MacDonald, Michael. "The Secularization of Suicide in England." *Past and Present* 111 (1986): 50–100.

McIntosh, John C. *Research on Suicide: A Bibliography*. Westport, CT: Greenwood Press, 1985.

MacIntyre, Alasdair. *After Virtue: A Study in Moral Theory*. 2d ed. Notre Dame, IN: Univ. of Notre Dame Press, 1984.

McKenzie, John L. *Second Isaiah*. The Anchor Bible. Garden City, NY: Doubleday, 1968.

McManners, John. *Death and the Enlightenment*. Oxford: Oxford Univ. Press, 1981.

Mair, A. W. "Suicide (Greek and Roman)." In *The Encyclopaedia of Religion and Ethics*, edited by J. Hastings, vol. 12, pp. 26–33. New York: Scribner's, 1922.

Margoliouth, G. "Suicide (Jewish)." In *The Encyclopaedia of Religion and Ethics*, edited by J. Hastings, vol. 12, pp. 37–38. New York: Scribner's, 1922.

Melling, David J. *Understanding Plato*. Oxford and New York: Oxford Univ. Press, 1987.

Miller, Fred D. "Epicurus on the Art of Dying." *Southern Journal of Philosophy* 14 (1976): 169–77.

Morselli, Enrico. *Il suicidio: Saggio di statistica morale*. 1879. Abridged English translation. *Suicide: An Essay on Comparative Moral Statistics*. London: Paul, 1881.

Müller, C. *Commentatio de locis quibusdam Epistolae Pauli ad Philippenses*. Hamburg: Meissner, 1843.

Musurillo, Herbert. *The Acts of the Christian Martyrs*. Oxford Early Christian Texts. Oxford: Clarendon, 1972.

Myers, Jacob M. *II Chronicles*. The Anchor Bible. Garden City, NY: Doubleday, 1965.

Neusner, Jacob. *Judaism: The Evidence of the Mishnah* (2d ed. Atlanta, GA: Scholars Press, 1987). Chicago: Univ. of Chicago Press, 1981.

———. *Judaism: The Classical Statement. The Evidence of Bavli*. Chicago: Univ. of Chicago Press, 1986.

Newell, Raymond R. "Suicide Accounts in Josephus: A Form Critical Study." In *Society of Biblical Literature Seminar Papers*, pp. 351–69. Missoula, MT: Scholars Press, 1982.

Nickelsburg, George E., Jr. *Resurrection, Immortality, and Eternal Life in Intertestamental Judaism*. Cambridge, MA: Harvard Univ. Press, 1972.

Nietzsche, F. *Twilight of the Idols*. Translated by R. J. Hollingdale. Harmondsworth: Penguin Books, 1968.

Nock, A. D. *Conversion: The Old and the New in Religion from Alexander the Great to Augustine of Hippo*. Oxford: Clarendon Press, 1933.

Novak, David. *Suicide and Morality: The Theories of Plato, Aquinas and Kant and Their Relevance for Suicidology*. New York: Scholars Studies Press, 1975.

Palmer, D. W. " 'To Die Is Gain' (Philippians i 21)." *Novum Testamentum* 17 (1975): 203–18.

Perls, A. "Der Selbstmord nach der Halacha." *Monatsschrift für Geschichte und Wissenschaft des Judentums* 55 (1911): 287–95.

Pope, Marvin H. *Job*. The Anchor Bible. Garden City, NY: Doubleday, 1973.

Prentice, Ann E. *Suicide: A Selective Bibliography of Over 2,200 Items*. Metuchen, NJ: Scarecrow Press, 1974.

Rabinowitz, Louis I., and Haim H. Cohn. "Suicide." In *The Encyclopaedia Judaica*, edited by C. Roth and G. Wigoder, vol. 15, pp. 489–91. Jerusalem: Keter Publishing House, 1972.

Reines, C. W. "The Jewish View of Suicide." *Judaism* 10 (1961): 160–70.

Riddle, Donald W. *The Martyrs: A Study in Social Control*. Chicago: Univ. of Chicago Press, 1931.

Rist, John M. *Plotinus: The Road to Reality*. Cambridge: Cambridge Univ. Press, 1967.

———. *Stoic Philosophy*. Cambridge: Cambridge Univ. Press, 1969.

———. *Epicurus: An Introduction*. Cambridge: Cambridge Univ. Press, 1972.

Rose, H. J. "Suicide (Introductory)." In *The Encyclopaedia of Religion and Ethics*, edited by J. Hastings, vol. 12, pp. 21–24. New York: Scribner's, 1922.

Rosner, Fred. "Suicide in Biblical, Talmudic, and Rabbinic Writings." *Tradition* 11 (1970): 25–40.

Sanders, E. P. *Jesus and Judaism.* Philadelphia: Fortress Press, 1985.

Scholten, Clemens. *Martyrium und Sophiamythos im Gnostizismus nach den Texten von Nag Hammadi.* Jahrbuch für Antike und Christentum Ergänzungsband, no. 14. Münster: Aschendorffsche Verlagsbuchhandlung, 1987.

Schweitzer, Albert. *The Mysticism of Paul the Apostle.* Translated by W. Montgomery. London: Adam & Charles Black, 1931.

———. *The Quest of the Historical Jesus.* Translated by W. Montgomery. London: Macmillan, 1968.

Scott, R. B. Y. *Proverbs-Ecclesiastes.* The Anchor Bible. Garden City, NY: Doubleday, 1965.

Seeley, David. *The Noble Death: Greco-Roman Martyrology and Paul's Concept of Salvation.* Journal for the Study of the New Testament Supplement Series, no. 28. Sheffield: JSOT, 1990.

Sevenster, J. N. *Paul and Seneca.* Supplements to Novum Testamentum, no. 4. Leiden: Brill, 1961.

Shneidman, E. S., N. L. Farberow, and R. E. Litman, eds. *The Psychology of Suicide.* New York: Science House, 1970.

Smith, D. Moody. *Johannine Christianity: Essays on Its Setting, Sources, and Theology.* Columbia: Univ. of South Carolina Press, 1984.

Smith, Jonathan Z. *Map Is Not Territory: Studies in the History of Religions.* Studies in Judaism in Late Antiquity, no. 23. Leiden: Brill, 1978.

———. *Imagining Religion: From Babylon to Jonestown.* Chicago: Univ. of Chicago Press, 1982.

Smith, Morton. "The Common Theology of the Ancient Near East." *Journal of Biblical Literature* 71 (1952): 135–47.

———. *Palestinian Parties and Politics That Shaped the Old Testament.* 2d ed. London: SCM Press, 1987.

Spero, Shubert. "In Defense of the Defenders of Masada." *Tradition* 11 (1970): 31–43.

Stahl, William H. *Macrobius: Commentary on the Dream of Scipio.* New York: Columbia Univ. Press, 1952.

Stone, M. E., and J. Strugnell. *The Books of Elijah: Parts 1–2.* Texts and Translations, no. 18, Pseudepigrapha Series, no. 8. Missoula, MT: Scholars Press, 1979.

Tabor, James D. "Resurrection and Immortality: Paul and Poimandres." In *Christian Teaching: Studies in Honor of LeMoine G. Lewis,* edited by Everett Ferguson, pp. 72–91. Abilene, TX: Abilene Christian Univ. Press, 1981.

———. *Things Unutterable: Paul's Ascent to Paradise in Its Greco-Roman, Judaic, and Early Christian Contexts.* Studies in Judaism. Lanham, MD: Univ. Press of America, 1986.

———. "Returning to the Divinity: Josephus's Portrayal of the Disappearances of Enoch, Elijah, and Moses." *Journal of Biblical Literature* 108 (1989): 225–38.

Tadic-Guilloteaux, N. "Sénèque face au suicide." *L'antiquité classique* 32 (1963): 541–51.

Tanner, R. G. "Martyrdom in Saint Ignatius of Antioch and the Stoic View of Suicide." In *Studia Patristica,* edited by E. A. Livingstone, pp. 201–5. Vol. 16.2. Texte und Untersuchungen, no. 129. Berlin: Akademie-Verlag, 1985.

Taylor, Steve. *Durkheim and the Study of Suicide.* London: Macmillan, 1982.

Tcherikover, Victor. *Hellenistic Civilization and the Jews.* Philadelphia: Magnes Press, 1959.

van der Horst, P. W. "A Pagan Platonist and a Christian Platonist on Suicide." *Vigiliae Christianae* 24 (1971): 282–88.

von Arnim, Hans. *Stoicorum Veterum Fragmenta.* 4 vols. Leipzig: Teubner, 1905–1924.

von Campenhausen, Hans. "Bearbeitungen und Interpretationen des Polykarp-martyriums." *Sitzungsberichte der Heidelberger Akademie der Wissenschaft,* Phil.-hist. Klasse. 3. Abh. (1957): 1–48.

Walzer, Richard. *Galen on Jews and Christians.* London: Oxford Univ. Press, 1949.

Watts, D. W. "The Books of Joel, Obadiah, Jonah, Nahum, Habakkuk and Zephaniah." *The Cambridge Bible Commentary.* Cambridge: Cambridge Univ. Press, 1975.

Williams, Glanville. *The Sanctity of Life and the Criminal Law.* New York: Knopf, 1957.

Williams, Sam K. *Jesus' Death as Saving Event: The Background and Origin of a Concept.* Harvard Dissertations in Religion, no. 2. Missoula, MT: Scholars Press, 1975.

Young, F. W. "Suicide." In *The Interpreter's Dictionary of the Bible,* edited by G. A. Buttrick, vol. 4, pp. 453–54. Nashville and New York: Abingdon Press, 1962.

Index